THE PENGUIN POETS

D 21

M LT

Milton: Poems

SELECTED
WITH AN INTRODUCTION BY
L. D. LERNER

★

PENGUIN BOOKS
MELBOURNE · LONDON · BALTIMORE

Penguin Books Ltd, Harmondsworth, Middlesex

U.S.A.: Penguin Books Inc ., 3300 Clipper Mill Road, Baltimore 11, Md
(*Educational Representative:*
D. C. Heath & Co., 285 Columbus Avenue, Boston 16, Mass)

AUSTRALIA: Penguin Books Pty Ltd, 200 Normanby Road,
Melbourne, S.C.5, Victoria

AGENT IN CANADA: Riverside Books Ltd, 47 Green Street,
Saint Lambert, Montreal, P.Q.

—

Made and printed in Great Britain by
The Whitefriars Press Ltd, Tonbridge

—

First published 1953

Contents

Prefatory Note	7
Introduction	9
Chronological Table	43
On the Morning of Christ's Nativity	47
On the Death of a Fair Infant Dying of a Cough	58
On Time	62
Upon the Circumcision	63
At a Solemn Music	64
On Shakespeare	65
L'Allegro	66
Il Penseroso	71
Sonnets:	
O Nightingale, that on yon bloomy spray	77
How soon hath time	77
When the Assault was Intended to the City	78
On the Detraction which Followed upon my Writing Certain Treatises	78
On the New Forcers of Conscience under the Long Parliament	79
On the Late Massacre in Piedmont	80
When I consider how my light is spent	80
Lawrence of virtuous father virtuous son	81
Cyriack, whose grandsire on the Royal Bench	81
Methought I saw my late espoused saint	82
To the Lord General Cromwell	82
To Mr Cyriack Skinner upon his Blindness	83
The Fifth Ode of Horace. Book I	84
Songs From Arcades	85
Lycidas	86
Comus	92
Paradise Lost	
Book I : Argument	125
Introductory	126

CONTENTS

Satan before the Council   127
The Architect of Pandemonium   129
Book II   130
Book III : Argument   162
Invocation to Light   163
Book IV : Argument   164
Satan's Soliloquy   165
Evening in Eden   168
Book V : Argument   168
The Morning Hymn of Adam and Eve   169
Abdiel   171
Book VI : Argument   172
Messiah Victorious   173
Book VII : Argument   175
Invocation   175
Book VIII : Argument   176
Book IX   177
Book X   213
Book XI : Argument   246
Michael tells Adam about Death   247
Book XII : Argument   248
The Departure from Eden   248
Paradise Regained
Book II
Satan Tempts Christ in the Wilderness: the Banquet   251
Book III
The Kingdoms of the World   252
Book IV
The Rejection of Classical Culture   255
Satan sets storms raging while Christ sleeps   259
Samson Agonistes   261

Suggestions for Reading   315

Prefatory Note

THE timelessness of great literature is a common platitude among
critics: the belief that it can be appreciated as easily after several
centuries as when it was first written. This is a comforting view,
since if true it would spare us a lot of hard work; and for some
kinds of literature, such as the love-lyric, it very nearly is true.
But to appreciate the work of a highly intelligent writer such as
Milton, keenly interested in the problems of his time, we cannot
rest in this easy assurance: we must teach ourselves the full significance of ideas which mean less to us to-day than they did to his
contemporaries, or which mean something different. The liberty
for which the Civil War was fought was not the liberty of John
Stuart Mill; original sin in the seventeenth century was not a
quaint relic of pre-scientific thinking, but the most important
element in human character: deposing a king was not a minor
consequence of a social revolution, but an act of desecration
against the anointed of God.

Unless we realize some of these things we shall read the great
writers of the past as foreigners. We need some knowledge of
medieval astronomy to understand

> then, listen I
> To the celestial sirens' harmony
> That sit upon the nine enfolded spheres.

And understanding on this obvious level is not all: we may think
we understand such a line as *Justify the ways of God to men* – we
may in fact know the meaning of each word – yet the full depth
of its significance will be quite lost on us unless we can think ourselves back to the religious outlook of the seventeenth century.

The following essay is an attempt to supply an introductory

sketch of the background of Milton's work. In order to achieve even this painfully inadequate sketch, I have felt it necessary to omit many topics that such an introduction might have dealt with. There is no account of Milton's life, though most of the important events are mentioned in the chronological table: and there is practically no literary criticism. This last I regret very much, since Milton has been the victim of some very intelligent destructive criticism in this century, and his defenders have on the whole shown themselves less acute than his attackers. However, literary criticism is something which the intelligent reader can supply for himself, whereas no-one can produce background knowledge, like a spider's web, from his own inside. So I have concentrated on what seemed the more important task; those who regard this decision as unpardonable must be referred apologetically to the Reading List.

Introduction

I

SOMEWHERE in the seventeenth century the modern world was
born. Our grandfathers were not at all puzzled about its birth:
they saw it springing like Pallas Athene, grown and fully armed,
from the head of its parent the Middle Ages. This event they
placed somewhere after the fall of Constantinople, and called it
the Renaissance. To-day historians find life more complicated
than that. 'The end of the Middle Ages' seems to mean something
different according as we look at politics, or religion, or econo-
mics, or literature: and these things all happened at different
times, and had remarkably little to do with one another.

There was politics, for instance. The medieval idea of Christendom was an attempt to view it as one community, in which the
chief division of authority was the vertical one between its
spiritual and temporal heads, Pope and Emperor. This is why
historians often say that the Middle Ages knew nothing of sovereignty: of the conception that Europe consisted of several inde-
pendent units, with a separate master supreme in each. Of course
theory and practice were ludicrously dissimilar, and neither Pope
nor Emperor, certainly not the latter, was really master over all
Europe: the Emperor for most of the time was merely a German
monarch. United Christendom was simply an ideal.

But about 1500 theory and practice began to get even more
dissimilar; and then the theory began to change. When Charles V
found himself, as no emperor had been for a long time, strong
enough to reassert the old idea of the Empire, that idea was too
antiquated to win him much support. Charles may have wanted
to build a new Holy Roman Empire of Christendom, but his
wars with Francis I of France, and his quarrels with the Pope,
are very like those of a modern nation state. The nation state, the

9

reality which corresponds to the theory of sovereignty, was in fact being born: though neither Henry VIII in England, nor Francis I of France, nor the German princes, had nearly as much control over their subjects' lives as our present government, or Napoleon, or even Louis XIV, yet they are a beginning.

One interesting consequence of this birth was in the field of political theory. The most formidable obstacle to the increasing power of the kings was the Papacy, which cherished the theory that since its power came from God it was, in the last resort, always the supreme authority. There was only one answer to this – kings had to claim that they too had their power from God. Hence the theory of the Divine Right of Kings. It was an old theory; the Emperors had developed it. But in the sixteenth century it received a new emphasis. Henry IV in France, James I in England, neither of them king by Papal sanction, both felt that they needed some such theoretical support.

The theory began as a weapon against the Papacy; but it was equally useful against subjects. In England the early Stuarts invoked it constantly against the claims of Parliament. Sovereignty being divine, neither Presbyterians, Scots, nor financiers need tell the king how to run Church and state. The answer to this was the theory of the social contract: that the monarch held his authority from an imagined (or even, some suggested, a real) contract between himself and his subjects. If he broke the contract, by ruling unjustly, for example, they could renounce their allegiance. Some writers, following the Jesuit Mariana, even suggested that they might kill him.

The real motives behind the execution of Charles I in 1649 may have been an unreasoning hatred of the Man of Blood; but the arguments used to defend it were quite reasonable and orthodox contract arguments. Milton wrote in *The Tenure of Kings and Magistrates*:

> It being thus manifest that the power of kings and magistrates is nothing else but what is only derivative,

transferred, and committed to them in trust from the people to the common good of them all, in whom the power yet remains fundamentally, and cannot be taken from them without a violation of their natural birthright ... then may the people, as oft as they shall judge it for the best, either choose him or reject him, retain him or depose him, though no tyrant, merely by the liberty and right of freeborn men to be governed as seems to them best.

*

Then there was religion. Here the birth of the modern world seems easy to find: was it not the Protestant Reformation? Certainly the importance of this was immeasurable, and certainly it got mixed up with the anti-Papalism of the new nation states — hence the 'Reformation' of Henry VIII who was a staunch Catholic, and hence also Luther's great success in Germany, where for an instant he united national feeling, hatred of Rome and its church, and the growing desire of the princes for power. As Luther thunders we can almost see a new Europe emerging.

Yet in some ways the Reformation belongs to the Middle Ages. Luther's mind is still that of a medieval theologian. And the one thing peculiarly modern about Church and state is probably religious toleration: that what each man believes is his own affair. This idea of course is as alien to Luther and Calvin (who burned Servetus with the approval of all Europe) as it is to the Roman Church. It was not born until the bloodshed resulting from warring religions in the same state suggested to cynical politicians like Henry IV the desirability of a compromise.

We can see this in Milton. No plea for liberty is more famous than his *Areopagitica*, written to attack the censorship of printing; yet even Milton can write:

I mean not tolerated Popery, and open superstition, which as it extirpates all religions and civil supremacies, so itself should be extirpate; ... that also which is impious or evil absolutely either against faith or manners no law can possibly permit.

Popery, being a political as much as a religious system, could hardly expect toleration in seventeenth-century England. But there is more to it than that. There are traces in this passage (and to this Milton owes some of his grave dignity) of 'the notion that it is one man's duty that another should be religious' which John Stuart Mill and other liberals found so abhorrent. Milton is clearly not pleading for the right to be wrong.

*

Most important, perhaps, there is the history of thought. Here there was a change in the seventeenth century far more important than the Renaissance: the break-up of the medieval synthesis. The Middle Ages had tried to unify knowledge in much the same way as it tried to unify Europe, but with more success. The work of St Thomas Aquinas and the Schoolmen is respected to-day in a way it was not for many centuries, since it has been seen not as a set of quibbles about angels sitting on the points of needles, but a courageous attempt to unite faith and reason in an ordered whole. The scholastic synthesis lasted a long time; it lasted through the Renaissance. You can find medieval astronomy in Milton:

> To the blank moon
> Her office they prescribed, to th'other five
> Their planetary motion and aspects
> In sextile, square, and trine and opposite,
> Of noxious efficacy, and when to join
> In synod unbenign, and taught the fixed
> Their influence malignant when to shower . . .

Medieval psychology is the very basis of Jonson's Humour plays: and there are medieval ideas of degree in Shakespeare:

> The Heavens themselves, the planets, and this centre
> Observe degree, priority, and place . . .

(Troilus and Cressida.)

To those who lived in the sixteenth and seventeenth centuries the most important intellectual movement seemed to be the new Platonism, or rather Neo-Platonism, since it stemmed from Plotinus and the Neo-Platonic philosophers of the third and fourth centuries A.D. The most famous English Platonists are those who worked at Cambridge in the mid seventeenth century, Cudworth, More, and Smith. But almost every leading thinker of the time has some traces of Platonism. Milton is impregnated with it.

But modern historians see something far more profound happening beneath the surface: the emergence of the lay mind, the scientific mind, the modern mind. The modern world was being born.

> And new philosophy calls all in doubt,
> The element of fire is quite put out;
> The sun is lost, and th'earth, and no man's wit
> Can well direct him where to look for it.
> And freely men confess that this world's spent,
> When in the planets and the firmament
> They seek so many new; then see that this
> Is crumbled out again to his atomies.
> 'Tis all in pieces, all coherence gone;
> All just supply, and all relation.
>
> (Donne: *An Anatomy of the World*.)

Donne noticed that something was happening; but it did not change his ways of thinking very deeply. Scientific and scholastic images jostle in his poetry, and either will usually do for his purpose. But different kinds of sensibility reacted differently.

The most famous apologist for the new scientific movement is Bacon. He wrote during the reign of James I, and died over thirty years before the Royal Society was founded; yet in his work we find all the enthusiasm for experiment, and suspicion of *a priori* thinking, that is associated with the scientific attitude. He has been called the *buccinator novi temporis* — the great publicist of the study of nature. He writes in the preface to the *De Augmentis*, his survey of all human learning:

> Those therefore who determine not to conjecture and guess, but to find out and know; not to invent fables and romances of worlds, but to look into and dissect the nature of this real world, must consult only things themselves.

As the century progressed, the tendency to think of all knowledge as drawn from experience grew, until eventually in Locke the scientific movement found an enthusiastic if not always consistent defender of the theoretical basis of its attitude. In the advanced intellectual circles of Restoration England we find that both the rationalist writings of men like Cudworth and the intuitive understanding of the 'inspired' Puritans are out of date: experiment is all.

But something else is needed for the growth of science — the emancipation from theology, the existence of each science in its own right, and not merely as a branch of a unified scheme of knowledge. The scheme which had served Europe for several centuries had been largely the creation of S. Thomas Aquinas; the seventeenth century witnessed the final discrediting of Thomism, so that thinkers as diverse as Hobbes, Milton, and Locke unite in their scorn of scholastic philosophy. Its replacement by what we can conveniently call a more secular way of thinking, however, raised difficulties.

Almost all the great seventeenth-century thinkers were religious, and none of them aimed to overthrow Christianity. But the rational and empirical standards towards which they were moving could not be applied to Christianity; and the question had to arise, What of Revelation? The answer lay in a dualism from which we have not yet completely recovered.

In its simplest form it is expressed by Bacon: 'It is therefore most wise soberly to render unto faith the things that are faith's.' This is a favourite idea in the seventeenth century: both Reason and Revelation should command our respect, but each in its own sphere, untouched by the other. Whether the aim is to protect religion from science or science from religion is a matter of individual emphasis; by the end of the century Reason (that is, philosophy and science) seemed to have become the more important. Locke wrote:

> Whatever God hath revealed is certainly true; no doubt can be made of it. This is the proper object of faith, *but whether it be a divine revelation or no, reason must judge.*

This is the point at which Christianity slides into Deism; often in the next century it is impossible to fix the dividing line:

> The spacious firmament on high,
> With all the blue ethereal sky,
> And spangled Heavens, a shining frame,
> Their Great Original proclaim . . .
>
> (Addison : *Hymn.*)

By the time we reach the age of Locke and Newton, Addison and Bolingbroke, it is clear that something has died in European culture. It is something far more complicated than can be shown in this short sketch; yet we might venture to give it a name, and call it Myth. A mythology is an attempt to unite and set forth all human knowledge, and it is more than that. It is an attempt to give that knowledge a narrative form, and so transpose it from the world of abstract reasoning to that of the imagination; and it is an attempt not by one individual, but by a whole society. The literary expression of a myth we call epic.

Paradise Lost is the last great epic in the language. When it was published the Royal Society was already formed, the Dissenters had left the Church, Locke and Dryden were writing. Yet it belongs almost wholly to the past, to the world that was going out. One illustration will suffice. Milton had met and admired Galileo. He appears in *Paradise Lost:*

> ... the moon, whose orb
> Through optic glass the Tuscan artist views
> At evening from the top of Fesole ...

He appears in *Areopagitica*, where Milton is very indignant at his silencing:

> I could recount what I have seen and heard in other countries, where this sort of inquisition tyrannizes; when I ... have been counted happy to be born in such a place of philosophic freedom, as they supposed England was, while they themselves did nothing but bemoan the servile condition into which learning amongst them was brought; ... There it was that I found and visited the famous Galileo, grown old a prisoner to the Inquisition for thinking in astronomy otherwise than the Franciscan and Dominican licensers thought.

Yet the true significance of what Galileo stood for seems unknown to Milton. We have seen that his cosmology is still medieval; and his attitude to scientific questioning is not that of Bacon or Newton or even Descartes, but what he puts into the mouth of the Archangel Raphael:

> ... the great Architect
> Did wisely to conceal and not divulge
> His secrets to be scanned by those who ought
> Rather admire ...

11

THE vast changes of the seventeenth century naturally affected men's sensibility, and these effects are seen in the literature of the time. Most obvious is the emergence of modern prose. The most famous passage in Sprat's *History of the Royal Society* describes how:

> They have exacted from all their members a close naked natural way of speaking; positive expressions, clear senses;

a native easiness; bringing all things as near to the mathe-
matical plainness as they can.

And Hobbes, though he despised the Royal Society, agreed with
them about the way to write. Among the causes of absurdity he
lists:

... the use of metaphors, tropes and other rhetorical
figures, instead of words proper ... In reckoning and
seeking of truth, such speeches are not to be admitted.

Here again, Milton clearly belongs to the world that is going out:

Methinks I see in my mind a noble and puissant nation
rousing herself like a strong man after sleep, and shaking her
invincible locks. Methinks I see her as an eagle mewing her
mighty youth, and kindling her undazzled eyes at the full
midday beam; purging and unscaling her long-abused
sight at the fountain itself of heavenly radiance.

The Royal Society would have found nothing to admire in the
magnificence of Milton's prose.

The seventeenth century was a Facing-Both-Ways age; perhaps no writer shows this more clearly than Sir Thomas Browne.
He himself believed that he belonged to the new world: 'in the
causes, nature and affections of the eclipses of the sun and moon,
there is most excellent speculation'. Though never a member of
the Royal Society, he was an enthusiastic scientist. He accepted
the contemporary dualism:

Thus there are two books from whence I collect my
Divinity; besides that written one of God, another of His
servant Nature, that universal and public manuscript, that
lies expansed unto the eyes of all.

Yet there was a point beyond which he would not go. For
Browne, the dualism is to protect faith rather than to protect
philosophy. He even enjoyed subjecting his reason to faith:

... and I think this is no vulgar part of Faith, to believe a
thing not only above but contrary to Reason, and against
the arguments of our proper senses.

And Browne's style: this is certainly not to the taste of the new movement:

> But man is a noble animal, splendid in ashes, and pompous in the grave, solemnizing Nativities and Deaths with equal lustre, nor omitting Ceremonies of bravery in the infamy of his nature.

This style deserves its fame: the magnificent rhythm, the assonance, the rolling Latinisms; and beneath them a vivid, astringent wit, a love of the concrete and the far-fetched ('Charles the Fifth can never hope to live within two Methuselahs of Hector'), an image that upsets the sonorous grandeur of a period in order to make it more impressive. In this way Browne reminds us of the metaphysical poets. He also shows how natural it was that the metaphysical style should have emerged during this transitional age.

Thanks chiefly to the insight of T. S. Eliot (though more perhaps to the similarity between our own age and the earlier seventeenth century) the metaphysical poets are better understood to-day than at any time since they wrote. We no longer find in Herbert 'a quaintness and carelessness of expression' or rebuke Donne for 'perplexing the mind of the fair sex with nice speculations of philosophy when he should engage their hearts, and entertain them with the softness of love'. The qualities peculiar to Donne, Herbert, Vaughan, and their contemporaries are not to be equated with their faults; to understand their poetry we must take the whole of it seriously.

Yet our enthusiasm for the metaphysicals is, in its way, as misleading as the lukewarmness of other times: it has led us into the natural human failing of remaking them in our own image. Some of the aims and opinions that have been fathered on Donne by his modern admirers would have puzzled and embarrassed him. Claims that he was really a sceptic, that his poetry reflects a tortured emotional state, that the metaphysicals use language like the symbolists, can all be shown to be false, or at least exaggerated:

yet to the twentieth-century reader these claims are part of the nature of metaphysical poetry. The reading of Donne, in fact, illustrates the complexity of the question of 'absolute' judgements in literature: the profound – and healthy – influence of metaphysical poetry on modern literature has resulted partly from a new understanding of it, and partly from a misunderstanding. The two can be – and are being – disentangled by historians of literature, but the effect on the modern mind cannot be undone. The following pages, like so much modern criticism, are a compromise: an attempt to see the subject through modern eyes, without making any assertions that are clearly unhistorical.

A good starting-point is Coleridge's epigram on Donne:

> With Donne, whose muse on dromedary trots,
> Wreathe iron pokers into true-love knots;
> Rhyme's sturdy cripple, fancy's maze and clue,
> Wit's forge and fire-blast, meaning's press and screw.

'Whose muse on dromedary trots': Donne's rhythms may, as his admirers claim, be masterly, but they are certainly not smooth. De Quincey suggested that his appalling ear came from having to listen constantly to such a concatenation of sounds as 'John Donne'. To-day we have changed our ideas on how his name was pronounced, and on the badness of his ear. A more profound explanation of his rhythms is the colloquial and dramatic interest in Donne and Herbert, the realism which reacted from the idealizing love poetry of the Elizabethans:

> Who says that fictions only and false hair
> Become a verse? Is there in truth no beauty? . . .

> Shepherds are honest people; let them sing:
> Riddle who list for me, and pull for Prime:
> I envy no man's nightingale or spring;
> Nor let them punish me with loss of rhyme,
> Who plainly say, My God, My King.

But trotting on a dromedary will not explain metaphysical poetry: it would exclude the impassioned Crashaw, or the stately Marvell. Nor need we take Herbert's plea for simplicity too literally; whatever the metaphysicals substituted for Elizabethan polish, it was not simplicity. Indeed the unusualness of their imagery is one of their most distinctive characteristics. The images startle because homely:

> ... That I might find
> What cordials make this curious broth,
> This broth of smells, that feeds and fats my mind.

or because far-fetched; Saint Mary Magdalen's eyes are

> ... two faithful fountains;
> Two walking baths, two weeping motions,
> Portable, and compendious oceans.

or because of the sudden revelation of a powerful, reasoning intellect:

> She's all states, and all Princes, I,
> Nothing else is.
> Princes do but play us; compared to this,
> All honour's mimic; all wealth alchemy.

This last suggests a further comment on Donne (and to a lesser extent on Marvell); the presence of a 'sequaciousness' in the thought: not merely a fondness for logical thinking, which underlies all Renaissance poetry, but a particularly brilliant, agile, and even saucy use of logic, which enables Donne to write of an ugly woman:

> All love is wonder; if we justly do
> Account her wonderful, why not lovely too?

T. S. Eliot saw all this when he propounded his theory – whose significance, of course, goes outside the field of literary criticism – of a split in sensibility: a dissociation between ratiocination and feeling which set in during the seventeenth century. 'Tennyson and Browning', he writes, 'are poets, and they think; but they do not feel their thought as immediately as the odour of a rose. A thought to Donne was an experience; it modified his sensibility.'

The theory is best illustrated by juxtaposition; and here is an example that may perhaps be added to those which Eliot gives:

> When with a sweet, though troubled look,
>   She first brake silence, saying, Dear friend,
>   O that our love might take no end,
> Or never had beginning took!
>
> I speak not this with a false heart,
>   (Wherewith his hand she gently strained)
>   Or that would change a love maintained
> With so much faith on either part . . .
>
> Only if love's fire with the breath
>   Of life be kindled, I doubt,
>   With our last air 'twill be breathed out,
> And quenched with the cold of death.
>
> (Lord Herbert of Cherbury's *Ode*.)

> . . . and hushed we sat
> As lovers to whom Time is whispering. . . .
> Well knew we that Life's greatest treasure lay
> With us, and of it was our talk. 'Ah yes!
> Love dies!' I said: I never thought it less.
> She yearned to me that sentence to unsay.
> Then when the fire domed blackening, I found
> Her cheek was salt against my kiss, and swift
> Up the sharp scale of sobs her breast did lift: —
> Now am I haunted by that taste! that sound!
>
> (Meredith: *Modern Love*.)

By the standards of his own age, Meredith is a more considerable poet than Lord Herbert. Yet in his poem quoted here there is something missing which is present in that of the older poet, something which it is tempting to call seriousness. This does not

mean that Lord Herbert is just philosophizing instead of writing
about people: taken in its context, the line in brackets is as
sympathetic and 'human' as anything in the Meredith. It means
rather that he takes his thinking seriously as thinking; he would
never use ideas as mere emotional counters in the way Meredith
uses the vast vaguenesses of Time and Life.

*

Where does Milton come in all this? The contrast between
Milton and the metaphysicals can certainly be driven too far. In
his youth Milton was something of a metaphysical. Professor
Grierson included the *Hymn on the Nativity* in his *Metaphysical
Lyrics and Poems; Upon the Circumcision* has suggestions of
Crashaw:

> Burn in your sighs, and borrow
> Seas wept for our deep sorrow.
> He who with all Heaven's heraldry whilere
> Entered the world, now bleeds to give us ease.

And Dr Leavis — no lover of Milton, and a great admirer of
Donne and Shakespeare — finds traces of their kind of writing in
Comus:

> And set to work millions of spinning worms,
> That in their green shops weave the smooth-haired silk.

But it is true that the general tendency of Milton's language was
away from the metaphysical. He declared himself a disciple of
Spenser; which, it has been pointed out, would be rather like
calling oneself a disciple of Tennyson to-day. He followed
neither of the main influences of the seventeenth century, Jonson
and Donne, but reverted to the less sophisticated poetry of an age
before. And at the same time he is seen by Eliot and other critics
to resemble the less sophisticated poetry of subsequent ages. Thus
there is a line through Spenser and Milton to Tennyson, a line
which misses out both of the two great 'schools' of Jonson and

Donne; and it is the excessive predominance of this non-ratio-cinative, non-witty poetry that Eliot deplored in his doctrine of the dissociation of sensibility: though he certainly seems to have exaggerated (as he himself has subsequently admitted) the influence of Milton in causing this.

Certainly 'meaning's press and screw' did not interest Milton much; he can enjoy writing poetry where for many lines meaning is subordinated more or less completely to sound:

> Him the Almighty Power
> Hurled headlong flaming from th'ethereal sky
> With hideous ruin and combustion down ·
> To bottomless perdition, there to dwell
> In adamantine chains and penal fire
> Who durst defy th'Omnipotent to arms.

That is magnificent, of course; yet the very readiness with which the 'of course' rises to our lips is betraying: the magnificence lies wholly in rhythm and sound; the epithets are wholly conventional.

There is a generalizing tendency in Milton which forms an obvious contrast to the sharp particularity of Donne. It is like the generalized painting of Poussin, and it increased as Milton got older. Laurence Binyon has pointed out that his rhythm and his imagery developed together: as the former became 'long drawn out', with effects spilling over the edge of many consecutive lines, so the pictures remind us more and more of a painter who subordinates details to the whole landscape, whose lines spill over the edge of the canvas. Mr Eliot complains that the imagery in *L'Allegro* is all general:

> While the ploughman near at hand,
> Whistles o'er the furrowed land,
> And the milkmaid singeth blithe,
> And the mower whets his scythe ...

There is detail ('whistles') – just enough of it. Yet on the whole Mr Eliot is obviously right, and this is poetry very different from

23

Shakespeare's. The more debatable point is whether it is disparagement to say that.

Milton is fond of mentioning philosophy in his poetry, as fond as Donne; but there is a difference. Donne writes:

> Have not all souls thought
> For many ages, that our body's wrought
> Of air and fire and other elements?
> And now they think of new ingredients,
> And one soul thinks one, and another way
> Another thinks, and 'tis an even lay.
>
> (Donne: *Second Anniversary*.)

Milton writes:

> How charming is divine philosophy!
> Not harsh and crabbed as dull fools suppose,
> But musical as is Apollo's lute,
> And a perpetual feast of nectared sweets.
>
> (*Comus*.)

Donne is philosophizing in his verse. In Milton (perhaps this is an unfairly obvious example) there is the beginning of a tendency to talk about philosophy.

Finally there is Milton's romanticism. This is a dangerous word for a critic to use, because it means so much. In one sense it refers simply to an interest in the suggestiveness of words as well as their statement; and this sense can apply as much to the metaphysicals as to anyone. When 'romantic' is used as a term of abuse it is usually commenting on the fact that nineteenth-century poets attached such importance to hints and suggestions that they forgot the hard core of meaning, so that many pages of Swinburne, for all their sound and fury, hardly seem to mean anything at all. Milton is certainly romantic in the first sense: one has only to think of the famous catalogues of proper names. And sometimes, in his early poetry, there are lines which seem to have little function except to suggest:

> Such sights as youthful poets dream,
> On summer eves, by haunted stream. . . .

> Through the soft silence of the listening night. . . .

These are lovely lines, and it is not Milton's fault that they resemble a lot of bad later poetry. But it is undeniable that there is no 'tough reasonableness beneath the slight lyric grace'.

One general comment can be made on Milton's language. In ideas, in general plan, in moral purpose, his poetry, we have seen, belongs to the past, to the world that was dying; but in execution it seems to belong to the future as much as to the past. Rhythm, metaphor, suggestion, imagery: Milton uses these in a way that sometimes reminds us more of the eighteenth and nineteenth centuries than of the sixteenth and seventeenth. Perhaps this is the explanation of his influence.

III

THE reign of the classics in European education is very impressive; only within the last hundred years have they been displaced. How far back does it go? The answer is: very nearly back to the classics themselves. By laying too much emphasis on the Renaissance, we tend to forget this. The very word Renaissance is misleading: you cannot have a rebirth unless there has been a death in between. There was, it is true, a vast unearthing, in the fifteenth century, of ancient authors whose work had long been lost; and the movement is important because it got mixed up with a new belief in the importance of man, the greatest creative outburst there has been in European painting, and the first tremulous beginnings of the new scientific movement. But it is quite false to imagine that the interest in the classics was something new. The Revival of Learning was the most typically medieval thing that the Middle Ages produced.

So when we find the seventeenth century dominated by the classics, we need not take this as evidence that it belongs to the modern world instead of the medieval, or that it belongs to the Renaissance instead of the modern world. Europe has always been dominated by the classics. It is true that science was at this time emancipating itself from Aristotle and learning to trust to experiment; but G. N. Clark points out that the classics gained a province for each one they lost, and the pseudo-Aristotelian doctrine of the unities was beginning its century of almost unchallenged rule over the theory and practice of drama. And this is the age in which the one supremely successful classical tragedy in English was written: *Samson Agonistes*.

To see how completely the classics ruled, we have only to look at Milton's small tract *On Education*. They are to form the basis of everything. The students are to hear 'some easy and delightful book of education' – Plutarch or Quintilian. They are to study agriculture – from Cato, Varro, and Columella; ethics – from Plato, Xenophon, and Cicero; and so on. And, of course, any dozen lines of Milton's own poetry will show us how completely the classics ran in his blood, how inevitable was the temptation to quote them.

Since they dominated education it was natural that they should dominate the arts. The Mannerist movement which followed the Renaissance meant among other things a rather stricter following of the ancients: thus anticipating the even greater strictness of the eighteenth century. As we move towards modern times we find the classics increasing their hold on the plastic arts, while at the same time they deaden the spirit which they had helped to quicken. But in the seventeenth century the Mannerist had given place to the Baroque, and the grip of the classics had momentarily loosened on architecture.

Of all literary forms, none haunted the minds of the sixteenth and seventeenth centuries more than the heroic poem; to demonstrate this it is only necessary to remember the popularity of the mock-heroic when the seventeenth century relaxed into the eighteenth. It was, like the unities, an idea which Europe got from the ancients via modern Italy. Homer and Vergil were the great models for heroic poets, more immediately Ariosto and Tasso (who influenced Milton deeply). Milton finally decided to write his great poem on a Christian theme; but it followed the classical epic in design: in beginning *in medias res*; in the Vergilian imagery (touched with Spenser) with which some books open:

> Now morn her rosy steps in th'Eastern clime
> Advancing, sowed the earth with orient pearl . . .

above all in the exordia, or introductions, to Books I, III, VII, and IX. They are simply classical invocations to the muse transposed into Christianity. The last two boast of this point:

> For thou art heavenly, she an empty dream.

And they boast of the change of subject:

> Sad task, yet argument
> Not less but more heroic than the wrath
> Of stern Achilles on his foe pursued
> Thrice fugitive about Troy wall; . . .
> Since first this subject for heroic song
> Pleased me long choosing and beginning late
> Not sedulous by nature to indite
> Wars, hitherto the only argument
> Heroic deemed . . .

Paradise Lost is very much a classical epic still; it is peopled with classical gods and themes, and every now and then the devils slide into identification with them. After the Council has dissolved in Book II, the infernal peers relax in very Greek occupations:

> – As at th'Olympian games, or Pythian fields.

Yet it is always the devils who are thus identified; and sometimes Milton is at pains to point out that the Greek names are simply an error by those who did not know their true infernal nature: as he does in the tale of Mulciber in Book I.

This attitude is a slight anticipation of what still to most readers comes as a shock in *Paradise Regained*: the utter rejection of classical learning. The case for Greek philosophy is put by Satan, but without the old enthusiasm of *Paradise Lost*:

> . . . teachers best
> Of moral prudence, with delight received
> In brief sententious precepts, while they treat
> Of fate and chance and change in human life;
> High actions, and high passions best describing.

This is tame when compared with the famous:

> Others apart sat on a Hill retired,
> In thoughts more elevate, and reasoned high,
> Of Providence, Foreknowledge, Will and Fate,
> Fixed Fate, free will, foreknowledge absolute,
> And found no end, in wandering mazes lost.

Christ, in his reply to Satan, is uncompromising: sophistry, materialism, humanism, are the marks of the classics; Hebrew literature is as beautiful as Greek, the Hebrew prophets finer than the Greek orators. Satan is abashed.

Whether this was Milton's own final verdict, or merely what he put into Christ's mouth, we cannot say; it probably does not matter much. The rejection, if it was his own, is not complete: when he came to write *Samson*, he modelled it on ancient tragedy, and wrote a preface to which Thomas Rhymer could not have objected. *Samson* is really an attempt to unite Greek and Christian cultures. In the preface, Milton defends ancient tragedy because 'the Apostle Paul himself thought it not unworthy to insert a verse of Euripides into the text of Holy Scripture'. So he chose a theme from the Old Testament, and mingled Greek rules with theological speculations. The result stands next to the Authorized Version as a completely successful union of all the elements that comprise our civilization.

M o s t fascinating, and most difficult to grasp, when one is study-
ing the culture of a period, are those critical terms which try to
cut across all the arts and define something which is common to
poetry, painting, and music. For the nineteenth century the term
'romantic' has become generally accepted as applying this way.
For the seventeenth, 'baroque' has long been used of architecture,
and almost as long of painting and sculpture. Lately many critics
have suggested that the word can be applied to the music of Bach,
and to a lot of seventeenth-century poetry, without losing all
meaning.

The best way to form an idea of the baroque, of course, is to
look at Bernini's St Teresa altarpiece at Rome, or the church of
Santa Maria della Salute at Venice; or at the paintings of Rubens
or Guido Reni or Tiepolo; or (for it is only the insular who
claim there is no baroque in England) at St Paul's cathedral.

The word has too complicated a meaning to be very susceptible
to accurate definition, but it is at least possible to suggest a few of
its attributes.

There is the state of mind, the emotion, which is portrayed.
This is extraordinarily private: ecstasy and agony, the most
intimate states there are, are the favourite themes of baroque
sculptors. Bernini's St Teresa (naturally a congenial subject: she
might almost be called a baroque saint) has been caught at the
most thrilling moment of a vision. But somehow, when the
sculptor has finished with it, it is no longer intimate: it has
become a public possession: the saints and martyrs who flaunt
their joys and griefs at us seem at their worst to be mere exhibi-
tionists.

The safest descriptions of baroque are probably those in terms
of its more formal elements; and these (metaphors apart) are, of
course, the only ones that can be commented on in baroque
architecture. Baroque is the predominance of the bold lines and

violent rhythms which as the sixteenth century closed began to appear in statues and church fronts, and which swirl round the church of San Carlo alle Quattro Fontane in Rome. In this sense the supreme baroque painter is probably Rubens; *The Rape of the Sabines* in the National Gallery, or *The Last Judgement*, among the Munich pictures, are full of crowded tumultuousness, energy, restless but rhythmical movement. What has happened to art when it becomes baroque is really an introduction of the dramatic and naturally the result is movement and contrast.

Everyone has remarked the baroque love of deception – the innumerable faked ceilings and false perspectives. There is the habit of sculpting not only a statue but also its setting, the pillars, the curtain, even the spectators, in an attempt to bridge the gap between the work of art and the world of the audience. Partly this is sheer delight in technical mastery, partly it is the energy of the baroque bursting through its very materials, so that enormous folds of curtaining must be made of stone. And partly, too, it is a conception of the overriding unity of a work of art (which Pevsner suggestively compares to the philosophy of Descartes), so that each piece of ornament owes its first duty to the whole, and only a secondary duty to its medium.

Then there is the strong sexual element in the baroque. Sometimes, as in Bernini's saints, it is open and unconcealed: more often it is implied in the portrayal of ecstasy. Borromini's façade of San Carlo is one of the most sensual things in architecture. But however sensuous, however materialistic, baroque is essentially a religious art: when divorced from its spiritual elements (heavy, emotionalistic, crude, but still spiritual) it turns into the light worldly pleasantry of the rococo. Whoever doubts that Guido Reni or Caravaggio is a religious painter has only to compare them with Boucher.

Now most of these qualities can be found in English poetry of the seventeenth century; and significantly, they are most pronounced in two Catholic poets, Southwell and Crashaw. Some of

This unswerving anti-Catholicism is interesting; for Milton travelled a long way from his early Puritanism, and part of the journey was in the direction of Rome.

Doctrinally, Milton may never have been a very ardent Calvinist; certainly in his last years he believed passionately in free will. In *Paradise Lost*, God is almost embarrassingly fulsome in his assurances that man is free:

> . . . no decree of mine
> Concurring to necessitate his fall,
> Or touch with lightest moment of impulse
> His free will, to her own inclining left
> In even scale . . .

On one doctrinal point, Milton moved even further. His long theological work, the *De Doctrina Christiana*, shows him to be an Arian; though in *Paradise Lost*, remembering perhaps that an epic is a social possession, he lays no emphasis on this personal aberration.

Milton was a true Puritan in his attitude towards culture; and that was an attitude he did not lose.

The Puritan achievement is one of the paradoxes of English culture. Sometimes Puritanism seems narrow, brutal, unlovely: the funereal Sundays, the broken glass of our cathedrals. Yet some of our greatest and most passionate literature is impregnated with it. Indeed, the passion seems to be generated by the tension set up between a deep sensitivity and love of this world on the one hand, and the instinct of renunciation on the other. Something of this tension is in Milton's sonnet, that most dignified of all invitations to dinner:

> Lawrence of virtuous father virtuous son,
> Now that the fields are dank, and ways are mire,
> Where shall we sometimes meet, and by the fire
> Help waste a sullen day; what may be won
> From the hard season gaining . . .
> He who of those delights can judge, and spare
> To interpose them oft, is not unwise.

B 2

There is no dissatisfaction with the pleasures in those last two lines. In rhythm and wording they are the perfect expression of the proud Puritan instinct of restraint, and fear of abandonment.

There is a lot to dislike in English Puritanism. Its hatred of pleasure is sometimes almost fanatical: Cromwell's major-generals, agents of virtue and despotism, seem to have deserved all the hatred they received. Its popularity among the commercial classes was remarked in the seventeenth century, and the connexion between the two, the responsibility of Puritanism for the spirit of money-making, has been discussed by Max Weber and a host of followers. From Wycliff to Lawrence the evangelical strain is strong in English culture; and so is the materialism that counts the Kingdom of Heaven in gold and jewels, and gives its heroes costly funerals.

Most hateful of all about Puritanism is the pride of its humility. George Fox wrote in his journal:

> I came and sate me down on the top of a rock, for the word of the Lord came to me, and I must go and sit down upon the rock in the mountain as Christ had done before.

Few men have ever had less of the milk of human kindness than Fox. If you can shift the responsibility for all your actions to the spirit of God within you, it doesn't matter what you do: there is no need for kindness: it is not your fault if the spirit keeps urging you into the limelight. It is amazing that this man should be the founder of the humble and well-named Society of Friends.

All these things are true; and yet the Puritan spirit is one of our glories. It is the spirit of Bunyan, humble and not proud of his humility; of Wordsworth, who has learned

> To look on Nature, not as in the hour
> Of thoughtless youth, but hearing oftentimes
> The still sad music of humanity . . .

of Marvell, whose most playful verse never loses the deep seriousness of its religious undertones; of Wesley, challenging the individual soul to find its own salvation; and above all of Milton, disillusioned and lonely, having learned the bitterest of all his lessons, that he was to serve God the way God chose, the way that brought no glory, and writing on this theme the greatest of his sonnets:

> Doth God exact day-labour, light denied,
> I fondly ask; but Patience to prevent
> That murmur, soon replies, God doth not need
> Either man's work or his own gifts, who best
> Bear his mild yoke, they serve him best. His state
> Is kingly. Thousands at his bidding speed
> And post o'er land and ocean without rest:
> They also serve who only stand and wait.

VI

IN a violent century, England did not escape her revolution. Like all revolutions, its causes and chances are complex – at one moment it seems amazing that war did not come in 1628, at another equally amazing that it came at all. Three main strands can be disentangled from the complications: the religious, the constitutional, the economic.

The religious quarrel was at first quite straightforward: the King's party was the Church party, the rebels were the Puritans, and their natural allies were the Presbyterian Scots, whom Charles had offended by trying to impose episcopacy on them. There was no dissension in the anti-Arminian ranks. But after a taste of Presbyterianism, the innumerable sects who made up Cromwell's New Model Army decided that 'New presbyter is but old priest writ large'. So there came the strange realignment of the second civil war. Charles, whose defeat in battle had in some ways strengthened his position, was being courted by all parties, and he eventually gave himself to the Scots, and they fought the army and were beaten; or, in religious terms, the Independents defeated the alliance of Anglican and Presbyterian.

The Independents were on the extreme left. They believed in
toleration: they had to, being composed of Baptists, Congrega-
tionalists, Fifth Monarchy Men, and dozens of other sects of
every size and opinion. They were uncompromisingly against
bishops and ritual, of course, and the famous Parliament of Saints
of 1653 came within an inch of abolishing tithes.

Then there was the political quarrel. Victorian historians,
eager to spot the emergence of English liberty – and liberalism –
probably paid too much attention to this. When we read the
literature of the time, the overwhelming impression is that most
men thought they were fighting about religion, not politics.
Certainly it was foolish to call the personal rule of Charles from
1629 to 1640 the Eleven Years' Tyranny: years which Evelyn
called 'that blessed halcyon time in England'. Yet in Parliament,
and among the classes represented in Parliament, there were continual grievances, magnificently set forth in the Petition of Right
of 1628, which the Whig historians placed with Magna Charta,
the Bill of Rights, and the Reform Act, the great documents of
English liberty. The Petition demanded: no extra-Parliamentary
taxation; no arbitrary imprisonment; no billeting; soldiers not to
be tried for ordinary offences by martial law – Parliament did not
love the king's army. The Long Parliament, during the first nine
months of its existence, set these and other grievances to rights;
thereafter things got so hectic that they were rather lost sight of.

And finally there may have been an economic quarrel. I say
'may have been', because Professor Trevelyan would have it that
'the causes of the war were not economic, and were only indi-
rectly social'. Directly opposed to this is the Marxist view that the
Civil War was England's bourgeois revolution – the most important step in the change-over from a medieval to a capitalist
economy. By this view it was a revolution of the commercial and
industrial classes, and its effect was the transference of political
power to the already economically preponderant class represented by the City of London. Purged of the over-simplifications

which Marxism is always prone to, this view has a lot to recommend it. Certainly it is true that Charles and his ministers were very interested, during the 'Eleven Years Tyranny', in the welfare of the working classes, and by their interference in industry they helped to alienate those who directed it. It is equally true that the City of London was more strongly anti-Royalist than any other part of England, and this cannot be mere coincidence. Under the Commonwealth, too, commercial interests began to influence foreign policy more strongly than ever before – as in the famous Navigation Acts of 1651. Marxists make a great deal of the sale and transference of landed property, but here the Civil War may not have made much difference to a process that had gone on for more than a century already.

But among the ranks of the rebels many ideologists besides the bourgeois are to be found. Peasants and workers could not have been very grateful for Charles' protection, since all the revolutionary social creeds of Levellers, Diggers, and the rest appear in the Parliamentary ranks. The Marxists have an answer to this too, of course; here it is, expressed by Marx:

> At this stage the proletarians do not fight their enemies, but the enemies of their enemies, the remnants of absolute monarchy, the landowners, etc. . . .

In other words, while the bourgeoisie are still overthrowing feudalism, the proletariat are still within their ranks. This argument may or may not be true; but some such argument is needed to explain the violent opinions that appear in the New Model Army.

And this leads us to the strangest thing about the Civil War: our extraordinary difficulty in judging its importance. To contemporaries, its events and ideas seemed both less and more important than they do to us. Less important, because we tend to forget how little everyday life was upset by the war – the improvement and maintenance of country houses went on undiminished, the courts were interrupted for only a few months; we are long before the days of total war. But also more important; because there are some things about the war that we tend to be over-confident about understanding.

In the five or ten years from 1645 onwards the Army spewed forth almost every revolutionary doctrine of the next three centuries, political, religious, social. Of course there was an idle army made up of enthusiasts, one of the best breeding grounds for dangerous doctrines, but somehow that does not seem explanation enough. The cautious historian, anxious to avoid anachronisms, is often tempted to believe in some apocalyptic theory that the war touched the amorphous raw material of history, and that responded with a vision of the future. Certainly it is strange to meet universal suffrage, religious toleration, and economic communism in the air, and then not meet them again for over a century. Lilburne and his Levellers are remarkable enough; there must have been others even further to the left. One Leveller manifesto disclaimed any intention to 'level men's estates, destroy property, or make all things common'. Why did they feel it necessary to say that?

No nation can stand extremism and fanaticism of more than a certain intensity, especially where it is Puritan and ascetic. Cromwell might have reconciled England to the death of Charles and the change of religion, but only because of the strong conservative elements in his character: opportunist in politics, right-wing on social questions, he was not on the extreme left even in religion, since he would not disestablish the Church. When he died it became clearer and clearer that everyone was tired of revolution, especially since many of the aims of the revolution were now safely achieved. So Charles II came back, and England has seldom been more pleased and more unanimous.

*

In 1640 Milton was thirty-two: at the height of his powers. The first tremors of the rebellion excited him wildly, and made him hurry home from Italy: 'I saw that a way was opening for the establishment of real liberty; that the foundation was laying for the deliverance of man from the yoke of slavery'. He had long been an opponent of episcopacy – ever since he had decided not to go into the Church. He was still a believer in the monarchy, and in the 1641 pamphlet *Of Reformation in England*, he attacked the 'no bishop, no king' argument by claiming that royal dignity, 'whose towering and steadfast height rests upon the unmovable foundations of justice and heroic virtue', did not need the support of episcopacy. Social and economic questions do not seem to have interested him.

The story of the next ten years in Milton's life is that of a steady interest in politics, and a gradual move towards the left. His first 'deviation' was the 1643 pamphlet in favour of divorce, which brought an outcry from all sides, not least the Presbyterians. Milton's reputation has never quite recovered from the rapidity with which this pamphlet followed after his own unfortunate marriage. Not long afterwards, as the gap widened between Parliament and the Army, between Presbyterianism and Independency, Milton found himself on the latter side. He lent his pen to the small band of fanatics who executed the king in 1649. Under the Commonwealth he became Secretary for Foreign Tongues, and this, and his studies, cost him his sight. Even after his blindness he worked steadily at his post until the verge of the Restoration; then, by some miracle, he escaped all punishment, and was allowed to retire into private life.

Long before 1660 his disillusion had begun. During the 1640's one party after another had disappointed him, and in the end even Cromwell, still refusing to disestablish the Church, had fallen in his eyes. Milton by 1660 is a bitter and disillusioned man; a deep pessimism runs through his last three great poems; and to it they owe some of their greatness. He had lost the wild hopes of his youth, and discovered Original Sin in his fellow men. His was the profound disillusion that only an ardent idealist can know, and it was so profoundly Christian that it never falls into mere despair. His tremendous sense of isolation finds its way into much of his later work, especially of course into the portrait of Samson. There is a lot of Milton himself, too, in the splendid figure of Abdiel in Book V of *Paradise Lost;* the eulogy on him is certainly what Milton would have liked for his own, but he was too fine an artist to write of himself so unblushingly:

> So spake the seraph Abdiel, faithful found
> Among the faithless, faithful only he;
> Among innumerable false, unmoved,
> Unshaken, unseduced, unterrified
> His loyalty he kept, his love, his zeal;
> Nor number nor example with him wrought
> To swerve from truth, or change his constant mind
> Though single.

Chronological Table

1603   (Accession of James I.)

1608   *John Milton born in Cheapside, son of a scrivener.*

1611   (Authorized Version of the Bible.)

1616   (Death of Shakespeare.)
       About this time, Milton went to St Paul's School.

1625   (Death of James I. Accession of Charles.)
       Milton entered Christ's College, Cambridge.
       'On The Death of a Fair Infant' *written.*

1626   (Death of Bacon.)

1628   (Petition of Right.)

1629   ('Eleven Years' Tyranny' of Charles I begins.)
       Milton takes his B.A.
       'Nativity Hymn' *written.*

1631   (Death of Donne.)
       'L'Allegro' *and* 'Il Penseroso' *written* (?).

1632   *Milton takes his M.A. Leaves Cambridge.*
       *Next six years at his father's house in Horton, Bucks, reading and
         studying.*
       *Second folio edition of Shakespeare's works published, containing
         Milton's sonnet.*

1633   (Donne's collected poems published.)
       (George Herbert's *The Temple* published.)
       'Arcades' *acted.*

1634   'Comus' *acted.*

1637   (Hampden's ship money case.)
       'Comus' *published.*
       Edward King drowned.

1638   *Obituary volume to Edward King published, including* 'Lycidas.'
       *Milton sets out on foreign tour. Next sixteen months spent chiefly
         in Italy.*

1639   (Hostilities begin between Charles I and the Scots.)

1640   (Short Parliament summoned: April.)

(Long Parliament summoned: November.)

(Death of Rubens.)

1641   (Execution of Strafford.)

Milton's first pamphlet, 'Of Reformation', published. Followed by many further pamphlets on ecclesiastical and political affairs during the next twenty years.

1642   (Civil War begins.)

(Closing of the Theatres.)

(Sir Thomas Browne's *Religio Medici* published.)

Milton's disastrous marriage to Mary Powell.

1643   *Milton's 'Doctrine and Discipline of Divorce.'*

1644   *Milton's 'Areopagitica'.*

1645   (Execution of Laud.)

(Battle of Naseby: final defeat of the Royalists.)

'Poems of Mr John Milton' *published.*

1646   (Charles surrenders.)

(Crashaw's *Steps to the Temple* and *Delights of the Muses*.)

1648   (Second Civil War.)

('Pride's Purge': Parliament cleared of Presbyterians.)

1649   (Execution of Charles I.)

Milton's 'Tenure of Kings and Magistrates'.

Milton secretary for Foreign Tongues to the Commonwealth.

1650   (Marvell's *Horatian Ode upon Cromwell's Return from Ireland*.)

1651   (Hobbes' *Leviathan* published.)

1652   (Crashaw's *Carmen Deo Nostro* published.)

Milton becomes totally blind.

1653   (Cromwell's dissolution of 'the Rump': the last remnant of the Long Parliament.)

1656   *Milton marries Katherine Woodcock (subject of 'Methought I saw my late espoused saint'.)*

1657   *Andrew Marvell becomes Milton's assistant in his official work.*

1658   (Death of Cromwell.)

Death of Milton's second wife.

1659   (Dryden's first publication: *On the Death of Oliver Cromwell*.)

1660   (Restoration of Charles II.)

(Royal Society founded.)

Milton retires into obscurity

44

1663   *Milton marries Elizabeth Minshull.*
1665   (Great Plague of London.)
       (Death of Poussin.)
1666   (Great Fire of London.)
1667   (Bernini's portico of St Peter's, Rome, built.)
       'Paradise Lost' *published.*
1671   'Paradise Regained' *and* 'Samson Agonistes' *published.*
1673   'Poems, &c, upon Several Occasions, by Mr John Milton'
       published: containing several political poems not in the 1645
       edition.
1674   *Death of Milton.*

On the Morning of Christ's Nativity

I

This is the month, and this the happy morn
Wherein the Son of Heaven's eternal King,
Of wedded maid and virgin mother born,
Our great redemption from above did bring;
For so the holy sages once did sing,
  That he our deadly forfeit should release,
And with his Father work us a perpetual peace.

II

That glorious form, that light unsufferable,
And that far-beaming blaze of majesty,
Wherewith he wont at Heaven's high council-table
To sit the midst of Trinal Unity,
He laid aside; and here with us to be,
  Forsook the courts of everlasting day,
And chose with us a darksome house of mortal clay.

III

Say Heavenly Muse, shall not thy sacred vein
Afford a present to the Infant God?
Hast thou no verse, no hymn, or solemn strain,
To welcome him to this his new abode,
Now while the heaven, by the sun's team untrod,
  Hath took no print of the approaching light,
And all the spangled host keep watch in squadrons bright?

IV

See how from far upon the eastern road
The star-led wizards haste with odours sweet.
O run, prevent them with thy humble ode,
And lay it lowly at his blessed feet;
Have thou the honour first thy Lord to greet.
    And join thy voice unto the Angel quire
From out his secret altar toucht with hallowed fire.

THE HYMN

I

IT was the winter wild,
While the Heaven-born child
All meanly wrapt in the rude manger lies;
Nature in awe to him
Had doffed her gaudy trim,
With her great Master so to sympathize:
It was no season then for her
To wanton with the sun, her lusty paramour.

II

Only with speeches fair
She woos the gentle air
To hide her guilty front with innocent snow,
And on her naked shame,
Pollute with sinful blame,
The saintly veil of maiden white to throw,
Confounded that her Maker's eyes
Should look so near upon her foul deformities.

III

But he her fears to cease,
Sent down the meek-eyed Peace,
She crowned with olive green came softly sliding
Down through the turning sphere
His ready harbinger,
With turtle wing the amorous clouds dividing,
And waving wide her myrtle wand
She strikes a universal peace through sea and land.

IV

No war, or battle's sound
Was heard the World around,
The idle spear and shield were high up hung;
The hooked chariot stood
Unstained with hostile blood,
The trumpet spake not to the armed throng;
And kings sat still with awful eye,
As if they surely knew their sovereign lord was by.

V

But peaceful was the night
Wherein the Prince of light
His reign of peace upon the earth began.
The winds with wonder whist
Smoothly the waters kissed,
Whispering new joys to the mild Ocean,
Who now hath quite forgot to rave,
While birds of calm sit brooding on the charmed wave.

VI

The stars with deep amaze
Stand fixed in steadfast gaze,
Bending one way their precious influence,
And will not take their flight,
For all the morning light,
Or Lucifer that often warned them thence;
But in their glimmering orbs did glow,
Until their Lord himself bespake and bid them go.

VII

And though the shady gloom
Had given day her room,
The sun himself withheld his wonted speed,
And hid his head for shame,
As his inferior flame
The new enlightened world no more should need;
He saw a greater sun appear
Than his bright throne or burning axletree could bear.

VIII

The shepherds on the lawn,
Or ere the point of dawn,
Sat simply chatting in a rustic row;
Full little thought they then
That the mighty Pan
Was kindly come to live with them below;
Perhaps their loves, or else their sheep,
Was all that did their silly thoughts so busy keep.

50

IX

When such music sweet
Their hearts and ears did greet,
As never was by mortal finger strook,
Divinely-warbled voice
Answering the stringed noise,
As all their souls in blissful rapture took.
The air such pleasure loth to lose
With thousand echoes still prolongs each heavenly close.

X

Nature that heard such sound
Beneath the hollow round
Of Cynthia's seat the airy region thrilling,
Now was almost won
To think her part was done
And that her reign had here its last fulfilling;
She knew such harmony alone
Could hold all Heaven and Earth in happier union.

XI

At last surrounds their sight
A globe of circular light,
That with long beams the shame-faced night arrayed;
The helmed cherubim
And sworded seraphim
Are seen in glittering ranks with wings displayed,
Harping in loud and solemn quire
With unexpressive notes to Heaven's new-born heir.

XII

Such music (as 'tis said)
Before was never made,
But when of old the sons of morning sung,
While the Creator great
His constellations set,
And the well-balanced world on hinges hung,
And cast the dark foundations deep,
And bid the weltering waves their oozy channel keep.

XIII

Ring out ye crystal spheres,
Once bless our human ears
(If ye have power to touch our senses so)
And let your silver chime
Move in melodious time;
And let the bass of Heaven's deep organ blow,
And with your ninefold harmony
Make up full consort to th'angelic symphony.

XIV

For if such holy song
Enwrap our fancy long,
Time will run back, and fetch the age of gold,
And speckled vanity
Will sicken soon and die,
And leprous sin will melt from earthly mould,
And Hell itself will pass away,
And leave her dolorous mansions to the peering day.

XV

Yea truth and justice then
Will down return to men,
Orbed in a rainbow; and like glories wearing
Mercy will sit between
Throned in celestial sheen,
With radiant feet the tissued clouds down steering,
And Heaven as at some festival,
Will open wide the gates of her high palace hall.

XVI

But wisest Fate says no,
This must not yet be so,
The babe lies yet in smiling infancy,
That on the bitter cross
Must redeem our loss;
So both himself and us to glorify.
Yet first to those ychained in sleep
The wakeful trump of doom must thunder through the deep,

XVII

With such a horrid clang
As on Mount Sinai rang
While the red fire and smouldering clouds out brake.
The aged earth aghast
With terror of that blast
Shall from the surface to the centre shake,
When at the world's last session
The dreadful Judge in middle air shall spread his throne.

XVIII

And then at last our bliss
Full and perfect is,
But now begins; for from this happy day
Th'old dragon underground
In straiter limits bound,
Not half so far casts his usurped sway,
And wrath to see his kingdom fail
Swindges the scaly horror of his folded tail.

XIX

The oracles are dumb,
No voice or hideous hum
Runs through the arched roof in words deceiving.
Apollo from his shrine
Can no more divine,
With hollow shriek the steep of Delphos leaving.
No nightly trance, or breathed spell,
Inspires the pale-eyed priest from the prophetic cell.

XX

The lonely mountains o'er,
And the resounding shore,
A voice of weeping heard and loud lament;
From haunted spring, and dale
Edged with poplar pale,
The parting genius is with sighing sent;
With flower-inwoven tresses torn
The nymphs in twilight shade of tangled thickets mourn.

XXI

In consecrated earth,
And on the holy hearth,
The Lars and Lemures moan with midnight plaint,
In urns and altars round,
A drear and dying sound
Affrights the flamens at their service quaint;
And the chill marble seems to sweat,
While each peculiar power forgoes his wonted seat.

XXII

Peor and Baalim
Forsake their temples dim,
With that twice-battered god of Palestine,
And mooned Ashtaroth,
Heaven's queen and mother both,
Now sits not girt with tapers' holy shine;
The Libyc Hammon shrinks his horn,
In vain the Tyrian maids their wounded Thammuz mourn.

XXIII

And sullen Moloch fled,
Hath left in shadows dread
His burning idol all of blackest hue;
In vain with cymbals' ring
They call the grisly king,
In dismal dance about the furnace blue;
The brutish gods of Nile as fast,
Isis and Orus and the dog Anubis haste.

XXIV

Nor is Osiris seen
In Memphian grove or green,
Trampling the unshowered grass with lowings loud;
Nor can he be at rest
Within his sacred chest,
Nought but profoundest Hell can be his shroud;
In vain with timbrelled anthems dark
The sable-stoled sorcerers bear his worshipped ark.

XXV

He feels from Juda's land
The dreaded infant's hand,
The rays of Bethlehem blind his dusky eyn;
Nor all the gods beside
Longer dare abide,
Not Typhon huge ending in snaky twine.
Our babe to show his godhead true
Can in his swaddling bands control the damned crew.

XXVI

So when the sun in bed,
Curtained with cloudy red,
Pillows his chin upon an orient wave,
The flocking shadows pale
Troop to th'infernal jail,
Each fettered ghost slips to his several grave,
And the yellow-skirted fays
Fly after the night-steeds, leaving their moon-loved maze.

XXVII

But see the Virgin blest
Hath laid her babe to rest.
Time is our tedious song should here have ending;
Heaven's youngest teemed star
Hath fixed her polished car,
Her sleeping Lord with handmaid lamp attending;
And all about the courtly stable
Bright-harnessed angels sit in order serviceable.

On the Death of a Fair Infant
Dying of a Cough

I

O FAIREST flower no sooner blown but blasted,
Soft silken primrose fading timelessly,
Summer's chief honour if thou hadst outlasted
Bleak winter's force that made thy blossom dry;
For he being amorous on that lovely dye
    That did thy cheek envermeil, thought to kiss
But killed alas, and then bewailed his fatal bliss.

II

For since grim Aquilo, his charioteer,
By boisterous rape th'Athenian damsel got,
He thought it touched his deity full near,
If likewise he some fair one wedded not,
Thereby to wipe away th'infamous blot,
    Of long-uncoupled bed, and childless eld,
Which 'mongst the wanton gods a foul reproach was held.

III

So mounting up in icy-pearled car,
Through middle empire of the freezing air
He wandered long, till thee he spied from far,
There ended was his quest, there ceased his care.
Down he descended from his snow-soft chair,
    But all unwares with his cold-kind embrace
Unhoused thy virgin soul from her fair biding place.

IV

Yet art thou not inglorious in thy fate;
For so Apollo, with unweeting hand
Whilom did slay his dearly-loved mate
Young Hyacinth born on Eurotas' strand,
Young Hyacinth the pride of Spartan land;
   But then transformed him to a purple flower
Alack that so to change thee winter hath no power.

V

Yet can I not persuade me thou art dead
Or that thy corse corrupts in earth's dark womb,
Or that thy beauties lie in wormy bed,
Hid from the world in a low delved tomb;
Could Heaven for pity thee so strictly doom?
   Oh no! for something in thy face did shine
Above mortality that shewed thou wast divine.

VI

Resolve me then Oh soul most surely blest
(If so it be that thou these plaints dost hear)
Tell me bright spirit where e'er thou hoverest
Whether above that high first-moving sphere
Or in the Elysian fields (if such there were.)
   Oh say me true if thou wert mortal wight
And why from us so quickly thou didst take thy flight.

VII

Wert thou some star which from the ruined roof
Of shaked Olympus by mischance didst fall;

Which careful Jove in nature's true behoof
Took up, and in fit place did reinstall?
Or did of late earth's sons besiege the wall
    Of sheeny Heaven, and thou some goddess fled
Amongst us here below to hide thy nectared head.

VIII

Or wert thou that just maid who once before
Forsook the hated earth, O tell me sooth
And cam'st again to visit us once more?
Or wert thou Mercy that sweet smiling youth!
Or that crowned matron sage white-robed Truth?
    Or any other of that heavenly brood
Let down in cloudy throne to do the world some good.

IX

Or wert thou of the golden winged host,
Who having clad thy self in human weed,
To earth from thy prefixed seat didst post,
And after short abode fly back with speed,
As if to shew what creatures Heaven doth breed,
    Thereby to set the hearts of men on fire
To scorn the sordid world, and unto Heaven aspire.

X

But oh why didst thou not stay here below
To bless us with thy heaven-loved innocence,
To slake his wrath whom sin hath made our foe
To turn swift-rushing black perdition hence,
Or drive away the slaughtering pestilence,
    To stand 'twixt us and our deserved smart?
But thou canst best perform that office where thou art.

XI

Then thou the mother of so sweet a child
Her false imagined loss cease to lament,
And wisely learn to curb thy sorrows wild;
Think what a present thou to God hast sent,
And render him with patience what he lent;
   This if thou do he will an offspring give,
That till the world's last-end shall make thy name to live.

On Time

FLY envious Time, till thou run out thy race,
Call on the lazy leaden-stepping hours,
Whose speed is but the heavy plummet's pace;
And glut thyself with what thy womb devours,
Which is no more than what is false and vain,
And merely mortal dross;
So little is our loss,
So little is thy gain.
For when as each thing bad thou hast entombed,
And last of all, thy greedy self consumed,
Then long eternity shall greet our bliss
With an individual kiss;
And joy shall overtake us as a flood,
When everything that is sincerely good
And perfectly divine,
With truth, and peace, and love shall ever shine
About the supreme throne
Of him t'whose happy-making sight alone,
When once our heavenly-guided soul shall climb,
Then all this earthly grossness quit,
Attired with stars, we shall for ever sit,
   Triumphing over death, and chance, and thee O Time.

Upon the Circumcision

Ye flaming powers, and winged warriors bright,
That erst with music, and triumphant song
First heard by happy watchful shepherds' ear,
So sweetly sung your joy the clouds along
Through the soft silence of the listening night;
Now mourn, and if sad share with us to bear
Your fiery essence can distill no tear,
Burn in your sighs, and borrow
Seas wept from our deep sorrow.
He who with all Heaven's heraldry whilere
Entered the world, now bleeds to give us ease.
Alas, how soon our sin.
     Sore doth begin
          His infancy to seize!

O more exceeding love or law more just?
Just law indeed, but more exceeding love!
For we by rightful doom remediless
Were lost in death, till he that dwelt above
High throned in secret bliss, for us frail dust
Emptied his glory, even to nakedness;
And that great covenant which we still transgress
Entirely satisfied,
And the full wrath beside
Of vengeful justice bore for our excess,
And seals obedience first with wounding smart
This day, but O ere long
Huge pangs and strong
     Will pierce more near his heart.

At a Solemn Music

BLEST pair of sirens, pledges of Heaven's joy,
Sphere-born harmonious sisters, Voice and Verse,
Wed your divine sounds, and mixed power employ
Dead things with inbreathed sense able to pierce,
And to our high-raised phantasy present
That undisturbed song of pure consent,
Aye sung before the sapphire-coloured throne
To him that sits thereon
With saintly shout and solemn jubilee,
Where the bright seraphim in burning row
Their loud up-lifted angel trumpets blow,
And the cherubic host in thousand quires
Touch their immortal harps of golden wires,
With those just spirits that wear victorious palms,
Hymns devout and holy psalms
Singing everlastingly;
That we on earth with undiscording voice
May rightly answer that melodious noise;
As once we did, till disproportioned sin
Jarred against nature's chime, and with harsh din
Broke the fair music that all creatures made
To their great Lord, whose love their motion swayed
In perfect diapason, whilst they stood
In first obedience, and their state of good.
O may we soon again renew that song,
And keep in tune with Heaven, till God ere long
To his celestial consort us unite,
To live with him, and sing in endless morn of light.

On Shakespeare

WHAT needs my Shakespeare for his honoured bones
The labour of an age in piled stones,
Or that his hallowed relics should be hid
Under a star-ypointing pyramid?
Dear son of memory, great heir of fame,
What needst thou such weak witness of thy name?
Thou in our wonder and astonishment
Hast built thyself a livelong monument.
For whilst to th'shame of slow-endeavouring art,
Thy easy numbers flow, and that each heart
Hath from the leaves of thy unvalued book
Those Delphic lines with deep impression took,
Then thou our fancy of itself bereaving,
Dost make us marble with too much conceiving;
And so sepulchered in such pomp dost lie,
That kings for such a tomb would wish to die.

L'Allegro

Hence loathed Melancholy
   Of Cerberus and blackest midnight born,
In Stygian cave forlorn
   'Mongst horrid shapes, and shrieks, and sights unholy,
Find out some uncouth cell,
   Where brooding darkness spreads his jealous wings,
And the night-raven sings;
   There under ebon shades, and low-browed rocks,
As ragged as thy locks,
   In dark Cimmerian desert ever dwell.
But come thou goddess fair and free,
In Heaven yclept Euphrosyne,
And by men, heart-easing Mirth,
Whom lovely Venus at a birth
With two sister Graces more
To ivy-crowned Bacchus bore;
Or whether (as some sager sing)
The frolic wind that breathes the spring,
Zephir with Aurora playing,
As he met her once a-Maying,
There on beds of violets blue,
And fresh blown roses washed in dew,
Filled her with thee a daughter fair,
So bucksome, blithe and debonair.
Haste thee nymph, and bring with thee
Jest and youthful Jollity,
Quips and Cranks, and wanton Wiles,
Nods, and Becks, and wreathed Smiles,
Such as hang on Hebe's cheek,
And love to live in dimple sleek;

Sport that wrinkled Care derides,
And Laughter, holding both his sides.
Come, and trip it as ye go
On the light fantastic toe,
And in thy right hand lead with thee,
The mountain nymph, sweet Liberty;
And if I give thee honour due,
Mirth, admit me of thy crew
To live with her and live with thee,
In unreproved pleasures free;
To hear the lark begin his flight,
And singing startle the dull night,
From his watch-tower in the skies,
Till the dappled dawn doth rise;
Then to come in spite of sorrow,
And at my window bid good-morrow,
Through the sweet-briar, or the vine,
Or the twisted eglantine.
While the cock with lively din,
Scatters the rear of darkness thin,
And to the stack, or the barn door,
Stoutly struts his dames before;
Oft listening how the hounds and horn
Cheerly rouse the slumbering morn,
From the side of some hoar hill,
Through the high wood echoing shrill.
Sometime walking not unseen
By hedgerow elms, on hillocks green,
Right against the eastern gate,
Where the great sun begins his state,
Robed in flames, and amber light,
The clouds in thousand liveries dight.
While the plowman near at hand,
Whistles o'er the furrowed land,

And the milkmaid singeth blithe,
And the mower whets his scythe,
And every shepherd tells his tale,
Under the hawthorn in the dale.
Straight mine eye hath caught new pleasures
Whilst the landscape round it measures,
Russet lawns, and fallows gray,
Where the nibbling flocks do stray,
Mountains on whose barren breast
The labouring clouds do often rest:
Meadows trim with daisies pied,
Shallow brooks, and rivers wide.
Towers, and battlements it sees
Bosomed high in tufted trees,
Where perhaps some beauty lies,
The cynosure of neighbouring eyes.
Hard by, a cottage chimney smokes,
From betwixt two aged oaks,
Where Corydon and Thyrsis met,
Are at their savoury dinner set
Of herbs, and other country messes,
Which the neat-handed Phillis dresses;
And then in haste her bower she leaves,
With Thestylis to bind the sheaves;
Or if the earlier season lead
To the tanned haycock in the mead,
Sometimes with secure delight
The upland hamlets will invite,
When the merry bells ring round
And the jocund rebecks sound
To many a youth and many a maid,
Dancing in the chequered shade;
And young and old come forth to play
On a sunshine holiday,

Till the livelong daylight fail;
Then to the spicy nut-brown ale,
With stories told of many a feat,
How fairy Mab the junkets ate;
She was pinched and pulled she said,
And he by Friar's lantern led .
Tells how the drudging goblin sweat
To earn his cream-bowl, duly set,
When in one night, ere glimpse of morn,
His shadowy flail hath threshed the corn
That ten day-labourers could not end,
Then lies him down, the lubber fiend,
And stretched out all the chimney's length,
Basks at the fire his hairy strength;
And crop-full out of doors he flings
Ere the first cock his matin rings.
Thus done the tales, to bed they creep,
By whispering winds soon lulled asleep.
Towered cities please us then,
And the busy hum of men,
Where throngs of knights and barons bold,
In weeds of peace high triumphs hold,
With store of ladies, whose bright eyes
Rain influence, and judge the prize
Of wit, or arms, while both contend
To win her grace, whom all commend.
There let Hymen oft appear
In saffron robe, with taper clear,
And pomp, and feast, and revelry,
With mask, and antique pageantry,
Such sights as youthful poets dream
On summer eves by haunted stream.
Then to the well-trod stage anon,
If Jonson's learned sock be on,

Or sweetest Shakespeare fancy's child,
Warble his native wood-notes wild,
And ever against eating cares
Lap me in soft Lydian airs,
Married to immortal verse
Such as the meeting soul may pierce
In notes, with many a winding bout
Of linked sweetness long drawn out,
With wanton heed, and giddy cunning,
The melting voice through mazes running;
Untwisting all the chains that tie
The hidden soul of harmony.
That Orpheus' self may heave his head
From golden slumber on a bed
Of heaped Elysian flowers, and hear
Such strains as would have won the ear
Of Pluto, to have quite set free
His half regained Eurydice.
These delights, if thou canst give,
Mirth with thee I mean to live.

Il Penseroso

HENCE vain, deluding joys,
   The brood of folly without father bred.
How little you bestead,
   Or fill the fixed mind with all your toys;
Dwell in some idle brain,
   And fancies fond with gaudy shapes possess,
As thick and numberless
   As the gay motes that people the sunbeams,
Or likest hovering dreams,
   The fickle pensioners of Morpheus' train.
But hail thou goddess, sage and holy,
Hail, divinest Melancholy,
Whose saintly visage is too bright
To hit the sense of human sight;
And therefore to our weaker view,
O'erlaid with black staid Wisdom's hue.
Black, but such as in esteem,
Prince Memnon's sister might beseem,
Or that starred Ethiope queen that strove
To set her beauty's praise above
The sea nymphs, and their powers offended.
Yet thou art higher far descended.
Thee bright-haired Vesta long of yore
To solitary Saturn bore;
His daughter she; (in Saturn's reign
Such mixture was not held a stain).
Oft in glimmering bowers and glades
He met her, and in secret shades
Of woody Ida's inmost grove,
While yet there was no fear of Jove.

Come pensive nun, devout and pure,
Sober, steadfast, and demure,
All in a robe of darkest grain,
Flowing with majestic train,
And sable stole of cypress lawn
Over thy decent shoulders drawn.
Come, but keep thy wonted state,
With even step and musing gait,
And looks commercing with the skies,
Thy rapt soul sitting in thine eyes:
There held in holy passion still,
Forget thyself to marble, till
With a sad leaden downward cast,
Thou fix them on the earth as fast.
And join with thee calm Peace, and Quiet,
Spare Fast, that oft with gods doth diet,
And hears the Muses in a ring,
Aye round about Jove's altar sing.
And add to these retired Leisure,
That in trim gardens takes his pleasure;
But first, and chiefest, with thee bring,
Him that yon soars on golden wing,
Guiding the fiery-wheeled throne,
The cherub Contemplation,
And the mute silence hist along
'Less Philomel will deign a song,
In her sweetest, saddest plight,
Smoothing the rugged brow of night,
While Cynthia checks her dragon yoke
Gently o'er th'accustomed oak;
Sweet bird that shunn'st the noise of folly,
Most musical, most melancholy!
Thee chauntress oft the woods among,
I woo to hear thy even-song;

And missing thee, I walk unseen
On the dry smooth-shaven green,
To behold the wandering moon,
Riding near her highest noon,
Like one that had been led astray
Through the Heaven's wide pathless way;
And oft as if her head she bowed,
Stooping through a fleecy cloud.
Oft on a plat of rising ground,
I hear the far-off curfew sound,
Over some wide-watered shore,
Swinging slow with sullen roar;
Or if the air will not permit,
Some still removed place will fit,
Where glowing embers through the room
Teach light to counterfeit a gloom.
Far from all resort of mirth,
Save the cricket on the hearth,
Or the bellman's drowsy charm,
To bless the doors from nightly harm;
Or let my lamp at midnight hour
Be seen in some high lonely tower,
Where I may oft out-watch the Bear,
With thrice great Hermes, or unsphere
The spirit of Plato to unfold
What worlds, or what vast regions hold
The immortal mind that hath forsook
Her mansion in this fleshly nook;
And of those demons that are found
In fire, air, flood, or under ground,
Whose power hath a true consent
With planet, or with element.
Some time let gorgeous tragedy
In sceptred pall come sweeping by,

Presenting Thebes, or Pelops' line,
Or the tale of Troy divine.
Or what (though rare) of later age
Ennobled hath the buskined stage.
But O sad virgin, that thy power
Might raise Musaeus from his bower,
Or bid the soul of Orpheus sing
Such notes as warbled to the string,
Drew iron tears down Pluto's cheek,
And made Hell grant what love did seek.
Or call up him that left half told
The story of Cambuscan bold,
Of Camball, and of Algarsife,
And who had Canacee to wife,
That owned the virtuous ring and glass,
And of the wondrous horse of brass,
On which the Tartar king did ride;
And if ought else great bards beside
In sage and solemn tunes have sung,
Of tourneys and of trophies hung;
Of forests and enchantments drear,
Where more is meant than meets the ear.
Thus night oft see me in thy pale career,
Till civil-suited morn appear,
Not tricked and frounced as she was wont,
With the Attic boy to hunt,
But kerchiefed in a comely cloud,
While rocking winds are piping loud,
Or ushered with a shower still,
When the gust hath blown his fill,
Ending on the rustling leaves,
With minute drops from off the eaves.
And when the sun begins to fling
His flaring beams, me goddess bring

To arched walks of twilight groves,
And shadows brown that Sylvan loves
Of pine, or monumental oak,
Where the rude axe with heaved stroke,
Was never heard the nymphs to daunt,
Or fright them from their hallowed haunt.
There in close covert by some brook,
Where no profaner eye may look,
Hide me from day's garish eye,
While the bee with honeyed thigh,
That at her flowery work doth sing,
And the waters murmuring
With such consort as they keep,
Entice the dewy-feathered sleep;
And let some strange mysterious dream,
Wave at his wings in airy stream,
Of lively portraiture displayed,
Softly on my eyelids laid.
And as I wake, sweet music breathe
Above, about, or underneath,
Sent by some spirit to mortals good,
Or th'unseen genius of the wood.
But let my due feet never fail
To walk the studious cloisters pale,
And love the high embowed roof,
With antique pillars massy proof,
And storied windows richly dight,
Casting a dim religious light.
There let the pealing organ blow,
To the full-voiced quire below,
In service high, and anthems clear,
As may with sweetness, through mine ear,
Dissolve me into ecstasies,
And bring all heaven before mine eyes.

And may at last my weary age
Find out the peaceful hermitage,
The hairy gown and mossy cell,
Where I may sit and rightly spell
Of every star that Heaven doth show,
And every herb that sips the dew
Till old experience do attain
To something like prophetic strain.
These pleasures Melancholy give,
And I with thee will choose to live.

Sonnets

O NIGHTINGALE, that on yon bloomy spray
    Warbl'st at eve, when all the woods are still,
    Thou with fresh hope the lover's heart dost fill,
    While the jolly hours lead on propitious May;
Thy liquid notes that close the eye of day,
    First heard before the shallow cuckoo's bill
    Portend success in love; O if Jove's will
    Have linked that amorous power to thy soft lay,
Now timely sing, ere the rude bird of hate
    Foretell my hopeless doom in some grove nigh:
    As thou from year to year hast sung too late
For my relief; yet hadst no reason why,
    Whether the Muse, or Love, call thee his mate,
    Both them I serve, and of their train am I.

How soon hath time, the subtle thief of youth,
    Stoln on his wing my three and twentieth year!
    My hasting days fly on with full career,
    But my late spring no bud or blossom shew'th.
Perhaps my semblance might deceive the truth,
    That I to manhood am arrived so near,
    And inward ripeness doth much less appear,
    That some more timely-happy spirits indu'th.
Yet be it less or more, or soon or slow,
    It shall be still in strictest measure even,
    To that same lot, however mean or high,

77

Toward which time leads me, and the will of Heaven;
    All is, if I have grace to use it so,
    As ever in my great Taskmaster's eye.

VIII

When the Assault was Intended to the City

Captain or colonel, or knight in arms,
    Whose chance on these defenceless doors may seize,
    If ever deed of honour did thee please,
    Guard them, and him within protect from harms.
He can requite thee, for he knows the charms
    That call fame on such gentle acts as these,
    And he can spread thy name o'er lands and seas,
    Whatever clime the sun's bright circle warms.
Lift not thy spear against the Muses' bower:
    The great Emathian conqueror bid spare
    The house of Pindarus, when temple and tower
Went to the ground: And the repeated air
    Of sad Electra's poet had the power
    To save th'Athenian walls from ruin bare.

XI

On the Detraction which Followed upon my Writing Certain Treatises

A book was writ of late called Tetrachordon;
    And woven close, both matter, form and style;
    The subject new; it walked the town awhile,
    Numbering good intellects; now seldom pored on.
Cries the stall-reader, bless us! what a word on
    A title page is this! and some in file
    Stand spelling false, while one might walk to Mile-
    End Green. Why is it harder Sirs than Gordon,

Colkitto, or Macdonnel, or Galasp?
   Those rugged names to our like mouths grow sleek
   That would have made Quintilian stare and gasp.
Thy age, like ours, O soul of Sir John Cheek,
   Hated not learning worse than toad or asp;
   When thou taught'st Cambridge, and King Edward Greek.

On the New Forcers of Conscience under the Long Parliament

Because you have thrown off your prelate lord,
   And with stiff vows renounced his liturgy,
   To seize the widowed whore Plurality
   From them whose sin ye envied, not abhorred,
Dare ye for this adjure the civil sword
   To force our consciences that Christ set free,
   And ride us with a classic hierarchy
   Taught ye by mere A.S. and Rutherford?
Men whose life, learning, faith and pure intent
   Would have been held in high esteem with Paul
   Must now be named and printed heretics
By shallow Edwards and Scotch what d'ye call:
   But we do hope to find out all your tricks,
   Your plots and packings worse than those of Trent,
                That so the Parliament
May with their wholesome and preventive shears
Clip your phylacteries, though baulk your ears,
                And succour our just fears
When they shall read this clearly in your charge
New presbyter is but old priest writ large.

XV

On the Late Massacre in Piedmont

Avenge O Lord thy slaughtered saints, whose bones
    Lie scattered on the Alpine mountains cold,
    Ev'n them who kept thy truth so pure of old
    When all our fathers worshipped stocks and stones,
Forget not: in thy book record their groans
    Who were thy sheep and in their ancient fold
    Slain by the bloody Piemontese that rolled
    Mother with infant down the rocks. Their moans
The vales redoubled to the hills, and they
    To Heaven. Their martyred blood and ashes sow
    O'er all th'Italian fields where still doth sway
The triple tyrant: that from these may grow
    A hundredfold, who having learnt thy way
    Early may fly the Babylonian woe.

XVI

When I consider how my light is spent
    Ere half my days in this dark world and wide,
    And that one talent which is death to hide,
    Lodged with me useless, though my soul more bent
To serve therewith my Maker, and present
    My true account, lest he returning chide,
    Doth God exact day-labour, light denied?
    I fondly ask; but Patience to prevent
That murmur, soon replies, God doth not need
    Either man's work or his own gifts; who best
    Bear his mild yoke, they serve him best. His state
Is kingly. Thousands at his bidding speed
    And post o'er land and ocean without rest:
    They also serve who only stand and wait.

XVII

Lawrence of virtuous father virtuous son,
    Now that the fields are dank, and ways are mire,
    Where shall we sometimes meet, and by the fire
    Help waste a sullen day; what may be won
From the hard season gaining: time will run
    On smoother, till Favonius re-inspire
    The frozen earth; and clothe in fresh attire
    The lily and rose, that neither sowed nor spun.
What neat repast shall feast us, light and choice,
    Of Attic taste, with wine, whence we may rise
    To hear the lute well touched, or artful voice
Warble immortal notes and Tuscan air?
    He who of those delights can judge, and spare
    To interpose them oft, is not unwise.

XVIII

Cyriack, whose grandsire on the Royal Bench
    Of British Themis, with no mean applause
    Pronounced and in his volumes taught our laws,
    Which others at their bar so often wrench:
To-day deep thoughts resolve with me to drench.
    In mirth, that after no repenting draws;
    Let Euclid rest, and Archimedes pause,
    And what the Swede intend, and what the French.
To measure life, learn thou betimes, and know
    Toward solid good what leads the nearest way;
    For other things mild Heaven a time ordains,
And disapproves that care, though wise in show,
    That with superfluous burden loads the day,
    And when God sends a cheerful hour, refrains.

XIX

Methought I saw my late espoused saint
   Brought to me like Alcestis from the grave,
   Whom Jove's great son to her glad husband gave,
   Rescued from death by force though pale and faint.
Mine as whom washed from spot of child-bed taint,
   Purification in the old law did save,
   And such, as yet once more I trust to have
   Full sight of her in Heaven without restraint,
Came vested all in white, pure as her mind.
   Her face was veiled, yet to my fancied sight,
   Love, sweetness, goodness, in her person shined
So clear, as in no face with more delight.
   But O as to embrace me she enclined
   I waked, she fled, and day brought back my night.

To the Lord General Cromwell

Cromwell, our chief of men, who through a cloud
   Not of war only, but detractions rude,
   Guided by faith and matchless fortitude
   To peace and truth thy glorious way hast ploughed,
And on the neck of crowned fortune proud
   Hast reared God's trophies, and his work pursued,
   While Darwen stream with blood of Scots imbrued,
   And Dunbar field resounds thy praises loud,
And Worcester's laureate wreath; yet much remains
   To conquer still; peace hath her victories
   No less renowned than war; new foes arise
Threatening to bind our souls with secular chains:
   Help us to save free conscience from the paw
   Of hireling wolves whose gospel is their maw.

To Mr Cyriack Skinner upon his Blindness

Cyriack, this three years' day these eyes, though clear
   To outward view, of blemish or of spot,
   Bereft of light their seeing have forgot,
   Nor to their idle orbs doth sight appear
Of sun or moon or star throughout the year,
   Or man or woman. Yet I argue not
   Against Heaven's hand or will, nor bate a jot
   Of heart or hope; but still bear up and steer
Right onward. What supports me, dost thou ask?
   The conscience, friend, to have lost them overplied
   In liberty's defence, my noble task,
Of which all Europe talks from side to side.
   This thought might lead me through the world's vain mask
   Content though blind, had I no better guide.

The Fifth Ode of Horace – Book I

Quis multa gracilis te puer in rosa, rendered almost word for word without rhyme according to the Latin measure, as near as the language will permit.

WHAT slender youth bedewed with liquid odours
Courts thee on roses in some pleasant cave,
   Pyrrha for whom bind'st thou
   In wreathes thy golden hair,
Plain in thy neatness; O how oft shall he
On faith and changed Gods complain: and seas
   Rough with black winds and storms
   Unwonted shall admire:
Who now enjoys thee credulous, all gold,
Who always vacant, always amiable
   Hopes thee; of flattering gales
   Unmindful. Hapless they
To whom thou untried seem'st fair. Me in my vowed
Picture the sacred wall declares t'have hung
   My dank and dropping weeds
   To the stern god of sea.

Songs from Arcades

I

O'ER the smooth enamelled green
Where no print of step hath been,
    Follow me as I sing,
    And touch the warbled string.
Under the shady roof
Of branching elm star-proof,
    Follow me,
I will bring you where she sits
Clad in splendour as befits
    Her deity.
Such a rural queen
All Arcadia hath not seen.

II

Nymphs and shepherds dance no more
    By sandy Ladon's lilied banks.
On old Lyaeus or Cyllene hoar,
    Trip no more in twilight ranks,
Though Erymanth your loss deplore,
    A better soil shall give ye thanks.
From the stony Maenalus,
Bring your flocks, and live with us,
Here ye shall have greater grace,
To serve the lady of this place.
    Though Syrinx your Pan's mistress were,
    Yet Syrinx well might wait on her.
        Such a rural queen
    All Arcadia hath not seen.

Lycidas

In this monody the author bewails a learned friend, unfortunately drowned in his passage from Chester on the Irish seas, 1637. And by occasion foretells the ruin of our corrupted clergy, then in their height.

YET once more, O ye laurels, and once more
Ye myrtles brown, with ivy never sere,
I come to pluck your berries harsh and crude,
And with forced fingers rude,
Shatter your leaves before the mellowing year.
Bitter constraint, and sad occasion dear,
Compels me to disturb your season due:
For Lycidas is dead, dead ere his prime
Young Lycidas, and hath not left his peer:
Who would not sing for Lycidas? He knew
Himself to sing, and build the lofty rhyme.
He must not float upon his watery bier
Unwept, and welter to the parching wind,
Without the meed of some melodious tear.
    Begin then, sisters of the sacred well
That from beneath the seat of Jove doth spring,
Begin, and somewhat loudly sweep the string.
Hence with denial vain, and coy excuse;
So may some gentle Muse
With lucky words favour my destined urn,
And as he passes turn,
And bid fair peace be to my sable shroud.
For we were nursed upon the self-same hill,
Fed the same flock, by fountain, shade, and rill.
    Together both, ere the high lawns appeared
Under the opening eyelids of the morn,
We drove afield, and both together heard

What time the gray-fly winds her sultry horn,
Battening our flocks with the fresh dews of night,
Oft till the star that rose at evening bright
Toward Heaven's descent had sloped his westering wheel.
Meanwhile the rural ditties were not mute,
Tempered to th'oaten flute;
Rough satyrs danced, and fauns with cloven heel,
From the glad sound would not be absent long,
And old Damoetas loved to hear our song.

But O the heavy change, now thou art gone,
Now thou art gone, and never must return!
Thee shepherd, thee the woods, and desert caves,
With wild thyme and the gadding vine o'ergrown,
And all their echoes mourn.
The willows, and the hazel copses green,
Shall now no more be seen,
Fanning their joyous leaves to thy soft lays.
As killing as the canker to the rose,
Or taint-worm to the weanling herds that graze,
Or frost to flowers that their gay wardrobe wear,
When first the white thorn blows;
Such, Lycidas, thy loss to shepherds' ear.

Where were ye nymphs when the remorseless deep
Closed o'er the head of your loved Lycidas?
For neither were ye playing on the steep,
Where your old Bards, the famous Druids lie,
Nor on the shaggy top of Mona high,
Nor yet where Deva spreads her wizard stream:
Ay me, I fondly dream!
Had ye been there – for what could that have done?
What could the Muse herself that Orpheus bore,
The Muse herself, for her inchanting son
Whom universal nature did lament,
When by the rout that made the hideous roar,

His gory visage down the stream was sent,
Down the swift Hebrus to the Lesbian shore.
　　Alas! What boots it with uncessant care
To tend the homely slighted shepherd's trade,
And strictly meditate the thankless muse,
Were it not better done as others use,
To sport with Amaryllis in the shade,
Or with the tangles of Neaera's hair?
Fame is the spur that the clear spirit doth raise
(That last infirmity of noble mind)
To scorn delights, and live laborious days;
But the fair guerdon when we hope to find,
And think to burst out into sudden blaze,
Comes the blind Fury with th'abhorred shears,
And slits the thin spun life. But not the praise,
Phoebus replied, and touched my trembling ears:
Fame is no plant that grows on mortal soil,
Nor in the glistering foil
Set off to th'world, nor in broad rumour lies,
But lives and spreads aloft by those pure eyes,
And perfect witness of all-judging Jove;
As he pronounces lastly on each deed,
Of so much fame in Heaven expect thy meed.
　　O fountain Arethuse, and thou honoured flood,
Smooth-sliding Mincius, crowned with vocal reeds,
That strain I heard was of a higher mood.
But now my oat proceeds,
And listens to the herald of the sea
That came in Neptune's plea;
He asked the waves, and asked the felon winds,
What hard mishap hath doomed this gentle swain?
And questioned every gust of rugged wings
That blows from off each beaked promontory;
They knew not of his story;

And sage Hippotades their answer brings,
That not a blast was from his dungeon strayed,
The air was calm, and on the level brine,
Sleek Panope with all her sisters played.
It was that fatal and perfidious bark
Built in th'eclipse, and rigged with curses dark,
That sunk so low that sacred head of thine.

    Next Camus, reverend sire, went footing slow,
His mantle hairy, and his bonnet sedge,
Inwrought with figures dim, and on the edge
Like to that sanguine flower inscribed with woe.
Ah! who hath reft (quoth he) my dearest pledge?
Last came and last did go,
The pilot of the Galilean lake,
Two massy keys he bore of metals twain,
(The golden opes, the iron shuts amain)
He shook his mitred locks, and stern bespake,
How well could I have spared for thee, young swain,
Enow of such as for their bellies' sake,
Creep and intrude, and climb into the fold?
Of other care they little reckoning make,
Than how to scramble at the shearers' feast,
And shove away the worthy bidden guest.
Blind mouths! That scarce themselves know how to hold
A sheep-hook, or have learned ought else the least
That to the faithful herdsman's art belongs!
What recks it them? What need they? They are sped;
And when they list, their lean and flashy songs
Grate on their scrannel pipes of wretched straw;
The hungry sheep look up, and are not fed,
But swoln with wind, and the rank mist they draw,
Rot inwardly, and foul contagion spread:
Besides what the grim wolf with privy paw
Daily devours apace, and nothing said.

But that two-handed engine at the door,
Stands ready to smite once, and smite no more.
   Return Alpheus, the dread voice is past,
That shrunk thy streams; return Sicilian muse,
And call the vales, and bid them hither cast
Their bells, and flowerets of a thousand hues.
Ye valleys low where the mild whispers use,
Of shades and wanton winds, and gushing brooks,
On whose fresh lap the swart star sparely looks,
Throw hither all your quaint enamelled eyes,
That on the green turf suck the honeyed showers,
And purple all the ground with vernal flowers.
Bring the rathe primrose that forsaken dies.
The tufted crow-toe, and pale jessamine,
The white pink, and the pansy freaked with jet,
The glowing violet.
The musk-rose, and the well attired woodbine.
With cowslips wan that hang the pensive head,
And every flower that sad embroidery wears:
Bid amaranthus all his beauty shed,
And daffadillies fill their cups with tears,
To strew the laureate hearse where Lycid lies.
For so to interpose a little ease,
Let our frail thoughts dally with false surmise.
Ay me! Whilst thee the shores, and sounding seas
Wash far away, where e'er thy bones are hurled,
Whether beyond the stormy Hebrides,
Where thou perhaps under the whelming tide
Visit'st the bottom of the monstrous world;
Or whether thou to our moist vows denied,
Sleepst by the fable of Bellerus old,
Where the great vision of the guarded mount
Looks toward Namancos and Bayona's hold;
Look homeward angel now, and melt with ruth.

And, O ye dolphins, waft the hapless youth.
    Weep no more, woeful shepherds, weep no more,
For Lycidas your sorrow is not dead,
Sunk though he be beneath the watery floor,
So sinks the day-star in the ocean bed,
And yet anon repairs his drooping head,
And tricks his beams, and with new spangled ore,
Flames in the forehead of the morning sky:
So Lycidas sunk low, but mounted high,
Through the dear might of him that walked the waves,
Where other groves, and other streams along,
With nectar pure his oozy locks he laves,
And hears the unexpressive nuptial song,
In the blest kingdoms meek of joy and love.
There entertain him all the saints above,
In solemn troops and sweet societies
That sing, and singing in their glory move,
And wipe the tears for ever from his eyes.
Now Lycidas the shepherds weep no more;
Henceforth thou art the genius of the shore,
In thy large recompense, and shalt be good
To all that wander in that perilous flood.
    Thus sang the uncouth swain to th'oaks and rills,
While the still morn went out with sandals gray;
He touched the tender stops of various quills,
With eager thought warbling his Doric lay:
And now the sun had stretched out all the hills,
And now was dropt into the western bay;
At last he rose, and twitched his mantle blue:
To-morrow to fresh woods, and pastures new.

Comus

A MASQUE

presented at Ludlow Castle, 1634; on Michaelmas night, before the Right Honourable John Earl of Bridgewater, Viscount Brackly, Lord President of Wales, and one of His Majesty's most honourable Privy Council

*

Eheu quid volui misero mihi! floribus austrum Perditus . . .

*

THE PERSONS

The attendant spirit, afterwards in the habit of Thyrsis
Comus with his crew
The lady
First Brother
Second Brother
Sabrina, the nymph

*

The first scene discovers a wild wood. The attendant spirit descends or enters.

BEFORE the starry threshold of Jove's court
My mansion is, where those immortal shapes
Of bright aerial spirits live insphered
In regions mild of calm and serene air,
Above the smoke and stir of this dim spot,
Which men call earth, and with low-thoughted care
Confined, and pestered in this pin-fold here,
Strive to keep up a frail and feverish being,
Unmindful of the crown that virtue gives
After this mortal change, to her true servants
Amongst the enthroned gods on sainted seats.

92

Yet some there be that by due steps aspire
To lay their just hands on that golden key
That opes the palace of eternity:
To such my errand is, and but for such,
I would not soil these pure ambrosial weeds,
With the rank vapours of this sin-worn mould.
    But to my task. Neptune besides the sway
Of every salt flood, and each ebbing stream,
Took in by lot 'twixt high and nether Jove,
Imperial rule of all the sea-girt isles
That like to rich and various gems inlay
The unadorned bosom of the deep,
Which he to grace his tributary gods
By course commits to several government,
And gives them leave to wear their sapphire crowns,
And wield their little tridents. But this isle,
The greatest and the best of all the main,
He quarters to his blue-haired deities,
And all this tract that fronts the falling sun
A noble peer of mickle trust and power
Has in his charge, with tempered awe to guide
An old and haughty nation, proud in arms:
Where his fair offspring nursed in princely lore,
Are coming to attend their father's state,
And new-entrusted sceptre, but their way
Lies through the perplexed paths of this drear wood,
The nodding horror of whose shady brows
Threats the forlorn and wandering passenger.
And here their tender age might suffer peril,
But that by quick command from sovereign Jove
I was dispatched for their defence and guard;
And listen why, for I will tell ye now
What never yet was heard in tale or song
From old, or modern bard in hall, or bower.

Bacchus that first from out the purple grape,
Crushed the sweet poison of misused wine,
After the Tuscan mariners transformed,
Coasting the Tyrrhene shore, as the winds listed,
On Circe's island fell (who knows not Circe
The daughter of the sun? Whose charmed cup
Whoever tasted, lost his upright shape,
And downward fell into a grovelling swine).
This nymph that gazed upon his clustering locks,
With ivy berries wreathed, and his blithe youth,
Had by him, ere he parted thence, a son
Much like his father, but his mother more,
Whom therefore she brought up and Comus named,
Who ripe, and frolic of his full grown age,
Roving the Celtic and Iberian fields,
At last betakes him to this ominous wood,
And in thick shelter of black shades imbowered,
Excels his mother at her mighty art,
Offering to every weary traveller
His orient liquor in a crystal glass,
To quench the drouth of Phoebus, which as they taste
(For most do taste through fond intemperate thirst)
Soon as the potion works, their human countenance,
Th'express resemblance of the gods, is changed
Into some brutish form of wolf, or bear,
Or ounce, or tiger, hog, or bearded goat,
All other parts remaining as they were,
And they, so perfect is their misery,
Not once perceive their foul disfigurement,
But boast themselves more comely than before,
And all their friends, and native home forget
To roll with pleasure in a sensual sty.
Therefore when any favoured of high Jove,
Chances to pass through this adventurous glade,

Swift as the sparkle of a glancing star,
I shoot from Heaven to give him safe convoy,
As now I do: But first I must put off
These my sky robes spun out of Iris' woof,
And take the weeds and likeness of a swain,
That to the service of this house belongs,
Who with his soft pipe, and smooth-dittied song,
Well knows to still the wild winds when they roar,
And hush the waving woods; nor of less faith,
And in this office of his mountain watch,
Likeliest, and nearest to the present aid
Of this occasion. But I hear the tread
Of hateful steps, I must be viewless now.

Comus enters with a charming rod in one hand, his glass in the other; with him a rout of monsters, headed like sundry sorts of wild beasts, but otherwise like men and women, their apparel glistening. They come in making a riotous and unruly noise, with torches in their hands.

Comus. The star that bids the shepherd fold,
Now the top of Heaven doth hold,
And the gilded car of day,
His glowing axle doth allay
In the steep Atlantic stream,
And the slope sun his upward beam
Shoots against the dusky pole,
Pacing towards the other goal
Of his chamber in the east.
Meanwhile welcome Joy, and Feast,
Midnight shout, and revelry,
Tipsy dance, and Jollity.
Braid your locks with rosy twine
Dropping odours, dropping wine.
Rigour now is gone to bed,
And Advice with scrupulous head,

Strict Age, and sour Severity,
With their grave saws in slumber lie.
We that are of purer fire
Imitate the starry quire,
Who in their nightly watchful spheres,
Lead in swift round the months and years.
The sounds and seas with all their finny drove
Now to the moon in wavering Morris move,
And on the tawny sands and shelves,
Trip the pert fairies and the dapper elves;
By dimpled brook, and fountain brim,
The wood-nymphs decked with daisies trim,
Their merry wakes and pastimes keep:
What hath night to do with sleep?
Night hath better sweets to prove,
Venus now wakes, and wakens love.
Come let us our rites begin,
'Tis only daylight that makes sin,
Which these dun shades will ne'er report.
Hail goddess of nocturnal sport
Dark veiled Cotytto, t' whom the secret flame
Of midnight torches burns; mysterious dame
That ne'er art called, but when the dragon womb
Of Stygian darkness spits her thickest gloom,
And makes one blot of all the air,
Stay thy cloudy ebon chair,
Wherein thou rid'st with Hecate, and befriend
Us thy vowed priests, till utmost end
Of all thy dues be done, and none left out,
Ere the blabbing eastern scout,
The nice morn on th' Indian steep,
From her cabined loophole peep,
And to the tell-tale sun descry
Our concealed solemnity.

Come, knit hands, and beat the ground,
In a light fantastic round.

The Measure

Break off, break off, I feel the different pace,
Of some chaste footing near about this ground.
Run to your shrouds, within these brakes and trees,
Our number may affright: some virgin sure
(For so I can distinguish by mine art)
Benighted in these woods. Now to my charms,
And to my wily trains; I shall ere long
Be well stocked with as fair a herd as grazed
About my mother Circe. Thus I hurl
My dazzling spells into the spongy air,
Of power to cheat the eye with blear illusion,
And give it false presentments, lest the place
And my quaint habits breed astonishment,
And put the damsel to suspicious flight,
Which must not be, for that's against my course;
I under fair pretence of friendly ends,
And well placed words of glozing courtesy
Baited with reasons not unplausible
Wind me into the easy-hearted man,
And hug him into snares. When once her eye
Hath met the virtues of this magic dust,
I shall appear some harmless villager
Whom thrift keeps up about his country gear.
But here she comes, I fairly step aside,
And hearken, if I may, her business here.

The Lady enters

This way the noise was, if mine ear be true,
My best guide now. Methought it was the sound
Of riot, and ill managed merriment,
Such as the jocund flute, or gamesome pipe

Stirs up among the loose unlettered hinds,
When for their teeming flocks, and granges full
In wanton dance they praise the bounteous Pan,
And thank the gods amiss. I should be loath
To meet the rudeness and swilled insolence
Of such late wassailers; yet O where else
Shall I inform my unacquainted feet
In the blind mazes of this tangled wood?
My brothers when they saw me wearied out
With this long way, resolving here to lodge
Under the spreading favour of these pines,
Stepped as they said to the next thicket side
To bring me berries, or such cooling fruit
As the kind hospitable woods provide.
They left me then, when the gray-hooded even
Like a sad votarist in palmer's weed
Rose from the hindmost wheels of Phoebus' wain.
But where they are, and why they came not back,
Is now the labour of my thoughts. 'Tis likeliest
They had engaged their wandering steps too far,
And envious darkness, ere they could return,
Had stole them from me, else O thievish night
Why shouldst thou, but for some felonious end,
In thy dark lantern thus close up the stars,
That nature hung in Heaven, and filled their lamps
With everlasting oil, to give due light
To the misled and lonely traveller?
This is the place, as well as I may guess,
Whence even now the tumult of loud mirth
Was rife, and perfect in my listening ear,
Yet nought but single darkness do I find.
What might this be? A thousand fantasies
Begin to throng into my memory
Of calling shapes, and beckoning shadows dire,

COMUS

And airy tongues, that syllable men's names
On sands, and shores, and desert wildernesses.
These thoughts may startle well, but not astound
The virtuous mind, that ever walks attended
By a strong siding champion, conscience. —
O welcome pure-eyed faith, white-handed hope,
Thou hovering angel girt with golden wings,
And thou unblemished form of chastity,
I see ye visibly, and now believe
That he, the supreme good, t' whom all things ill
Are but as slavish officers of vengeance,
Would send a glistering guardian if need were
To keep my life and honour unassailed.
Was I deceived, or did a sable cloud
Turn forth her silver lining on the night?
I did not err, there does a sable cloud
Turn forth her silver lining on the night,
And casts a gleam over this tufted grove.
I cannot hallow to my brothers, but
Such noise as I can make to be heard farthest
I'll venture, for my new enlivened spirits
Prompt me; and they perhaps are not far off.

Song

Sweet Echo, sweetest nymph that liv'st unseen
    Within thy airy shell
    By slow Meander's margent green,
And in the violet-embroidered vale
    Where the lovelorn nightingale
Nightly to thee her sad song mourneth well.
Canst thou not tell me of a gentle pair
    That likest thy Narcissus are?
        O if thou have

99

D2

Hid them in some flowery cave,
    Tell me but where
Sweet queen of parley, daughter of the sphere,
So mayest thou be translated to the skies,
And give resounding grace to all Heaven's harmonies.

Comus. Can any mortal mixture of earth's mould
Breathe such divine enchanting ravishment?
Sure something holy lodges in that breast,
And with these raptures moves the vocal air
To testify his hidden residence;
How sweetly did they float upon the wings
Of silence, through the empty-vaulted night
At every fall smoothing the raven down
Of darkness till it smiled: I have oft heard
My mother Circe with the sirens three,
Amidst the flowery-kirtled Naiades
Culling their potent herbs, and baleful drugs,
Who as they sung, would take the prisoned soul,
And lap it in Elysium; Scylla wept,
And chid her barking waves into attention,
And fell Charybdis murmured soft applause.
Yet they in pleasing slumber lulled the sense,
And in sweet madness robbed it of itself;
But such a sacred, and homefelt delight,
Such sober certainty of waking bliss
I never heard till now. I'll speak to her
And she shall be my queen. Hail foreign wonder
Whom certain these rough shades did never breed
Unless the goddess that in rural shrine
Dwell'st here with Pan, or Silvan, by blest song
Forbidding every bleak unkindly fog
To touch the prosperous growth of this tall wood.
  Lady. Nay gentle shepherd, ill is lost that praise

COMUS

That is addressed to unattending ears.
Not any boast of skill, but extreme shift
How to regain my severed company
Compelled me to awake the courteous echo
To give me answer from her mossy couch.

 Comus. What chance good lady hath bereft you thus?
 Lady. Dim darkness, and this leavy labyrinth.
 Comus. Could that divide you from near-ushering guides?
 Lady. They left me weary on a grassy turf.
 Comus. By falsehood, or discourtesy, or why?
 Lady. To seek i' th' valley some cool friendly spring.
 Comus. And left your fair side all unguarded lady?
 Lady. They were but twain, and purposed quick return.
 Comus. Perhaps forestalling night prevented them.
 Lady. How easy my misfortune is to hit!
 Comus. Imports their loss, beside the present need?
 Lady. No less than if I should my brothers lose.
 Comus. Were they of manly prime, or youthful bloom?
 Lady. As smooth as Hebe's their unrazored lips.
 Comus. Two such I saw, what time the laboured ox
In his loose traces from the furrow came,
And the swinkt hedger at his supper sat;
I saw them under a green mantling vine
That crawls along the side of yon small hill,
Plucking ripe clusters from the tender shoots;
Their port was more than human, as they stood;
I took it for a faery vision
Of some gay creatures of the element
That in the colours of the rainbow live
And play i' th' plighted clouds. I was awe-strook,
And as I passed, I worshipped: if those you seek
It were a journey like the path to Heaven,
To help you find them.
 Lady.   Gentle villager

What readiest way would bring me to that place?

Comus. Due west it rises from this shrubby point.

Lady. To find out that, good shepherd, I suppose,
In such a scant allowance of starlight,
Would overtask the best land-pilot's art,
Without the sure guess of well-practised feet.

Comus. I know each lane, and every alley green,
Dingle, or bushy dell of this wild wood,
And every bosky bourn from side to side,
My daily walks and ancient neighbourhood,
And if your stray attendance be yet lodged,
Or shroud within these limits, I shall know
Ere morrow wake, or the low roosted lark
From her thatched pallet rouse; if otherwise
I can conduct you lady to a low
But loyal cottage, where you may be safe
Till further quest.

Lady   Shepherd I take thy word,
And trust thy honest offered courtesy,
Which oft is sooner found in lowly sheds
With smoky rafters, than in tapstry halls
And courts of princes, where it first was named,
And yet is most pretended. In a place
Less warranted than this, or less secure
I cannot be, that I should fear to change it.
Eye me, blest providence, and square my trial
To my proportioned strength. Shepherd lead on. –

The two Brothers

Elder Brother. Unmuffle ye faint stars, and thou fair moon
That wontst to love the traveller's benison,
Stoop thy pale visage through an amber cloud,
And disinherit chaos, that reigns here
In double night of darkness, and of shades;

Or if your influence be quite dammed up
With black usurping mists, some gentle taper,
Though a rush candle from the wicker hole
Of some clay habitation visit us
With thy long levelled rule of streaming light,
And thou shalt be our star of Arcady,
Or Tyrian cynosure.

   Second Brother.   Or if our eyes
Be barred that happiness, might we but hear
The folded flocks penned in their wattled cotes,
Or sound of pastoral reed with oaten stops,
Or whistle from the lodge, or village cock
Count the night watches to his feathery dames,
'Twould be some solace yet, some little cheering
In this close dungeon of innumerous boughs.
But O that hapless virgin our lost sister,
Where may she wander now, whither betake her
From the chill dew, amongst rude burrs and thistles?
Perhaps some cold bank is her bolster now
Or 'gainst the rugged bark of some broad elm
Leans her unpillowed head fraught with sad fears.
What if in wild amazement, and affright,
Or while we speak within the direful grasp
Of savage hunger, or of savage heat?

   Elder Brother. Peace, brother, be not over-exquisite
To cast the fashion of uncertain evils;
For grant they be so, while they rest unknown,
What need a man forestall his date of grief,
And run to meet what he would most avoid?
Or if they be but false alarms of fear,
How bitter is such self-delusion!
I do not think my sister so to seek,
Or so unprincipled in virtue's book,
And the sweet peace that goodness bosoms ever,

As that the single want of light and noise
(Not being in danger, as I trust she is not)
Could stir the constant mood of her calm thoughts,
And put them into misbecoming plight.
Virtue could see to do what virtue would
By her own radiant light, though sun and moon
Were in the flat sea sunk. And Wisdom's self
Oft seeks to sweet retired solitude,
Where with her best nurse Contemplation
She plumes her feathers, and lets grow her wings
That in the various bustle of resort
Were all too ruffled, and sometimes impaired.
He that has light within his own clear breast
May sit i' th' centre, and enjoy bright day,
But he that hides a dark soul, and foul thoughts
Benighted walks under the midday sun;
Himself is his own dungeon.

    Second Brother.   'Tis most true
That musing meditation most affects
The pensive secrecy of desert cell,
Far from the cheerful haunt of men, and herds,
And sits as safe as in a senate house,
For who would rob a hermit of his weeds,
His few books, or his beads, or maple dish,
Or do his grey hairs any violence?
But beauty like the fair Hesperian tree
Laden with blooming gold, had need the guard
Of dragon watch with unenchanted eye,
To save her blossoms, and defend her fruit
From the rash hand of bold incontinence.
You may as well spread out the unsunned heaps
Of miser's treasure by an outlaw's den,
And tell me it is safe, as bid me hope
Danger will wink on opportunity,

And let a single helpless maiden pass
Uninjured in this wild surrounding waste.
Of night, or loneliness it recks me not,
I fear the dread events that dog them both,
Lest some ill greeting touch attempt the person
Of our unowned sister.

    Elder Brother. I do not, brother,
Infer as if I thought my sister's state
Secure without all doubt, or controversy;
Yet where an equal poise of hope and fear
Does arbitrate th' event, my nature is
That I incline to hope, rather than fear,
And gladly banish squint suspicion.
My sister is not so defenceless left
As you imagine, she has a hidden strength
Which you remember not.

    Second Brother.   What hidden strength,
Unless the strength of Heaven, if you mean that?

    Elder Brother. I mean that too, but yet a hidden strength
Which if Heaven gave it, may be termed her own:
'Tis chastity, my brother, chastity:
She that has that, is clad in complete steel,
And like a quivered nymph with arrows keen
May trace huge forests, and unharboured heaths,
Infamous hills, and sandy perilous wilds,
Where through the sacred rays of chastity,
No savage fierce, bandit, or mountaineer
Will dare to soil her virgin purity;
Yea there, where very desolation dwells
By grots and caverns shagged with horrid shades,
She may pass on with unblenched majesty,
Be it not done in pride, or in presumption.
Some say no evil thing that walks by night
In fog, or fire, by lake, or moorish fen,

Blue meagre hag, or stubborn unlaid ghost,
That breaks his magic chains at curfew time,
No goblin, or swart faery of the mine,
Hath hurtful power o'er true virginity.
Do ye believe me yet, or shall I call
Antiquity from the old schools of Greece
To testify the arms of chastity?
Hence had the huntress Dian her dread bow
Fair silver-shafted queen for ever chaste,
Wherewith she tamed the brinded lioness
And spotted mountain pard, but set at nought
The frivolous bolt of Cupid; gods and men
Feared her stern frown, and she was queen o' th' woods.
What was that snaky-headed Gorgon shield
That wise Minerva wore, unconquered virgin,
Wherewith she freezed her foes to congealed stone?
But rigid looks of chaste austerity,
And noble grace that dashed brute violence
With sudden adoration, and blank awe.
So dear to Heaven is saintly chastity,
That when a soul is found sincerely so,
A thousand liveried angels lackey her,
Driving far off each thing of sin and guilt,
And in clear dream, and solemn vision
Tell her of things that no gross ear can hear,
Till oft converse with heavenly habitants
Begin to cast a beam on th' outward shape,
The unpolluted temple of the mind,
And turns it by degrees to the soul's essence,
Till all be made immortal: but when lust
By unchaste looks, loose gestures and foul talk,
But most by lewd and lavish act of sin,
Lets in defilement to the inward parts,
The soul grows clotted by contagion,

Imbodies, and imbrutes, till she quite lose
The divine property of her first being.
Such are those thick and gloomy shadows damp
Oft seen in charnel vaults, and sepulchres,
Lingering, and sitting by a new-made grave,
As loath to leave the body that it loved,
And linked itself by carnal sensualty
To a degenerate and degraded state.

   Second Brother. How charming is divine philosophy!
Not harsh, and crabbed as dull fools suppose,
But musical as is Apollo's lute,
And a perpetual feast of nectared sweets,
Where no crude surfeit reigns.

   Elder Brother.   List, list, I hear
Some far off hallow break the silent air.

   Second Brother. Methought so too; what should it be?

   Elder Brother.   For certain
Either someone like us night-foundered here,
Or else some neighbour woodman, or at worst,
Some roving robber calling to his fellows.

   Second Brother. Heaven keep my sister. Again, again and near;
Best draw, and stand upon our guard.

   Elder Brother.   I'll hallow;
If he be friendly he comes well, if not,
Defence is a good cause, and Heaven be for us.

       The attendant Spirit habited like a shepherd

That hallow I should know, what are you? speak;
Come not too near, you fall on iron stakes else.

   Spirit. What voice is that, my young lord? speak again.

   Second Brother. O brother, 'tis my father's shepherd sure.

   Elder Brother. Thyrsis, whose artful strains have oft delayed
The huddling brook to hear his madrigal,
And sweetened every muskrose of the dale,

How cam'st thou here, good swain? Hath any ram
Slipped from the fold, or young kid lost his dam,
Or straggling wether the pent flock forsook?
How couldst thou find this dark sequestered nook?
 Spirit. O my loved master's heir, and his next joy,
I came not here on such a trivial toy
As a strayed ewe, or to pursue the stealth
Of pilfering wolf; not all the fleecy wealth
That doth enrich these downs, is worth a thought
To this my errand, and the care it brought.
But O my virgin lady, where is she?
How chance she is not in your company?
 Elder Brother. To tell thee sadly shepherd, without blame,
Or our neglect, we lost her as we came.
 Spirit. Ay me unhappy then my fears are true.
 Elder Brother. What fears, good Thyrsis? Prythee briefly show
 Spirit. I'll tell ye, 'tis not vain or fabulous,
(Though so esteemed by shallow ignorance)
What the sage poets, taught by the heavenly Muse,
Storied of old in high immortal verse
Of dire Chimeras and enchanted isles,
And rifted rocks whose entrance leads to hell,
For such there be, but unbelief is blind.
 Within the navel of this hideous wood,
Immured in cypress shades a sorcerer dwells
Of Bacchus and of Circe born, great Comus,
Deep skilled in all his mother's witcheries,
And here to every thirsty wanderer,
By sly enticement gives his baneful cup,
With many murmurs mixt, whose pleasing poison
The visage quite transforms of him that drinks,
And the inglorious likeness of a beast
Fixes instead, unmoulding reason's mintage
Charactered in the face; this have I learned

Tending my flocks hard by i' th' hilly crofts,
That brow this bottom glade, whence night by night
He and his monstrous rout are heard to howl
Like stabled wolves, or tigers at their prey,
Doing abhorred rites to Hecate
In their obscured haunts of inmost bowers.
Yet have they many baits, and guileful spells
To inveigle and invite the unwary sense
Of them that pass unweeting by the way.
This evening late, by then the chewing flocks
Had ta'en their supper on the savoury herb
Of knot-grass dew-besprent, and were in fold,
I sat me down to watch upon a bank
With ivy canopied, and interwove
With flaunting honeysuckle, and began
Wrapt in a pleasing fit of melancholy
To meditate my rural minstrelsy,
Till fancy had her fill; but ere a close
The wonted roar was up amidst the woods,
And filled the air with barbarous dissonance,
At which I ceased, and listened them a while,
Till an unusual stop of sudden silence
Gave respite to the drowsy frighted steeds
That draw the litter of close-curtained sleep.
At last a soft and solemn breathing sound
Rose like a steam of rich distilled perfumes,
And stole upon the air, that even silence
Was took ere she was ware, and wished she might
Deny her nature, and be never more
Still to be so displaced. I was all ear,
And took in strains that might create a soul
Under the ribs of death, but O ere long
Too well I did perceive it was the voice
Of my most honoured lady, your dear sister.

Amazed I stood, harrowed with grief and fear,
And O poor hapless nightingale thought I
How sweet thou sing'st, how near the deadly snare!
Then down the lawns I ran with headlong haste
Through paths and turnings often trod by day,
Till guided by mine ear I found the place
Where that damned wizard, hid in sly disguise
(For so by certain signs I knew) had met
Already, ere my best speed could prevent,
The aidless innocent lady his wished prey,
Who gently asked if he had seen such two,
Supposing him some neighbour villager;
Longer I durst not stay, but soon I guessed
Ye were the two she meant; with that I sprung
Into swift flight, till I had found you here,
But further know I not.

    Second Brother.   O night and shades,
How are ye joined with hell in triple knot
Against th'unarmed weakness of one virgin
Alone and helpless! Is this the confidence
You gave me brother?

    Elder Brother.   Yes, and keep it still,
Lean on it safely, not a period
Shall be unsaid for me. Against the threats
Of malice or of sorcery, or that power
Which erring men call chance, this I hold firm,
Virtue may be assailed, but never hurt,
Surprised by unjust force, but not enthralled,
Yea even that which mischief meant most harm,
Shall in the happy trial prove most glory.
But evil on itself shall back recoil,
And mix no more with goodness, when at last
Gathered like scum, and settled to itself
It shall be in eternal restless change

Self-fed and self-consum'd. If this fail,
The pillared firmament is rottenness,
And earth's base built on stubble. But come let's on.
Against th'opposing will and arm of Heaven
May never this just sword be lifted up,
But for that damned magician, let him be girt
With all the grisly legions that troop
Under the sooty flag of Acheron,
Harpies and Hydras, or all the monstrous forms
'Twixt Africa and Ind, I'll find him out,
And force him to restore his purchase back,
Or drag him by the curls, to a foul death,
Cursed as his life.

    Spirit.   Alas, good venturous youth,
I love thy courage yet, and bold emprise,
But here thy sword can do thee little stead;
Far other arms and other weapons must
Be those that quell the might of hellish charms;
He with his bare wand can unthread thy joints,
And crumble all thy sinews.

    Elder Brother.   Why prithee shepherd
How durst thou then thyself approach so near
As to make this relation?

    Spirit.   Care and utmost shifts
How to secure the lady from surprisal,
Brought to my mind a certain shepherd lad
Of small regard to see to, yet well skilled
In every virtuous plant and healing herb
That spreads her verdant leaf to th' morning ray.
He loved me well, and oft would beg me sing,
Which when I did, he on the tender grass
Would sit, and hearken even to ecstasy,
And in requital ope his leathern scrip,
And show me simples of a thousand names

Telling their strange and vigorous faculties;
Amongst the rest a small unsightly root,
But of divine effect, he culled me out;
The leaf was darkish, and had prickles on it,
But in another country, as he said,
Bore a bright golden flower, but not in this soil:
Unknown, and like esteemed, and the dull swain
Treads on it daily with his clouted shoon,
And yet more med'cinal is it than that moly
That Hermes once to wise Ulysses gave;
He called it Haemony, and gave it me,
And bade me keep it as of sovereign use
'Gainst all enchantments, mildew blast, or damp
Or ghastly fury's apparition.
I pursed it up, but little reck'ning made,
Till now that this extremity compelled,
But now I find it true; for by this means
I knew the foul enchanter though disguised,
Entered the very lime-twigs of his spells,
And yet came off: if you have this about you
(As I will give you when we go) you may
Boldly assault the necromancer's hall;
Where if he be, with dauntless hardihood,
And brandished blade rush on him, break his glass,
And shed the luscious liquor on the ground;
But seize his wand, though he and his curst crew
Fierce sign of battle make, and menace high,
Or like the sons of Vulcan vomit smoke,
Yet will they soon retire, if he but shrink.
   Elder Brother. Thyrsis lead on apace, I'll follow thee,
And some good angel bear a shield before us.

The scene changes to a stately palace, set out with all manner of deliciousness;
soft music, tables spread with all dainties. Comus appears with his rabble, and the
lady set in an enchanted chair, to whom he offers his glass, which she puts by, and
goes about to rise.

112

Comus. Nay lady sit; if I but wave this wand,
Your nerves are all chained up in alabaster,
And you a statue; or as Daphne was,
Root-bound, that fled Apollo.

  Lady.   Fool do not boast,
Thou canst not touch the freedom of my mind
With all thy charms, although this corporal rind
Thou hast inmanacled, while Heaven sees good.

  Comus. Why are you vext lady? Why do you frown?
Here dwell no frowns, nor anger; from these gates
Sorrow flies far: see here be all the pleasures
That fancy can beget on youthful thoughts,
When the fresh blood grows lively, and returns
Brisk as the April buds in primrose-season.
And first behold this cordial julep here
That flames and dances in his crystal bounds
With spirits of balm, and fragrant syrups mixed.
Not that Nepenthes which the wife of Thone,
In Egypt gave to Jove-born Helena,
Is of such power to stir up joy as this,
To life so friendly, or so cool to thirst.
Why should you be so cruel to yourself,
And to those dainty limbs which nature lent
For gentle usage, and soft delicacy?
But you invert the covenants of her trust,
And harshly deal, like an ill borrower,
With that which you received on other terms,
Scorning the unexempt condition
By which all mortal frailty must subsist,
Refreshment after toil, ease after pain,
That have been tired all day without repast,
And timely rest have wanted. But fair virgin,
This will restore all soon.

  Lady.   'Twill not false traitor,

'Twill not restore the truth and honesty
That thou hast banished from thy tongue with lies.
Was this the cottage, and the safe abode
Thou told'st me of? What grim aspects are these,
These oughly-headed monsters? Mercy guard me!
Hence with thy brewed enchantments, foul deceiver,
Hast thou betrayed my credulous innocence
With visored falsehood, and base forgery,
And wouldst thou seek again to trap me here
With liquorish baits fit to ensnare a brute?
Were it a draft for Juno when she banquets,
I would not taste thy treasonous offer; none
But such as are good men can give good things,
And that which is not good, is not delicious
To a well-governed and wise appetite.

    Comus. O foolishness of men! That lend their ears
To those budge doctors of the stoic fur,
And fetch their precepts from the cynic tub,
Praising the lean and sallow abstinence.
Wherefore did nature pour her bounties forth,
With such a full and unwithdrawing hand,
Covering the earth with odours, fruits, and flocks,
Thronging the seas with spawn innumerable,
But all to please, and sate the curious taste?
And set to work millions of spinning worms,
That in their green shops weave the smooth-haired silk
To deck her sons, and that no corner might
Be vacant of her plenty, in her own loins
She hutched th'all worshipped ore, and precious gems
To store her children with; if all the world
Should in a pet of temperance feed on pulse,
Drink the clear stream, and nothing wear but frieze,
Th'all giver would be unthanked, would be unpraised,
Not half his riches known, and yet despised,

And we should serve him as a grudging master,
As a penurious niggard of his wealth,
And live like nature's bastards, not her sons,
Who would be quite surcharged with her own weight,
And strangled with her waste fertility;
Th'earth cumbered, and the winged air darkt with plumes,
The herds would over-multitude their lords,
The sea o'erfraught would swell, and th'unsought diamonds
Would so emblaze the forehead of the deep,
And so bestud with stars, that they below
Would grow inured to light, and come at last
To gaze upon the sun with shameless brows.
List lady be not coy, and be not cozened
With that same vaunted name virginity;
Beauty is nature's coin, must not be hoarded,
But must be current, and the good thereof
Consists in mutual and partaken bliss,
Unsavoury in the enjoyment of itself.
If you let slip time, like a neglected rose
It withers on the stalk with languished head.
Beauty is nature's brag, and must be shown
In courts, at feasts, and high solemnities
Where most may wonder at the workmanship;
It is for homely features to keep home,
They had their name thence; coarse complexions
And cheeks of sorry grain will serve to ply
The sampler, and to tease the huswife's wool.
What need a vermeil-tinctured lip for that
Love-darting eyes, or tresses like the morn?
There was another meaning in these gifts;
Think what, and be advised, you are but young yet.

    Lady. I had not thought to have unlocked my lips
In this unhallowed air, but that this juggler
Would think to charm my judgement, as mine eyes,

Obtruding false rules pranked in reason's garb.
I hate when vice can bolt her arguments,
And virtue has no tongue to check her pride:
Impostor do not charge most innocent nature,
As if she would her children should be riotous
With her abundance; she good cateress
Means her provision only to the good
That live according to her sober laws,
And holy dictate of spare temperance:
If every just man that now pines with want
Had but a moderate and beseeming share
Of that which lewdly-pampered luxury
Now heaps upon some few with vast excess,
Nature's full blessings would be well dispensed
In unsuperfluous even proportion,
And she no whit encumbered with her store;
And then the giver would be better thanked,
His praise due paid; for swinish gluttony
Ne'er looks to Heaven amidst his gorgeous feast,
But with besotted base ingratitude
Crams, and blasphemes his feeder. Shall I go on?
Or have I said enough? To him that dares
Arm his profane tongue with contemptuous words
Against the sun-clad power of chastity,
Fain would I something say, yet to what end?
Thou hast nor ear, nor soul to apprehend
The sublime notion, and high mystery
That must be uttered to unfold the sage
And serious doctrine of virginity,
And thou art worthy that thou should'st not know
More happiness than this thy present lot.
Enjoy your dear wit, and gay rhetoric
That hath so well been taught her dazzling fence;
Thou art not fit to hear thyself convinced;

Yet should I try, the uncontrolled worth
Of this pure cause would kindle my rapt spirits
To such a flame of sacred vehemence,
That dumb things would be moved to sympathize,
And the brute earth would lend her nerves, and shake,
Till all thy magic structures reared so high,
Were shattered into heaps o'er thy false head.

Comus. She fables not, I feel that I do fear
Her words set off by some superior power;
And though not mortal, yet a cold shuddering dew
Dips me all o'er, as when the wrath of Jove
Speaks thunder, and the chains of Erebus
To some of Saturn's crew. I must dissemble,
And try her yet more strongly. Come, no more,
This is mere moral babble, and direct
Against the canon laws of our foundation;
I must not suffer this, yet 'tis but the lees
And settlings of a melancholy blood;
But this will cure all straight, one sip of this
Will bathe the drooping spirits in delight
Beyond the bliss of dreams. Be wise, and taste. —

*The Brothers rush in with swords drawn, wrest his glass out of his hand, and
break it against the ground; his rout make sign of resistance, but are all driven in;
the attendant spirit comes in.*

Spirit. What, have you let the false enchanter 'scape?
O ye mistook, ye should have snatched his wand
And bound him fast; without his rod reversed,
And backward mutters of dissevering power,
We cannot free the lady that sits here
In stony fetters fixt, and motionless;
Yet stay, be not disturbed, now I bethink me,
Some other means I have which may be used,
Which once of Meliboeus old I learnt,

The soothest shepherd that e'er piped on plains.
  There is a gentle nymph not far from hence,
That with moist curb sways the smooth Severn stream;
Sabrina is her name, a virgin pure;
Whilom she was the daughter of Locrine,
That had the sceptre from his father Brute.
The guiltless damsel, flying the mad pursuit
Of her enraged stepdame Gwendolen,
Commended her fair innocence to the flood
That stayed her flight with his cross-flowing course;
The water nymphs that in the bottom played,
Held up their pearled wrists and took her in,
Bearing her straight to aged Nereus' hall,
Who piteous of her woes, reared her lank head,
And gave her to his daughters to imbathe
In nectared lavers strewed with asphodel,
And through the porch and inlet of each sense
Dropt in ambrosial oils till she revived,
And underwent a quick immortal change
Made goddess of the river; still she retains
Her maiden gentleness, and oft at eve
Visits the herds along the twilight meadows,
Helping all urchin blasts, and ill luck signs
That the shrewd meddling elf delights to make,
Which she with precious vialed liquors heals.
For which the shepherds at their festivals
Carol her goodness loud in rustic lays,
And throw sweet garland wreaths into her stream
Of pansies, pinks, and gaudy daffodils.
And, as the old swain said, she can unlock
The clasping charm, and thaw the numbing spell,
If she be right invoked in warbled song,
For maidenhood she loves, and will be swift
To aid a virgin, such as was herself,

In hard besetting need; this will I try
And add the power of some adjuring verse.

Song

Sabrina fair
    Listen where thou art sitting
Under the glassy, cool, translucent wave,
    In twisted braids of lilies knitting
The loose train of thy amber-dropping hair;
    Listen for dear honour's sake,
    Goddess of the silver lake,
      Listen and save.

Listen and appear to us
In name of great Oceanus,
By the earth-shaking Neptune's mace,
And Tethys' grave majestic pace,
By hoary Nereus wrinkled look,
And the Carpathian wizard's hook,
By scaly Triton's winding shell,
And old sooth-saying Glaucus' spell,
By Leucothea's lovely hands,
And her son that rules the strands,
By Thetis' tinsel-slippered feet,
And the songs of sirens sweet,
By dead Parthenope's dear tomb,
And fair Ligea's golden comb,
Wherewith she sits on diamond rocks
Sleeking her soft alluring locks,
By all the nymphs that nightly dance
Upon thy streams with wily glance,
Rise, rise, and heave thy rosy head
From thy coral-paven bed,

And bridle in thy headlong wave,
Till thou our summons answered have.
  Listen and save.

Sabrina rises, attended by water-nymphs, and sings

By the rushy-fringed bank,
Where grows the willow and the osier dank,
 My sliding chariot stays,
Thick set with agate, and the azurn sheen
Of turquois blue, and emerald green
 That in the channel strays;
Whilst from off the waters fleet
Thus I set my printless feet
O'er the cowslip's velvet head,
That bends not as I tread;
Gentle swain at thy request
 I am here.
Spirit. Goddess dear
We implore thy powerful hand
To undo the charmed band
Of true virgin here distrest,
Through the force, and through the wile
Of unblest enchanter vile.
 Sabrina. Shepherd 'tis my office best
To help ensnared chastity;
Brightest lady look on me;
Thus I sprinkle on thy breast
Drops that from my fountain pure,
I have kept of precious cure;
Thrice upon thy fingers' tip,
Thrice upon thy rubied lip;
Next this marbled venomed seat
Smeared with gums of glutinous heat
I touch with chaste palms moist and cold.

Now the spell hath lost his hold;
And I must haste ere morning hour
To wait in Amphitrite's bower.

Sabrina descends, and the lady rises out of her seat

Spirit. Virgin, daughter of Locrine,
Sprung of old Anchises line,
May thy brimmed waves for this
Their full tribute never miss
From a thousand petty rills,
That tumble down the snowy hills:
Summer drouth, or singed air
Never scorch thy tresses fair,
Nor wet October's torrent flood
Thy molten crystal fill with mud,
May thy billows roll ashore
The beryl, and the golden ore,
May thy lofty head be crowned
With many a tower and terrace round,
And here and there thy banks upon
With groves of myrrh, and cinnamon.
    Come lady while Heaven lends us grace
Let us fly this cursed place,
Lest the sorcerer us entice
With some other new device.
Not a waste, or needless sound
Till we come to holier ground;
I shall be your faithful guide
Through this gloomy covert wide,
And not many furlongs thence
Is your father's residence,
Where this night are met in state
Many a friend to gratulate
His wished presence, and beside

All the swains that there abide
With jigs, and rural dance resort;
We shall catch them at their sport,
And our sudden coming there
Will double all their mirth and cheer.
Come let us haste, the stars grow high,
But night sits monarch yet in the mid sky.

The scene changes, presenting Ludlow town and the president's castle, then come in country-dancers, after them the attendant Spirit, with the two Brothers and the Lady.

Song

Spirit. Back shepherds, back, enough your play,
Till next sunshine holiday.
Here be without duck or nod
Other trippings to be trod
Of lighter toes, and such court guise
As Mercury did first devise
With the mincing Dryades
On the lawns and on the leas.

This second song presents them to their father and mother

Noble lord, and lady bright,
I have brought ye new delight.
Here behold so goodly grown
Three fair branches of your own;
Heaven hath timely tried their youth,
Their faith, their patience, and their truth.
And sent them here through hard assays
With a crown of deathless praise,
    To triumph in victorious dance
O'er sensual folly, and intemperance.

The dances ended, the Spirit epiloguises

Spirit. To the ocean now I fly,
And those happy climes that lie
Where day never shuts his eye,
Up in the broad fields of the sky:
There I suck the liquid air
All amidst the gardens fair
Of Hesperus, and his daughters three
That sing about the golden tree:
Along the crisped shades and bowers
Revels the spruce and jocund spring;
The graces, and the rosy-bosomed hours,
Thither all their bounties bring,
That there eternal summer dwells,
And west winds, with musky wing
About the cedarn alleys fling
Nard, and Cassia's balmy smells.
Iris there with humid bow,
Waters the odorous banks that blow
Flowers of more mingled hue
Than her purfled scarf can show,
And drenches with Elysian dew
(List mortals, if your ears be true)
Beds of Hyacinth, and roses
Where young Adonis oft reposes,
Waxing well of his deep wound
In slumber soft, and on the ground
Sadly sits th'Assyrian queen;
But far above in spangled sheen
Celestial Cupid her famed son advanced,
Holds his dear Psyche sweet entranced
After her wandering labours long,
Till free consent the gods among

Make her his eternal bride,
And from her fair unspotted side
Two blissful twins are to be born,
Youth and Joy; so Jove hath sworn.

    But now my task is smoothly done,
I can fly, or I can run
Quickly to the green earth's end,
Where the bowed welkin slow doth bend,
And from thence can soar as soon
To the corners of the moon.

    Mortals that would follow me,
Love virtue, she alone is free;
She can teach you how to climb
Higher than the sphery chime;
Or if virtue feeble were,
Heaven itself would stoop to her.

Paradise Lost

BOOK I

The Argument

THIS first book proposes first in brief the whole subject, Man's disobedience, and the loss thereupon of Paradise, wherein he was placed: then touches the prime cause of his fall, the serpent, or rather Satan in the serpent; who revolting from God, and drawing to his side many legions of angels, was by the command of God driven out of Heaven with all his crew into the great deep. Which action passed over, the poem hastes into the midst of things, presenting Satan wtih his angels now fallen into Hell, described here, not in the centre (for Heaven and earth may be supposed as yet not made, certainly not yet accursed) but in a place of utter darkness, fitliest called chaos: here Satan with his angels lying on the burning lake, thunder-struck and astonished, after a certain space recovers, as from confusion, calls up him who next in order and dignity lay by him; they confer of their miserable fall. Satan awakens all his legions, who lay till then in the same manner confounded; they rise, their numbers, array of battle, their chief leaders named, according to the idols known afterwards in Canaan and the countries adjoining. To these Satan directs his speech, comforts them with hope yet of regaining Heaven, but tells them lastly of a new world and new kind of creature to be created, according to an ancient prophecy or report in Heaven; for that angels were long before this visible creation was the opinion of many ancient Fathers. To find out the truth of this prophecy, and what to determine thereon, he refers to a full council. What his associates thence attempt. Pandemonium, the palace of Satan rises, suddenly built out of the deep: the infernal peers there sit in council.

Introductory

Of Man's first disobedience, and the fruit
Of that forbidden tree, whose mortal taste
Brought death into the world, and all our woe,
With loss of Eden, till one greater man
Restore us, and regain the blissful seat,
Sing Heavenly Muse, that on the secret top
Of Oreb, or of Sinai, didst inspire
That shepherd who first taught the chosen seed,
In the beginning how the Heavens and earth
Rose out of chaos: or if Sion hill
Delight thee more, and Siloa's brook that flowed
Fast by the oracle of God; I thence
Invoke thy aid to my adventurous song,
That with no middle flight intends to soar
Above th'Aonian mount, while it pursues
Things unattempted yet in prose or rhyme.
And chiefly thou O spirit, that dost prefer
Before all temples th'upright heart and pure,
Instruct me, for thou know'st; thou from the first
Wast present, and with mighty wings outspread
Dovelike satst brooding on the vast abyss
And madst it pregnant: what in me is dark
Illumine, what is low raise and support;
That to the highth of this great argument
I may assert eternal providence,
And justify the ways of God to men.

(Lines 1–26)

Satan before the Counsil

                        Thus far these beyond
Compare of mortal prowess, yet observed
Their dread commander: he above the rest
In shape and gesture proudly eminent
Stood like a tower; his form had yet not lost
All her original brightness, nor appeared
Less than archangel ruined, and th'excess
Of glory obscured: as when the sun new risen
Looks through the horizontal misty air
Shorn of his beams, or from behind the moon
In dim eclipse disastrous twilight sheds
On half the nations, and with fear of change
Perplexes monarchs. Darkened so, yet shone
Above them all th'arch angel: but his face
Deep scars of thunder had intrenched, and care
Sat on his faded cheek, but under brows
Of dauntless courage, and considerate pride
Waiting revenge: cruel his eye, but cast
Signs of remorse and passion to behold
The fellows of his crime, the followers rather
(Far other once beheld in bliss) condemned
For ever now to have their lot in pain,
Millions of spirits for his fault amerced
Of Heaven, and from eternal splendours flung
For his revolt, yet faithful how they stood,
Their glory withered. As when Heaven's fire
Hath scathed the forest oaks, or mountain pines,
With singed top their stately growth though bare
Stands on the blasted heath. He now prepared
To speak; whereat their doubled ranks they bend
From wing to wing, and half enclose him round
With all his peers: attention held them mute.

Thrice he assayed, and thrice in spite of scorn,
Tears such as angels weep, burst forth: at last
Words interwove with sighs found out their way.

    O myriads of immortal Spirits, O Powers
Matchless, but with th'Almighty, and that strife
Was not inglorious, though th'event was dire,
As this place testifies, and this dire change
Hateful to utter: but what power of mind
Foreseeing or presaging, from the depth
Of knowledge past or present, could have feared,
How such united force of Gods, how such
As stood like these, could ever know repulse?
For who can yet believe, though after loss,
That all these puissant legions, whose exile
Hath emptied Heaven, shall fail to reascend
Self-raised, and repossess their native seat?
For me, be witness all the host of Heaven,
If counsels different, or danger shunned
By me, have lost our hopes. But he who reigns
Monarch in Heaven, till then as one secure
Sat on his throne, upheld by old repute,
Consent or custom, and his regal state
Put forth at full, but still his strength concealed,
Which tempted our attempt, and wrought our fall.
Henceforth his might we know, and know our own
So as not either to provoke, or dread
New war, provoked; our better part remains
To work in close design, by fraud or guile
What force effected not: that he no less
At length from us may find, who overcomes
By force, hath overcome but half his foe.
Space may produce new worlds; whereof so rife
There went a fame in Heaven that he ere long
Intended to create, and therein plant

A generation, whom his choice regard
Should favour equal to the sons of Heaven:
Thither, if but to pry, shall be perhaps
Our first eruption, thither or elsewhere:
For this infernal pit shall never hold
Celestial spirits in bondage, nor the abyss
Long under darkness cover. But these thoughts
Full counsel must mature: peace is despaired,
For who can think submission! War then, war
Open or understood must be resolved.

He spake: and to confirm his words, out-flew
Millions of flaming swords, drawn from the thighs
Of mighty cherubim; the sudden blaze
Far round illumined Hell: highly they raged
Against the Highest, and fierce with grasped arms
Clashed on their sounding shields the din of war,
Hurling defiance toward the vault of Heaven.

(Lines 587–669)

The Architect of Pandemonium

The hasty multitude
Admiring entered, and the work some praise
And some the architect; his hand was known
In Heaven by many a towered structure high,
Where sceptred angels held their residence,
And sat as princes, whom the supreme king
Exalted to such power, and gave to rule,
Each in his hierarchy, the orders bright.
Nor was his name unheard or unadored
In ancient Greece; and in Ausonian land
Men called him Mulciber; and how he fell
From Heaven, they fabled, thrown by angry Jove
Sheer o'er the crystal battlements: from morn

To noon he fell, from noon to dewy eve,
A summer's day; and with the setting sun
Dropt from the zenith like a falling star,
On Lemnos th'Aegean isle: thus they relate,
Erring; for he with this rebellious rout
Fell long before; nor aught availed him now
To have built in Heaven high towers; nor did he scape
By all his engines, but was headlong sent
With his industrious crew to build in Hell.

(Lines 730–751)

*

BOOK II

The Argument

THE consultation begun, Satan debates whether another battle
be to be hazarded for the recovery of Heaven: some advise it,
others dissuade: a third proposal is preferred, mentioned before by
Satan, to search the truth of that prophecy or tradition in Heaven
concerning another world, and another kind of creature equal or
not much inferior to themselves, about this time to be created:
their doubt who shall be sent on this difficult search: Satan their
chief undertakes alone the voyage, is honoured and applauded.
The council thus ended, the rest betake them several ways and to
several employments, as their inclinations lead them, to entertain
the time till Satan return. He passes on his journey to Hell gates,
finds them shut, and who sat there to guard them, by whom at
length they are opened, and discover to him the great gulf
between Hell and Heaven; with what difficulty he passes
through, directed by Chaos, the power of that place, to the sight
of this new world which he sought.

HIGH on a throne of royal state, which far
Outshone the wealth of Ormus and of Ind,
Or where the gorgeous east with richest hand
Showers on her kings barbaric pearl and gold,
Satan exalted sat, by merit raised
To that bad eminence; and from despair
Thus high uplifted beyond hope, aspires
Beyond thus high, insatiate to pursue
Vain war with Heaven, and by success untaught
His proud imaginations thus displayed.

Powers and Dominions, Deities of Heaven,
For since no deep within her gulf can hold
Immortal vigour, though oppressed and fall'n,
I give not Heaven for lost. From this descent
Celestial virtues rising will appear
More glorious and more dread than from no fall,
And trust themselves to fear no second fate:
Me though just right, and the fixed laws of Heaven
Did first create your leader, next, free choice,
With what besides, in council or in fight,
Hath been achieved of merit, yet this loss
Thus far at least recovered, hath much more
Established in a safe unenvied throne
Yielded with full consent. The happier state
In Heaven, which follows dignity, might draw
Envy from each inferior; but who here
Will envy whom the highest place exposes
Foremost to stand against the Thunderer's aim
Your bulwark, and condemns to greatest share
Of endless pain? Where there is then no good
For which to strive, no strife can grow up there
From faction; for none sure will claim in Hell
Precedence, none, whose portion is so small
Of present pain, that with ambitious mind

Will covet more. With this advantage then
To union, and firm faith, and firm accord,
More than can be in Heaven, we now return
To claim our just inheritance of old,
Surer to prosper than prosperity
Could have assured us; and by what best way,
Whether of open war or covert guile,
We now debate; who can advise, may speak.

He ceased, and next him Moloch, sceptered king
Stood up, the strongest and the fiercest spirit
That fought in Heaven; now fiercer by despair:
His trust was with th'Eternal to be deemed
Equal in strength, and rather than be less
Cared not to be at all; with that care lost
Went all his fear: of God, or Hell, or worse
He recked not, and these words thereafter spake.

My sentence is for open war: of wiles,
More unexpert, I boast not: them let those
Contrive who need, or when they need, not now.
For while they sit contriving, shall the rest,
Millions that stand in arms, and longing wait
The signal to ascend, sit lingering here
Heaven's fugitives, and for their dwelling place
Accept this dark opprobrious den of shame,
The prison of his tyranny who reigns
By our delay? No, let us rather choose,
Armed with Hell flames and fury, all at once
O'er Heaven's high towers to force resistless way,
Turning our tortures into horrid arms
Against the torturer; when to meet the noise
Of his almighty engine he shall hear
Infernal thunder, and for lightning see
Black fire and horror shot with equal rage
Among his angels; and his throne itself

Mixed with Tartarean sulphur, and strange fire,
His own invented torments. But perhaps
The way seems difficult and steep to scale
With upright wing against a higher foe.
Let such bethink them, if the sleepy drench
Of that forgetful lake benumb not still,
That in our proper motion we ascend
Up to our native seat: descent and fall
To us is adverse. Who but felt of late,
When the fierce foe hung on our broken rear
Insulting, and pursued us through the deep,
With what compulsion and laborious flight
We sunk thus low? Th'ascent is easy then;
Th'event is feared? should we again provoke
Our stronger, some worse way his wrath may find
To our destruction? If there be in Hell
Fear to be worse destroyed: what can be worse
Than to dwell here, driven out from bliss, condemned
In this abhorred deep to utter woe;
Where pain of unextinguishable fire
Must exercise us without hope of end
The vassals of his anger, when the scourge
Inexorably, and the torturing hour
Calls us to penance? More destroyed than thus
We should be quite abolished and expire.
What fear we then? What doubt we to incense
His utmost ire? Which to the highth enraged,
Will either quite consume us, and reduce
To nothing this essential, happier far
Than miserable to have eternal being:
Or if our substance be indeed divine,
And cannot cease to be, we are at worst
On this side nothing; and by proof we feel
Our power sufficient to disturb his Heaven,

And with perpetual inroads to alarm,
Though inaccessible, his fatal throne:
Which if not victory is yet revenge.

    He ended frowning, and his look denounced
Desperate revenge, and battle dangerous
To less than gods. On th'other side up rose
Belial, in act more graceful and humane;
A fairer person lost not Heaven; he seemed
For dignity composed and high exploit:
But all was false and hollow; though his tongue
Dropt manna, and could make the worse appear
The better reason, to perplex and dash
Maturest counsels: for his thoughts were low;
To vice industrious, but to nobler deeds
Timorous and slothful: yet he pleased the ear,
And with persuasive accent thus began.

    I should be much for open war, O peers,
As not behind in hate; if what was urged
Main reason to persuade immediate war,
Did not dissuade me most, and seem to cast
Ominous conjecture on the whole success:
When he who most excels in fact of arms,
In what he counsels, and in what excels
Mistrustful, grounds his courage on despair
And utter disolution, as the scope
Of all his aim, after some dire revenge.
First, what revenge? the towers of Heaven are filled
With armed watch, that render all access
Impregnable; oft on the bordering deep
Encamp their legions, or with obscure wing
Scout far and wide into the realm of night,
Scorning surprise. Or could we break our way
By force, and at our heels all Hell should rise
With blackest insurrection, to confound

134

Heaven's purest light, yet our great enemy
All incorruptible would on his throne
Sit unpolluted, and th'ethereal mould
Incapable of stain would soon expel
Her mischief, and purge off the baser fire
Victorious. Thus repulsed, our final hope
Is flat despair; we must exasperate
Th'almighty victor to spend all his rage,
And that must end us, that must be our cure,
To be no more; — sad cure, for who would lose,
Though full of pain, this intellectual being,
Those thoughts that wander through eternity,
To perish rather, swallowed up and lost
In the wide womb of uncreated night,
Devoid of sense and motion? and who knows,
Let this be good, whether our angry foe
Can give it, or will ever? How he can
Is doubtful; that he never will is sure.
Will he, so wise, let loose at once his ire,
Belike through impotence, or unaware,
To give his enemies their wish, and end
Them in his anger, whom his anger saves
To punish endless? Wherefore cease we then?
Say they who counsel war, we are decreed,
Reserved and destined to eternal woe;
Whatever doing, what can we suffer more,
What can we suffer worse? Is this then worst,
Thus sitting, thus consulting, thus in arms?
What when we fled amain, pursued and strook
With Heaven's afflicting thunder, and besought
The deep to shelter us? This Hell then seemed
A refuge from those wounds: or when we lay
Chained on the burning lake? That sure was worse.
What if the breath that kindled those grim fires

Awaked should blow them into sevenfold rage
And plunge us in the flames? Or from above
Should intermitted vengeance arm again
His red right hand to plague us? What if all
Her stores were opened, and this firmament
Of Hell should spout her cataracts of fire,
Impendent horrors, threatening hideous fall
One day upon our heads; while we perhaps
Designing or exhorting glorious war,
Caught in a fiery tempest shall be hurled
Each on his rock transfixed, the sport and prey
Of racking whirlwinds, or for ever sunk
Under yon boiling ocean, wrapped in chains;
There to converse with everlasting groans,
Unrespited, unpitied, unreprieved,
Ages of hopeless end; this would be worse.
War therefore, open or concealed, alike
My voice dissuades; for what can force or guile
With him, or who deceive his mind, whose eye
Views all things at one view? He from Heaven's highth
All these our motions vain, sees and derides;
Not more almighty to resist our might
Than wise to frustrate all our plots and wiles.
Shall we then live thus vile, the race of Heaven
Thus trampled, thus expelled to suffer here
Chains and these torments? Better these than worse
By my advice; since fate inevitable
Subdues us, and omnipotent decree,
The victor's will. To suffer, as to do,
Our strength is equal, nor the law unjust
That so ordains: this was at first resolved,
If we were wise, against so great a foe
Contending, and so doubtful what might fall.
I laugh, when those who at the spear are bold

And venturous, if that fail them, shrink and fear
What yet they know must follow, to endure
Exile, or ignominy, or bonds, or pain,
The sentence of their conqueror: This is now
Our doom; which if we can sustain and bear,
Our supreme foe in time may much remit
His anger, and perhaps thus far removed
Not mind us not offending, satisfied
With what is punished; whence these raging fires
Will slacken, if his breath stir not their flames.
Our purer essence then will overcome
Their noxious vapour, or inured not feel,
Or changed at length, and to the place conformed
In temper and in nature, will receive
Familiar the fierce heat, and void of pain;
This horror will grow mild, this darkness light,
Besides what hope the never-ending flight
Of future days may bring, what chance, what change
Worth waiting, since our present lot appears
For happy though but ill, for ill not worst,
If we procure not to ourselves more woe.
      Thus Belial with words clothed in reason's garb
Counselled ignoble ease and peaceful sloth,
Not peace: and after him thus Mammon spake:
      Either to disenthrone the King of Heaven
We war, if war be best, or to regain
Our own right lost: him to unthrone we then
May hope, when everlasting fate shall yield
To fickle chance, and chaos judge the strife.
The former vain to hope argues as vain
The latter: for what place can be for us
Within Heaven's bound, unless Heaven's Lord supreme
We overpower? Suppose he should relent
And publish grace to all, on promise made

Of new subjection; with what eyes could we
Stand in his presence humble, and receive
Strict laws imposed, to celebrate his throne
With warbled hymns, and to his godhead sing
Forced Halleluiahs; while he lordly sits
Our envied sovereign, and his altar breathes
Ambrosial odours and ambrosial flowers,
Our servile offerings. This must be our task
In Heaven, this our delight; how wearisome
Eternity so spent in worship paid
To whom we hate. Let us not then pursue
By force impossible, by leave obtained
Unacceptable, though in Heaven, our state
Of spendid vassalage, but rather seek
Our own good from ourselves, and from our own
Live to ourselves, though in this vast recess,
Free, and to none accountable, preferring
Hard liberty before the easy yoke
Of servile pomp. Our greatness will appear
Then most conspicuous, when great things of small,
Useful of hurtful, prosperous of adverse
We can create, and in what place so e'er
Thrive under evil, and work ease out of pain
Through labour and endurance. This deep world
Of darkness do we dread? How oft amidst
Thick clouds and dark doth Heaven's all-ruling sire
Choose to reside, his glory unobscured,
And with the majesty of darkness round
Covers his throne; from whence deep thunders roar,
Mustering their rage, and Heaven resembles Hell?
As he our darkness, cannot we his light
Imitate when we please? This desert soil
Wants not her hidden lustre, gems and gold;
Nor want we skill or art, from whence to raise

Magnificence; and what can Heaven show more?
Our torments also may in length of time
Become our elements, these piercing fires
As soft as now severe, our temper changed
Into their temper; which must needs remove
The sensible of pain. All things invite
To peaceful counsels, and the settled state
Of order, how in safety best we may
Compose our present evils, with regard
Of what we are and where, dismissing quite
All thoughts of war; ye have what I advise.

　　He scarce had finished, when such murmur filled
Th'assembly, as when hollow rocks retain
The sound of blustering winds, which all night long
Had roused the sea, now with hoarse cadence lull
Sea-faring men o'erwatched, whose bark by chance
Or pinnace anchors in a craggy bay
After the tempest; such applause was heard
As Mammon ended, and his sentence pleased,
Advising peace; for such another field
They dreaded worse than Hell: — so much the fear
Of thunder and the sword of Michael
Wrought still within them; and no less desire
To found this nether empire, which might rise
By policy, and long process of time,
In emulation opposite to Heaven.
Which when Beëlzebub perceived, than whom,
Satan except, none higher sat, with grave
Aspect he rose, and in his rising seemed
A pillar of state; deep on his front engraven
Deliberation sat and public care;
And princely counsel in his face yet shone,
Majestic though in ruin: sage he stood
With Atlantean shoulders fit to bear

The weight of mightiest monarchies; his look
Drew audience and attention still as night
Or summer's noon-tide air, while thus he spake.
    Thrones and imperial Powers, offspring of Heaven,
Ethereal Virtues; or these titles now
Must we renounce, and changing style be called
Princes of Hell? For so the popular vote
Inclines, here to continue, and build up here
A growing empire. Doubtless; while we dream,
And know not that the King of Heaven hath doomed
This place our dungeon, not our safe retreat
Beyond his potent arm, to live exempt
From Heaven's high jurisdiction, in new league
Banded against his throne, but to remain
In strictest bondage, though thus far removed,
Under th'inevitable curb, reserved
His captive multitude: For he, be sure,
In highth or depth, still first and last will reign
Sole King, and of his kingdom lose no part
By our revolt, but over Hell extend
His empire, and with iron sceptre rule
Us here, as with his golden those in Heaven.
What sit we then projecting peace and war?
War hath determined us, and foiled with loss
Irreparable; terms of peace yet none
Vouchsafed or sought; for what peace will be given
To us enslaved, but custody severe,
And stripes, and arbitrary punishment
Inflicted? and what peace can we return,
But to our power hostility and hate,
Untamed reluctance, and revenge though slow,
Yet ever plotting how the conqueror least
May reap his conquest, and may least rejoice
In doing what we most in suffering feel;

Nor will occasion want, nor shall we need
With dangerous expedition to invade
Heaven, whose high walls fear no assault or seige,
Or ambush from the deep. What if we find
Some easier enterprise? There is a place
(If ancient and prophetic fame in Heaven
Err not) another world, the happy seat
Of some new race called Man, about this time
To be created like to us, though less
In power and excellence, but favoured more
Of him who rules above; so was his will
Pronounced among the gods, and by an oath,
That shook Heaven's whole circumference, confirmed.
Thither let us bend all our thoughts, to learn
What creatures there inhabit, of what mould,
Or substance, how endued, and what their power,
And where their weakness, how attempted best,
By force or subtlety: though Heaven be shut,
And Heaven's high Arbitrator sit secure
In his own strength, this place may lie exposed,
The utmost border of his kingdom, left
To their defence who hold it: here perhaps
Some advantageous act may be achieved
By sudden onset, either with Hell fire
To waste his whole creation, or possess
All as our own, and drive as we were driven,
The puny habitants, or if not drive,
Seduce them to our party, that their God
May prove their foe, and with repenting hand
Abolish his own works. This would surpass
Common revenge, and interrupt his joy
In our confusion, and our joy upraise
In his disturbance; when his darling sons
Hurled headlong to partake with us, shall curse

Their frail originals, and faded bliss,
Faded so soon. Advise if this be worth
Attempting, or to sit in darkness here
Hatching vain empires. Thus Beëlzebub
Pleaded his devilish counsel, first devised
By Satan, and in part proposed: for whence,
But from the author of all ill could spring
So deep a malice, to confound the race
Of mankind in one root, and earth with Hell
To mingle and involve, done all to spite
The great Creator? But their spite still serves
His glory to augment. The bold design
Pleased highly those infernal states, and joy
Sparkled in all their eyes; with full assent
They vote: whereat his speech he thus renews.

    Well have ye judged, well ended long debate,
Synod of gods, and like to what ye are,
Great things resolved; which from the lowest deep
Will once more lift us up, in spite of fate,
Nearer our ancient seat; perhaps in view
Of those bright confines, whence with neighbouring arms
And opportune excursion we may chance
Re-enter Heaven; or else in some mild zone
Dwell not unvisited of Heaven's fair light,
Secure, and at the brightening orient beam
Purge off this gloom; the soft delicious air,
To heal the scar of these corrosive fires
Shall breathe her balm. But first whom shall we send
In search of this new world, whom shall we find
Sufficient? Who shall tempt with wandering feet
The dark unbottomed infinite abyss
And through the palpable obscure find out
His uncouth way, or spread his airy flight
Upborn with indefatigable wings

Over the vast abrupt, ere he arrive
The happy isle; what strength, what art can then
Suffice, or what evasion bear him safe
Through the thick senteries and stations thick
Of angels watching round? Here he had need
All circumspection, and we now no less
Choice in our suffrage; for on whom we send,
The weight of all and our last hope relies.

   This said, he sat; and expectation held
His look suspense, awaiting who appeared
To second, or oppose, or undertake
The perilous attempt; but all sat mute,
Pondering the danger with deep thoughts; and each
In others' countenance read his own dismay
Astonished; none among the choice and prime
Of those Heaven-warring champions could be found
So hardy as to proffer or accept
Alone the dreadful voyage; till at last
Satan, whom now transcendent glory raised
Above his fellows, with monarchal pride
Conscious of highest worth, unmoved thus spake.

   O progeny of Heaven, empyreal Thrones,
With reason hath deep silence and demur
Seized us, though undismayed: long is the way
And hard, that out of Hell leads up to light;
Our prison strong, this huge convex of fire,
Outrageous to devour, immures us round
Ninefold, and gates of burning adamant
Barred over us prohibit all egress.
These past, if any pass, the void profound
Of unessential night receives him next
Wide gaping, and with utter loss of being
Threatens him, plunged in that abortive gulf.
If thence he scape into whatever world,

Or unknown region, what remains him less
Than unknown dangers and as hard escape.
But I should ill become this throne, O peers,
And this imperial sovereignty, adorned
With splendour, armed with power, if aught proposed
And judged of public moment, in the shape
Of difficulty or danger could deter
Me from attempting. Wherefore do I assume
These royalties, and not refuse to reign,
Refusing to accept as great a share
Of hazard as of honour, due alike
To him who reigns, and so much to him due
Of hazard more, as he above the rest
High honoured sits? Go therefore mighty Powers,
Terror of Heaven, though fallen; intend at home
While here shall be our home, what best may ease
The present misery, and render Hell
More tolerable; if there be cure or charm
To respite or deceive, or slack the pain
Of this ill mansion: intermit no watch
Against a wakeful foe, while I abroad
Through all the coasts of dark destruction seek
Deliverance for us all: this enterprise
None shall partake with me. Thus saying rose
The monarch, and prevented all reply,
Prudent, lest from his resolution raised
Others among the chief might offer now
(Certain to be refused) what erst they feared;
And so refused might in opinion stand
His rivals, winning cheap the high repute
Which he through hazard huge must earn. But they
Dreaded not more th'adventure than his voice
Forbidding; and at once with him they rose;
Their rising all at once was as the sound

Of thunder heard remote. Towards him they bend
With awful reverence prone; and as a god
Extol him equal to the highest in Heaven:
Nor failed they to express how much they praised,
That for the general safety he despised
His own: for neither do the spirits damned
Lose all their virtue; lest bad men should boast
Their specious deeds on earth, which glory excites,
Or close ambition varnished o'er with zeal.
Thus they their doubtful consultations dark
Ended rejoicing in their matchless chief:
As when from mountain tops the dusky clouds
Ascending, while the north wind sleeps, o'erspread
Heaven's cheerful face, the lowering element
Scowls o'er the darkened landscape snow or shower;
If chance the radiant sun with farewell sweet
Extend his evening beam, the fields revive,
The birds their notes renew, and bleating herds
Attest their joy, that hill and valley rings.
O shame to men! Devil with devil damned
Firm concord holds, men only disagree
Of creatures rational, though under hope
Of Heavenly grace; and God proclaiming peace,
Yet live in hatred, enmity, and strife
Among themselves, and levy cruel wars,
Wasting the earth, each other to destroy:
As if (which might induce us to accord)
Man had not hellish foes enow besides,
That day and night for his destruction wait.

    The Stygian council thus dissolved; and forth
In order came the grand infernal Peers,
Midst came their mighty Paramount, and seemed
Alone th'Antagonist of Heaven, nor less
Than Hell's dread emperor with pomp supreme,

And godlike imitated state; him round
A globe of fiery seraphim enclosed
With bright emblazonry, and horrent arms.
Then of their session ended they bid cry
With trumpets' regal sound the great result:
Toward the four winds four speedy cherubim
Put to their mouths the sounding alchemy
By herald's voice explained: the hollow abyss
Heard far and wide, and all the host of Hell
With deafening shout, returned them loud acclaim.
Thence more at ease their minds and somewhat raised
By false presumptuous hope, the ranged powers
Disband, and wandering each his several way
Pursues, as inclination or sad choice
Leads him perplext, where he may likeliest find
Truce to his restless thoughts, and entertain
The irksome hours, till his great chief return.
Part on the plain, or in the air sublime
Upon the wing, or in swift race contend,
As at th'Olympian games or Pythian fields;
Part curb their fiery steeds, or shun the goal
With rapid wheels, or fronted brigades form.
As when to warn proud cities war appears
Waged in the troubled sky, and armies rush
To battle in the clouds; before each van
Prick forth the airy knights, and couch their spears
Till thickest legions close: with feats of arms
From either end of Heaven the welkin burns.
Others with vast Typhoean rage more fell
Rend up both rocks and hills, and ride the air
In whirlwind; Hell scarce holds the wild uproar.
As when Alcides from Oealia crowned
With conquest, felt th' envenomed robe, and tore
Through pain up by the roots Thessalian pines,

And Lichas from the top of Oeta threw
Into th'Euboic sea. Others more mild,
Retreated in a silent valley, sing
With notes angelical to many a harp
Their own heroic deeds and hapless fall
By doom of battle; and complain that Fate
Free virtue should enthrall to force or chance.
Their song was partial, but the harmony
(What could it less when spirits immortal sing?)
Suspended Hell, and took with ravishment
The thronging audience. In discourse more sweet
(For eloquence the soul, song charms the sense)
Others apart sat on a hill retired,
In thoughts more elevate, and reasoned high
Of providence, foreknowledge, will, and fate,
Fixed fate, free will, foreknowledge absolute,
And found no end, in wandering mazes lost.
Of good and evil much they argued then,
Of happiness and final misery,
Passion and apathy, and glory and shame,
Vain wisdom all, and false philosophy:
Yet with a pleasing sorcery could charm
Pain for a while or anguish, and excite
Fallacious hope, or arm th'obdured breast
With stubborn patience as with triple steel.
Another part in squadrons and gross bands
On bold adventure to discover wide
That dismal world, if any clime perhaps
Might yield them easier habitation, bend
Four ways their flying march, along the banks
Of four infernal rivers that disgorge
Into the burning lake their baleful streams;
Abhorred Styx, the flood of deadly hate,
Sad Acheron of sorrow, black and deep;

Cocytus, named of lamentation loud
Heard on the rueful stream; fierce Phlegeton
Whose waves of torrent fire inflame with rage.
Far off from these a slow and silent stream,
Lethe the river of oblivion rolls
Her watery labyrinth, whereof who drinks,
Forthwith his former state and being forgets,
Forgets both joy and grief, pleasure and pain.
Beyond this flood a frozen continent
Lies dark and wild, beat with perpetual storms
Of whirlwind and dire hail, which on firm land
Thaws not, but gathers heap, and ruin seems
Of ancient pile; all else deep snow and ice,
A gulf profound as that Serbonian bog
Betwixt Damiata and mount Casius old,
Where armies whole have sunk: the parching air
Burns frore, and cold performs th'effect of fire.
Thither by harpy-footed furies hailed,
At certain revolutions all the damned
Are brought: and feel by turns the bitter change
Of fierce extremes, extremes by change more fierce,
From beds of raging fire to starve in ice
Their soft ethereal warmth, and there to pine
Immovable, infixed, and frozen round,
Periods of time, thence hurried back to fire
They ferry over this Lethean sound
Both to and fro, their sorrow to augment,
And wish and struggle, as they pass, to reach
The tempting stream, with one small drop to lose
In sweet forgetfulness all pain and woe,
All in one moment, and so near the brink;
But fate withstands, and to oppose th'attempt
Medusa with Gorgonian terror guards
The ford, and of itself the water flies

All taste of living wight, as once it fled
The lips of Tantalus. Thus roving on
In confused march forlorn, th'adventurous bands
With shuddering horror pale, and eyes aghast
Viewed first their lamentable lot, and found
No rest: through many a dark and dreary vale
They passed, and many a region dolorous,
O'er many a frozen, many a fiery Alp,
Rocks, caves, lakes, fens, bogs, dens, and shades of death,
A universe of death, which God by curse
Created evil, for evil only good,
Where all life dies, death lives, and nature breeds,
Perverse, all monstrous, all prodigious things,
Abominable, inutterable, and worse
Than fables yet have feigned, or fear conceived,
Gorgons and Hydras, and Chimeras dire.

Meanwhile the adversary of God and Man,
Satan with thoughts inflamed of highest design,
Puts on swift wings, and toward the gates of Hell
Explores his solitary flight; sometimes
He scours the right hand coast, sometimes the left,
Now shaves with level wing the deep, then soars
Up to the fiery conclave touring high.
As when far off at sea a fleet descried
Hangs in the clouds, by equinoctial winds
Close sailing from Bengala, or the isles
Of Ternate and Tidore, whence merchants bring
Their spicy drugs: they on the trading flood
Through the wide Ethiopian to the Cape
Ply stemming nightly toward the pole. So seemed
Far off the flying fiend: at last appear
Hell bounds high reaching to the horrid roof,
And thrice threefold the gates; three folds were brass,
Three iron, three of adamantine rock,

Impenetrable, impaled with circling fire,
Yet unconsumed. Before the gates there sat
On either side a formidable shape;
The one seemed woman to the waist, and fair,
But ended foul in many a scaly fold
Voluminous and vast, a serpent armed
With mortal sting: about her middle round
A cry of Hell hounds never-ceasing barked
With wide Cerberean mouths full loud, and rung
A hideous peal: yet, when they list, would creep,
If aught disturbed their noise, into her womb,
And kennel there, yet there still barked and howled
Within unseen. Far less abhorred than these
Vexed Scylla bathing in the sea that parts
Calabria from the hoarse Trinacrian shore:
Nor uglier follow the night-hag, when called
In secret, riding through the air she comes
Lured with the smell of infant blood, to dance
With Lapland witches, while the labouring moon
Eclipses at their charms. The other shape,
If shape it might be called that shape had none
Distinguishable in member, joint, or limb,
Or substance might be called that shadow seemed,
For each seemed either; black it stood as night,
Fierce as ten furies, terrible as Hell,
And shook a dreadful dart; what seemed his head
The likeness of a kingly crown had on.
Satan was now at hand, and from his seat
The monster moving onward came as fast,
With horrid strides; Hell trembled as he strode.
Th'undaunted fiend what this might be admired,
Admired, not feared; God and his son except,
Created thing nought valued he nor shunned;
And with disdainful look thus first began.

Whence and what art thou, execrable shape,
That dar'st, though grim and terrible, advance
Thy miscreated front athwart my way
To yonder gates? Through them I mean to pass,
That be assured, without leave asked of thee:
Retire, or taste thy folly, and learn by proof,
Hell-born, not to contend with spirits of Heaven.

To whom the goblin full of wrath replied,
Art thou that traitor angel, art thou he,
Who first broke peace in Heaven, and faith, till then
Unbroken, and in proud rebellious arms
Drew after him the third part of Heaven's sons
Conjured against the highest, for which both thou
And they, outcast from God, are here condemned
To waste eternal days in woe and pain?
And reck'n'st thou thyself with spirits of Heaven,
Hell-doomed, and breath'st defiance here and scorn,
Where I reign king, and to enrage thee more,
Thy king and lord? Back to thy punishment,
False fugitive, and to thy speed add wings,
Lest with a whip of scorpions I pursue
Thy ling'ring, or with one stroke of this dart
Strange horror seize thee, and pangs unfelt before.

So spake the grisly terror, and in shape,
So speaking and so threatening, grew tenfold
More dreadful and deform: on th'other side
Incensed with indignation Satan stood
Unterrified, and like a comet burned
That fires the length of Ophiucus huge
In th'Arctic sky, and from his horrid hair
Shakes pestilence and war. Each at the head
Levelled his deadly aim; their fatal hands
No second stroke intend, and such a frown
Each cast at th'other, as when two black clouds

With Heaven's artillery fraught, come rattling on
Over the Caspian, then stand front to front
Hovering a space, till winds the signal blow
To join their dark encounter in mid air:
So frowned the mighty combatants, that Hell
Grew darker at their frown, so matched they stood;
For never but once more was either like
To meet so great a foe: and now great deeds
Had been achieved, whereof all Hell had rung,
Had not the snaky sorceress that sat
Fast by Hell gate, and kept the fatal key,
Ris'n, and with hideous outcry rushed between.

O father what intends thy hand, she cried,
Against thy only son? What fury O son,
Possesses thee to bend that mortal dart
Against thy father's head? And know'st for whom?
For him who sits above and laughs the while
At thee ordained his drudge, to execute
Whate'er his wrath, which he calls Justice, bids,
His wrath which one day will destroy ye both.

She spake, and at her words the hellish pest
Forbore, then these to her Satan returned:

So strange thy outcry; and thy words so strange
Thou interposest, that my sudden hand
Prevented spares to tell thee yet by deeds
What it intends; till first I know of thee,
What thing thou art, thus double-formed, and why
In this infernal vale first met thou call'st
Me father, and that phantasm call'st my son?
I know thee not, nor ever saw till now
Sight more detestable than him and thee.

T' whom thus the portress of Hell gate replied:
Hast thou forgot me then, and do I seem
Now in thine eye so foul, once deemed so fair

In Heaven, when at th'assembly, and in sight
Of all the seraphim with thee combined
In bold conspiracy against Heaven's king,
All on a sudden miserable pain
Surprised thee, dim thine eyes, and dizzy swum
In darkness, while thy head flames thick and fast
Threw forth, till on the left side opening wide,
Likest to thee in shape and countenance bright,
Then shining heavenly fair, a goddess armed
Out of thy head I sprung; amazement seized
All th'host of Heaven; back they recoiled afraid
At first, and called me Sin, and for a sign
Portentous held me; but familiar grown,
I pleased, and with attractive graces won
The most averse, thee chiefly, who full oft
Thyself in me thy perfect image viewing
Becam'st enamoured, and such joy thou took'st
With me in secret, that my womb conceived
A growing burden.   Meanwhile war arose,
And fields were fought in Heaven; wherein remained
(For what could else) to our almighty Foe
Clear victory, to our part loss and rout
Through all the empyrean: down they fell
Driven headlong from the pitch of Heaven, down
Into this deep, and in the general fall
I also; at which time this powerful key
Into my hand was given, with charge to keep
These gates for ever shut, which none can pass
Without my opening. Pensive here I sat
Alone, but long I sat not, till my womb
Pregnant by thee, and now excessive grown
Prodigious motion felt, and rueful throes.
At last this odious offspring whom thou seest
Thine own begotten, breaking violent way

Tore through my entrails, that with fear and pain
Distorted, all my nether shape thus grew
Transformed: but he my inbred enemy
Forth issued, brandishing his fatal dart
Made to destroy. I fled, and cried out Death;
Hell trembled at the hideous name, and sighed
From all her caves, and back resounded Death.
I fled, but he pursued, (though more, it seems,
Inflamed with lust than rage) and swifter far,
Me overtook his mother all dismayed,
And in embraces forcible and foul
Engendering with me, of that rape begot
These yelling monsters that with ceaseless cry
Surround me, as thou sawest, hourly conceived
And hourly born, with sorrow infinite
To me, for when they list into the womb
That bred them they return, and howl and gnaw
My bowels, their repast; then bursting forth
Afresh with conscious terrors vex me round,
That rest or intermission none I find.
Before mine eyes in opposition sits
Grim Death my son and foe, who sets them on,
And me his parent would full soon devour
For want of other prey, but that he knows
His end with mine involved; and knows that I
Should prove a bitter morsel, and his bane,
Whenever that shall be; so fate pronounced.
But thou O father, I forewarn thee, shun
His deadly arrow; neither vainly hope
To be invulnerable in those bright arms,
Though tempered heavenly, for that mortal dint,
Save he who reigns above, none can resist.
    She finished, and the subtle fiend his lore
Soon learned, now milder, and thus answered smooth.

Dear daughter, since thou claimest me for thy sire,
And my fair son here showst me, the dear pledge
Of dalliance had with thee in Heaven, and joys
Then sweet, now sad to mention, through dire change
Befallen us unforeseen, unthought of, know
I come no enemy, but to set free
From out this dark and dismal house of pain,
Both him and thee, and all the Heavenly host
Of spirits that in our just pretences armed
Fell with us from on high: from them I go
This uncouth errand sole, and one for all
Myself expose, with lonely steps to tread
Th'unfounded deep, and through the void immense
To search with wandering quest a place foretold
Should be, and, by concurring signs, ere now
Created vast and round, a place of bliss
In the purlieus of Heaven, and therein placed
A race of upstart creatures, to supply
Perhaps our vacant room, though more removed,
Lest Heaven surcharged with potent multitude
Might hap to move new broils: be this or aught
Than this more secret now designed, I haste
To know, and this once known, shall soon return,
And bring ye to the place where thou and Death
Shall dwell at ease, and up and down unseen
Wing silently the buxom air, imbalmed
With odours; there ye shall be fed and filled
Immeasurably, all things shall be your prey.
He ceased, for both seemed highly pleased, and Death
Grinned horrible a ghastly smile, to hear
His famine should be filled, and blest his maw
Destined to that good hour: no less rejoiced
His mother bad, and thus bespake her sire.
    The key of this infernal pit by due,

And by command of Heaven's all-powerful king
I keep, by him forbidden to unlock
These adamantine gates; against all force
Death ready stands to interpose his dart,
Fearless to be o'ermatched by living might.
But what owe I to his commands above
Who hates me, and hath hither thrust me down
Into this gloom of Tartarus profound,
To sit in hateful office here confined,
Inhabitant of Heaven, and heavenly-born,
Here in perpetual agony and pain,
With terrors and with clamours compassed round
Of mine own brood that on my bowels feed:
Thou art my father, thou my author, thou
My being gav'st me; whom should I obey
But thee, whom follow? thou wilt bring me soon
To that new world of light and bliss, among
The gods who live at ease, where I shall reign
At thy right hand voluptuous, as beseems
Thy daughter and thy darling, without end.

    Thus saying, from her side the fatal key,
Sad instrument of all our woe, she took;
And towards the gate rolling her bestial train,
Forthwith the huge portcullis high up drew,
Which but herself not all the Stygian powers
Could once have moved; then in the key-hole turns
Th'intricate wards, and every bolt and bar
Of massy iron or solid rock with ease
Unfastens: on a sudden open fly
With impetuous recoil and jarring sound
Th'infernal doors, and on their hinges grate
Harsh thunder, that the lowest bottom shook
Of Erebus. She opened, but to shut
Excelled her power; the gates wide open stood,

That with extended wings a bannered host
Under spread ensigns marching might pass through
With horse and chariots ranked in loose array;
So wide they stood, and like a furnace mouth
Cast forth redounding smoke and ruddy flame.
Before their eyes in sudden view appear
The secrets of the hoary deep, a dark
Illimitable ocean without bound,
Without dimension, where length, breadth, and highth,
And time and place are lost; where eldest Night
And Chaos, ancestors of nature, hold
Eternal anarchy, amidst the noise
Of endless wars, and by confusion stand.
For hot, cold, moist, and dry, four champions fierce
Strive here for mastery, and to battle bring
Their embryon atoms; they around the flag
Of each his faction, in their several clans,
Light-armed or heavy, sharp, smooth, swift or slow,
Swarm populous, unnumbered as the sands
Of Barca or Cyrene's torrid soil,
Levied to side with warring winds, and poise
Their lighter wings. To whom these most adhere,
He rules a moment; Chaos umpire sits,
And by decision more imbroils the fray
By which he reigns: next him high arbiter
Chance governs all. Into this wild abyss,
The womb of nature and perhaps her grave,
Of neither sea, nor shore, nor air, nor fire,
But all these in their pregnant causes mixed
Confus'dly, and which thus must ever fight,
Unless th'Almighty Maker them ordain
His dark materials to create more worlds.
Into this wild abyss the wary fiend
Stood on the brink of Hell and looked awhile,

Pondering his voyage: for no narrow frith
He had to cross. Nor was his ear less pealed
With noises loud and ruinous (to compare
Great things with small) than when Bellona storms,
With all her battering engines bent to raze
Some capital city, or less than if this frame
Of Heaven were falling, and these elements
In mutiny had from her axle torn
The steadfast earth. At last his sail-broad vans
He spreads for flight, and in the surging smoke
Uplifted spurns the ground, thence many a league
As in a cloudy chair ascending rides
Audacious, but that seat soon failing, meets
A vast vacuity: all unawares
Fluttering his pennons vain plumb down he drops
Ten thousand fathom deep, and to this hour
Down had been falling, had not by ill chance
The strong rebuff of some tumultuous cloud
Instinct with fire and nitre hurried him
As many miles aloft: that fury stayed,
Quenched in a boggy Syrtis, neither sea,
Nor good dry land: nigh foundered on he fares,
Treading the crude consistence, half on foot,
Half flying; behoves him now both oar and sail.
As when a gryfon through the wilderness
With winged course o'er hill or moory dale,
Pursues the Arimaspian, who by stealth
Had from his wakeful custody purloined
The guarded gold: so eagerly the fiend
O'er bog or steep, through strait, rough, dense, or rare,
With head, hands, wings, or feet pursues his way,
And swims, or sinks, or wades, or creeps, or flies.
At length a universal hubbub wild
Of stunning sounds and voices all confused

Borne through the hollow dark assaults his ear
With loudest vehemence: thither he plies,
Undaunted to meet there whatever power
Or spirit of the nethermost abyss
Might in that noise reside, of whom to ask
Which way the nearest coast of darkness lies
Bordering on light; when straight behold the throne
Of Chaos, and his dark pavilion spread
Wide on the wasteful deep; with him enthroned
Sat sable-vested Night, eldest of things,
The consort of his reign; and by them stood
Orcus and Ades, and the dreaded name
Of Demogorgon; Rumour next and Chance,
And Tumult and Confusion all embroiled.
And Discord with a thousand various mouths.

   T'whom Satan turning boldly, thus. Ye Powers
And spirits of this nethermost abyss,
Chaos and ancient Night, I come no spy,
With purpose to explore or to disturb
The secrets of your realm, but by constraint
Wandering this darksome desert, as my way
Lies through your spacious empire up to light,
Alone, and without guide, half lost, I seek
What readiest path leads where your gloomy bounds
Confine with Heaven; or if some other place
From your dominion won, th'ethereal king
Possesses lately, thither to arrive
I travel this profound; direct my course.
Directed, no mean recompense it brings
To your behoof, if I that region lost,
All usurpation thence expelled, reduce
To her original darkness, and your sway
(Which is my present journey) and once more
Erect the standard there of ancient Night;

Yours be th'advantage all, mine the revenge.
   Thus Satan; and him thus the anarch old
With faltering speech and visage incomposed
Answered. I know thee, stranger, who thou art,
That mighty leading angel, who of late
Made head against Heaven's king, though overthrown.
I saw and heard, for such a numerous host
Fled not in silence through the frighted deep
With ruin upon ruin, rout on rout,
Confusion worse confounded; and Heaven gates
Poured out by millions her victorious bands
Pursuing. I upon my frontiers here
Keep residence; if all I can will serve,
That little which is left so to defend
Encroached on still through our intestine broils
Weakening the sceptre of old Night; first Hell
Your dungeon stretching far and wide beneath;
Now lately Heaven and earth, another world
Hung o'er my realm, linked in a golden chain
To that side Heaven from whence your legions fell:
If that way be your walk, you have not far;
So much the nearer danger; go and speed;
Havoc and spoil and ruin are my gain.
   He ceased; and Satan stayed not to reply,
But glad that now his sea should find a shore,
With fresh alacrity and force renewed
Springs upward like a pyramid of fire
Into the wild expanse, and through the shock
Of fighting elements, on all sides round
Environed wings his way; harder beset
And more endangered, than when Argo passed
Through Bosphorus betwixt the justling rocks:
Or when Ulysses on the larboard shunned
Charybdis, and by th'other whirlpool steered.

So he with difficulty and labour hard
Moved on, with difficulty and labour he;
But he once past, soon after when man fell,
Strange alteration! Sin and Death amain
Following his track, such was the will of Heaven,
Paved after him a broad and beaten way
Over the dark abyss, whose boiling gulf
Tamely endured a bridge of wondrous length
From Hell continued reaching th'utmost orb
Of this frail world; by which the spirits perverse
With easy intercourse pass to and fro
To tempt or punish mortals, except whom
God and good angels guard by special grace.
But now at last the sacred influence
Of light appears, and from the walls of Heaven
Shoots far into the bosom of dim Night
A glimmering dawn; here Nature first begins
Her farthest verge, and Chaos to retire.
As from her outmost works a broken foe
With tumult less and with less hostile din,
That Satan with less toil, and now with ease
Wafts on the calmer wave by dubious light
And like a weather-beaten vessel holds
Gladly the port, though shrouds and tackle torn;
Or in the emptier waste, resembling air,
Weighs his spread wings, at leisure to behold
Far off th'empyreal Heaven, extended wide
In circuit, undetermined square or round,
With opal towers and battlements adorned
Of living sapphire, once his native seat;
And fast by hanging in a golden chain
This pendant world, in bigness as a star
Of smallest magnitude close by the moon.
Thither full fraught with mischievous revenge,
Accurst, and in a cursed hour he hies.

BOOK III

The Argument

God sitting on his throne sees Satan flying towards this world, then newly created; shews him to the Son who sat at his right hand; foretells the success of Satan in perverting mankind; clears his own justice and wisdom from all imputation, having created man free and able enough to have withstood his tempter; yet declares his purpose of grace towards him, in regard he fell not of his own malice, as did Satan, but by him seduced. The Son of God renders praises to his Father for the manifestation of his gracious purpose towards man; but God again declares, that grace cannot be extended towards man without the satisfaction of divine justice; man hath offended the majesty of God by aspiring to godhead, and therefore with all his progeny devoted to death must die, unless some one can be found sufficient to answer for his offence, and undergo his punishment. The Son of God freely offers himself a ransom for man: the Father accepts him, ordains his incarnation, pronounces his exaltation above all names in Heaven and earth; commands all the angels to adore him; they obey, and hymning to their harps in full quire, celebrate the Father and the Son. Meanwhile Satan alights upon the bare convex of this world's outermost orb; where wandering he first finds a place since called the Limbo of Vanity; what persons and things fly up thither; thence comes to the gate of Heaven, described ascending by stairs, and the waters above the firmament that flow about it: His passage thence to the orb of the sun; he finds there Uriel the regent of that orb, but first changes himself into the shape of a meaner angel; and pretending a zealous desire to behold the new creation and man whom God had placed here, inquires of him the place of his habitation, and is directed; alights first on Mount Niphates.

Invocation to Light

HAIL holy light, offspring of Heaven first-born,
Or of th'eternal coeternal beam
May I express thee unblamed? since God is light,
And never but in unapproached light
Dwelt from eternity, dwelt then in thee,
Bright effluence of bright essence increate.
Or hear'st thou rather pure ethereal stream,
Whose fountain who shall tell? Before the sun,
Before the Heavens thou wert, and at the voice
Of God as with a mantle didst invest
The rising world of waters dark and deep,
Won from the void and formless infinite.
Thee I revisit now with bolder wing,
Escaped the Stygian pool, though long detained
In that obscure sojourn, while in my flight
Through utter and through middle darkness borne
With other notes than to th'Orphean lyre
I sung of Chaos and eternal Night,
Taught by the Heavenly Muse to venture down
The dark descent, and up to reascend,
Though hard and rare. Thee I revisit safe,
And feel thy sovereign vital lamp; but thou
Revisit'st not these eyes, that roll in vain
To find thy piercing ray, and find no dawn;
So thick a drop serene hath quenched their orbs,
Or dim suffusion veiled. Yet not the more
Cease I to wander where the Muses haunt
Clear spring, or shady grove, or sunny hill,
Smit with the love of sacred song; but chief
Thee Sion and the flowery brooks beneath
That wash thy hallowed feet, and warbling flow,
Nightly I visit: nor sometimes forget

F 2

Those other two equalled with me in fate,
So were I equalled with them in renown,
Blind Thamyris and blind Maeonides,
And Tiresias and Phineus prophets old.
Then feed on thoughts, that voluntary move
Harmonious numbers; as the wakeful bird
Sings darkling, and in shadiest covert hid
Tunes her nocturnal note. Thus with the year
Seasons return, but not to me returns
Day, or the sweet approach of even or morn,
Or sight of vernal bloom, or summer's rose,
Or flocks, or herds, or human face divine;
But cloud instead, and ever-during dark
Surrounds me, from the cheerful ways of men
Cut off, and for the book of knowledge fair
Presented with a universal blank
Of nature's works to me expunged and razed,
And wisdom at one entrance quite shut out.
So much the rather thou celestial light
Shine inward, and the mind through all her powers
Irradiate, there plant eyes, all mist from thence
Purge and disperse, that I may see and tell
Of things invisible to mortal sight.

*

BOOK IV

The Argument

SATAN now in prospect of Eden, and nigh the place where he
must now attempt the bold enterprise which he undertook alone
against God and man, falls into many doubts with himself, and
many passions, fear, envy, and despair; but at length confirms

himself in evil, journeys on to Paradise, whose outward prospect and situation is described, overleaps the bounds, sits in the shape of a cormorant on the Tree of Life, as highest in the garden to look about him. The garden described; Satan's first sight of Adam and Eve; his wonder at their excellent form and happy state, but with resolution to work their fall; overhears their discourse, thence gathers that the Tree of Knowledge was forbidden them to eat of, under penalty of death; and thereon intends to found his temptation, by seducing them to transgress: then leaves them a while, to know further of their state by some other means. Meanwhile Uriel descending on a sunbeam warns Gabriel, who had in charge the gate of Paradise, that some evil spirit had escaped the deep, and passed at noon by his sphere in the shape of a good angel down to Paradise, discovered after by his furious gestures in the mount. Gabriel promises to find him out ere morning. Night coming on, Adam and Eve discourse of going to their rest: their bower described; their evening worship. Gabriel drawing forth his bands of night-watch to walk the round of Paradise, appoints two strong angels to Adam's bower, lest the evil spirit should be there doing some harm to Adam or Eve sleeping; there they find him at the ear of Eve, tempting her in a dream, and bring him, though unwilling, to Gabriel; by whom questioned, he scornfully answers, prepares resistance, but hindered by a sign from Heaven, flies out of Paradise.

Satan's Soliloquy

O THOU that with surpassing glory crowned,
Look'st from thy sole dominion like the god
Of this new world; at whose sight all the stars
Hide their diminished heads; to thee I call,
But with no friendly voice, and add thy name
O Sun to tell thee how I hate thy beams
That bring to my remembrance from what state

I fell, how glorious once above thy sphere;
Till pride and worse ambition threw me down
Warring in Heaven against Heaven's matchless King:
Ah wherefore! He deserved no such return
From me, whom he created what I was
In that bright eminence, and with his good
Upbraided none; nor was his service hard.
What could be less than to afford him praise,
The easiest recompense, and pay him thanks,
How due! Yet all his good proved ill in me,
And wrought but malice; lifted up so high
I sdeind subjection, and thought one step higher
Would set me highest, and in a moment quit
The debt immense of endless gratitude,
So burthensome, still paying, still to owe;
Forgetful what from him I still received,
And understood not that a grateful mind
By owing owes not, but still pays, at once
Indebted and discharged; what burden then?
O had his powerful destiny ordained
Me some inferior angel, I had stood
Then happy; no unbounded hope had raised
Ambition. Yet why not? some other power
As great might have aspired, and me though mean
Drawn to his part; but other powers as great
Fell not, but stand unshaken, from within
Or from without, to all temptations armed.
Hadst thou the same free will and power to stand?
Thou hadst: whom hast thou then or what to accuse,
But Heaven's free love dealt equally to all?
Be then his love accurst, since love or hate,
To me alike, it deals eternal woe.
Nay cursed be thou; since against his thy will
Chose freely what it now so justly rues.

Me miserable! Which way shall I fly
Infinite wrath, and infinite despair?
Which way I fly is Hell; myself am Hell;
And in the lowest deep a lower deep
Still threatening to devour me opens wide,
To which the Hell I suffer seems a Heaven.
O then at last relent: is there no place
Left for repentance, none for pardon left?
None left but by submission; and that word
Disdain forbids me, and my dread of shame
Among the spirits beneath, whom I seduced
With other promises and other vaunts
Than to submit, boasting I could subdue
Th'omnipotent. Ay me, they little know
How dearly I abide that boast so vain,
Under what torments inwardly I groan:
While they adore me on the throne of Hell,
With diadem and sceptre high advanced
The lower still I fall, only supreme
In misery; such joy ambition finds.
But say I could repent and could obtain
By act of grace my former state; how soon
Would highth recall high thoughts, how soon unsay
What feigned submission swore; ease would recant
Vows made in pain, as violent and void.
For never can true reconcilement grow
Where wounds of deadly hate have pierced so deep:
Which would but lead me to a worse relapse,
And heavier fall: so should I purchase dear
Short intermission bought with double smart.
This knows my punisher; therefore as far
From granting he, as I from begging peace:
All hope excluded thus, behold instead
Of us outcast, exiled, his new delight,

Mankind created, and for him this world.
So farewell hope, and with hope farewell fear,
Farewell remorse; all good to me is lost;
Evil be thou my good; by thee at least
Divided empire with Heaven's king I hold
By thee, and more than half perhaps will reign;
As man ere long, and this new world shall know.

(Lines 32–113)

Evening in Eden

Now came still evening on, and twilight gray
Had in her sober livery all things clad;
Silence accompanied, for beast and bird,
They to their grassy couch, these to their nests
Were slunk, all but the wakeful nightingale;
She all night long her amorous descant sung:
Silence was pleased: now glowed the firmament
With living sapphires. Hesperus that led
The starry host, rode brightest, till the moon
Rising in clouded majesty, at length
Apparent queen unveiled her peerless light,
And o'er the dark her silver mantle threw.

(Lines 598–609)

*

BOOK V

The Argument

MORNING approached, Eve relates to Adam her troublesome dream; he likes it not, yet comforts her: they come forth to their day labours: their morning hymn at the door of their bower. God to render man inexcusable sends Raphael to admonish him of his obedience, of his free estate, of his enemy near at hand; who he is, and why his enemy, and whatever else may avail Adam to know. Raphael comes down to Paradise, his appearance described, his coming discerned by Adam afar off sitting at the door of his bower; he goes out to meet him, brings him to his lodge, entertains him with the choicest fruits of Paradise got together by Eve; their discourse at table: Raphael performs his message, minds Adam of his state and of his enemy; relates at Adam's request who that enemy is, and how he came to be so, beginning from his first revolt in Heaven, and the occasion thereof; how he drew his legions after him to the parts of the north, and there incited them to rebel with him, persuading all but only Abdiel a seraph, who in argument dissuades and opposes him, then forsakes him.

The Morning Hymn of Adam and Eve

THESE are thy glorious works, parent of good,
Almighty, thine this universal frame,
Thus wondrous fair; thyself how wondrous then!
Unspeakable, who sitst above these Heavens
To us invisible or dimly seen
In these thy lowest works, yet these declare
Thy goodness beyond thought, and power divine.
Speak ye who best can tell, ye sons of light,
Angels for ye behold him, and with songs
And choral symphonies, day without night,
Circle his throne rejoicing, ye in Heaven;
On earth join all ye creatures to extol
Him first, him last, him midst, and without end.
Fairest of stars, last in the train of night,
If better thou belong not to the dawn,
Sure pledge of day, that crownst the smiling morn
With thy bright circlet, praise him in thy sphere
While day arises, that sweet hour of prime.

169

Thou sun, of this great world both eye and soul,
Acknowledge him thy greater, sound his praise
In thy eternal course, both when thou climb'st,
And when high noon hast gained, and when thou fallst.
Moon, that now meetst the orient sun, now fli'st
With the fixt stars, fixt in their orb that flies,
And ye five other wandering fires that move
In mystic dance not without song, resound
His praise, who out of darkness called up light.
Air, and ye elements the eldest birth
Of nature's womb, that in quaternion run
Perpetual circle, multiform; and mix
And nourish all things, let your ceaseless change
Vary to our great Maker still new praise.
Ye mists and exhalations that now rise
From hill or steaming lake, dusky or grey,
Till the sun paint your fleecy skirts with gold,
In honour to the world's great author rise,
Whether to deck with clouds the uncoloured sky,
Or wet the thirsty earth with falling showers,
Rising or falling still advance his praise.
His praise ye winds, that from four quarters blow,
Breathe soft or loud; and wave your tops, ye pines,
With every plant, in sign of worship wave.
Fountains and ye, that warble, as ye flow,
Melodious murmurs, warbling tune his praise.
Join voices all ye living souls, ye birds,
That singing up to Heaven gate ascend,
Bear on your wings and in your notes his praise;
Ye that in waters glide, and ye that walk
The earth, and stately tread, or lowly creep;
Witness if I be silent, morn or even,
To hill or valley, fountain, or fresh shade
Made vocal by my song, and taught his praise.

Hail universal lord, be bounteous still
To give us only good; and if the night
Have gathered aught of evil or concealed,
Disperse it, as now light dispels the dark.

(Lines 153–208)

Abdiel

He said, and as the sound of waters deep
Hoarse murmur echoed to his words applause
Through the infinite host, nor less for that
The flaming seraph fearless, though alone
Encompassed round with foes, thus answered bold.

    O alienate from God, O spirit accurst,
Forsaken of all good: I see thy fall
Determined, and thy hapless crew involved
In this perfidious fraud, contagion spread
Both of thy crime and punishment: henceforth
No more be troubled how to quit the yoke
Of God's Messiah: those indulgent laws
Will not now be vouchsafed, other decrees
Against thee are gone forth without recall;
That golden sceptre which thou didst reject
Is now an iron rod to bruise and break
Thy disobedience. Well thou didst advise,
Yet not for thy advice or threats I fly
These wicked tents devoted, lest the wrath
Impendent, raging into sudden flame
Distinguish not: for soon expect to feel
His thunder on thy head, devouring fire.
Then who created thee lamenting learn,
When who can uncreate thee thou shalt know.
    So spake the seraph Abdiel, faithful found,
Among the faithless, faithful only he;

Among innumerable false, unmoved,
Unshaken, unseduced, unterrified,
His loyalty he kept, his love, his zeal;
Nor number nor example with him wrought
To swerve from truth, or change his constant mind
Though single. From amidst them forth he passed,
Long way through hostile scorn, which he sustained
Superior, nor of violence feared aught;
And with retorted scorn his back he turned
On those proud towers to swift destruction doomed.

(Lines 869–904)

*

BOOK VI

The Argument

RAPHAEL continues to relate how Michael and Gabriel were sent forth to battle against Satan and his angels. The first fight described: Satan and his powers retire under night: He calls a council, invents devilish engines, which in the second day's fight put Michael and his angels to some disorder; but they at length pulling up mountains overwhelmed both the force and machines of Satan: Yet the tumult not so ending, God on the third day sends Messiah his Son, for whom he had reserved the glory of that victory: he in the power of his Father coming to the place, and causing all his legions to stand still on either side, with his chariot and thunder driving into the midst of his enemies, pursues them unable to resist towards the wall of Heaven; which opening, they leap down with horror and confusion into the place of punishment prepared for them in the deep: Messiah returns with triumph to his Father.

Messiah Victorious

So spake the Son, and into terror changed
His countenance too severe to be beheld
And full of wrath bent on his enemies.
At once the four spread out their starry wings
With dreadful shade contiguous, and the orbs
Of his fierce chariot rolled, as with the sound
Of torrent floods, or of a numerous host.
He on his impious foes right onward drove,
Gloomy as night; under his burning wheels
The steadfast empyrean shook throughout,
All but the throne itself of God. Full soon
Among them he arrived; in his right hand
Grasping ten thousand thunders, which he sent
Before him, such as in their minds infixed
Plagues; they astonished all resistance lost,
All courage; down their idle weapons dropped;
O'er shields and helms, and helmed heads he rode
Of thrones and mighty seraphim prostrate,
That wished the mountains now might be again
Thrown on them as a shelter from his ire.
Nor less on either side tempestuous fell
His arrows, from the fourfold-visaged four,
Distinct with eyes, and from the living wheels,
Distinct alike with multitude of eyes,
One spirit in them ruled, and every eye
Glared lightning, and shot forth pernicious fire
Among th'accurst, that withered all their strength,
And of their wonted vigour left them drained,
Exhausted, spiritless, afflicted, fallen.
Yet half his strength he put not forth, but checked
His thunder in mid volley, for he meant
Not to destroy, but root them out of Heaven:

The overthrown he raised, and as a herd
Of goats or timorous flock together thronged
Drove them before him thunderstruck, pursued
With terrors and with furies to the bounds
And crystal wall of Heaven, which opening wide,
Rolled inward, and a spacious gap disclosed
Into the wasteful deep; the monstrous sight
Strook them with horror backward, but far worse
Urged them behind; headlong themselves they threw
Down from the verge of Heaven, eternal wrath
Burnt after them to the bottomless pit.

　　Hell heard th'insufferable noise, Hell saw
Heaven ruining from Heaven, and would have fled
Affrighted; but strict fate had cast too deep
Her dark foundations, and too fast had bound.
Nine days they fell; confounded Chaos roared,
And felt tenfold confusion in their fall
Through his wild anarchy, so huge a rout
Incumbered him with ruin: Hell at last
Yawning received them whole, and on them closed,
Hell their fit habitation fraught with fire
Unquenchable, the house of woe and pain.
Disburdened Heaven rejoiced, and soon repaired
Her mural breach, returning whence it rolled.
Sole victor from th'expulsion of his foes
Messiah his triumphal chariot turned:
To meet him all his saints, who silent stood
Eye witnesses of his almighty acts,
With jubilee advanced; and as they went,
Shaded with branching palm, each order bright
Sung triumph, and him sung victorious King,
Son, Heir and Lord, to him dominion given,
Worthiest to reign: he celebrated rode
Triumphant through mid Heaven, into the courts

And temple of his mighty Father throned
On high; who into glory him received,
Where now he sits at the right hand of bliss.

(Lines 824–892)

*

BOOK VII

The Argument

RAPHAEL at the request of Adam relates how and wherefore this
world was first created; that God, after the expelling of Satan and
his angels out of Heaven, declared his pleasure to create another
world and other creatures to dwell therein; sends his Son with
glory and attendance of angels to perform the work of creation in
six days: the angels celebrate with hymns the performance thereof, and his reascension into Heaven.

Invocation

DESCEND from Heaven Urania, by that name
If rightly thou art called, whose voice divine
Following, above th'Olympian hill I soar,
Above the flight of Pegasean wing.
The meaning, not the name I call: for thou
Nor of the Muses nine, nor on the top
Of old Olympus dwellst, but heavenly born,
Before the hills appeared, or fountain flowed,
Thou with eternal wisdom didst converse,
Wisdom thy sister, and with her didst play
In presence of th'almighty Father, pleased
With thy celestial song. Up led by thee
Into the Heaven of Heavens I have presumed,
An earthly guest, and drawn empyreal air,

Thy tempering; with like safety guided down
Return me to my native element:
Lest from this flying steed unreined, (as once
Bellerophon, though from a lower clime)
Dismounted, on th'Aleian field I fall
Erroneous, there to wander and forlorn.
Half yet remains unsung, but narrower bound
Within the visible diurnal sphere;
Standing on earth, not rapt above the pole,
More safe I sing with mortal voice, unchanged
To hoarse or mute, though fall'n on evil days,
On evil days though fall'n, and evil tongues;
In darkness, and with dangers compassed round,
And solitude; yet not alone, while thou
Visit'st my slumbers nightly, or when morn
Purples the east: still govern thou my song,
Urania, and fit audience find, though few.
But drive far off the barbarous dissonance
Of Bacchus and his revellers, the race
Of that wild rout that tore the Thracian bard
In Rhodope, where woods and rocks had ears
To rapture, till the savage clamour drowned
Both harp and voice; nor could the Muse defend
Her son. So fail not thou, who thee implores:
For thou art heavenly, she an empty dream.

(Lines 1–39)

*

BOOK VIII

The Argument

ADAM inquires concerning celestial motions, is doubtfully
answered, and exhorted to search rather things more worthy of

knowledge: Adam assents, and still desirous to detain Raphael, relates to him what he remembered since his own creation, his placing in Paradise, his talk with God concerning solitude and fit society, his first meeting and nuptials with Eve, his discourse with the angel thereupon; who after admonitions repeated departs.

*

BOOK IX

The Argument

SATAN having compassed the earth, with meditated guile returns as a mist by night into Paradise, enters into the serpent sleeping. Adam and Eve in the morning go forth to their labours, which Eve proposes to divide in several places, each labouring apart: Adam consents not, alleging the danger, lest that enemy, of whom they were forewarned, should attempt her found alone: Eve loth to be thought not circumspect or firm enough, urges her going apart, the rather desirous to make trial of her strength; Adam at last yields: the serpent finds her alone; his subtle approach, first gazing, then speaking, with much flattery extolling Eve above all other creatures. Eve wondering to hear the serpent speak, asks how he attained to human speech and such understanding not till now; the serpent answers that by tasting of a certain tree in the garden he attained both to speech and reason, till then void of both: Eve requires him to bring her to that tree, and finds it to be the Tree of Knowledge forbidden: the serpent now grown bolder, with many wiles and arguments induces her at length to eat; she pleased with the taste deliberates awhile whether to impart thereof to Adam or not, at last brings him of the fruit, relates what persuaded her to eat thereof: Adam at first amazed, but perceiving her lost, resolves through vehemence of love to perish with her; and extenuating the trespass, eats also of the fruit: the effects thereof in them both; they seek to cover their nakedness; then fall to variance and accusation of one another.

No more of talk where God or angel guest
With man, as with his friend, familiar used
To sit indulgent, and with him partake
Rural repast, permitting him the while
Venial discourse unblamed: I now must change
Those notes to tragic; foul distrust, and breach
Disloyal on the part of man, revolt,
And disobedience: on the part of Heaven
Now alienated, distance and distaste,
Anger and just rebuke, and judgement given,
That brought into this world a world of woe,
Sin and her shadow death, and misery
Death's harbinger: sad task, yet argument
Not less but more heroic than the wrath
Of stern Achilles on his foe pursued
Thrice fugitive about Troy wall; or rage
Of Turnus for Lavinia disespoused,
Or Neptune's ire or Juno's, that so long
Perplexed the Greek and Cytherea's son;
If answerable style I can obtain
Of my celestial patroness, who deigns
Her nightly visitation unimplored,
And dictates to me slumbering, or inspires
Easy my unpremeditated verse:
Since first this subject for heroic song
Pleased me long choosing, and beginning late,
Not sedulous by nature to indite
Wars, hitherto the only argument
Heroic deemed, chief mastery to dissect
With long and tedious havoc fabled knights

In battles feigned; the better fortitude
Of patience and heroic martyrdom
Unsung; or to describe races and games,
Or tilting furniture, emblazoned shields,
Impresses quaint, caparisons and steeds;
Bases and tinsel trappings, gorgeous knights
At joust and tournament; then marshalled feast
Served up in hall with sewers, and seneschals;
The skill of artifice or office mean,
Not that which justly gives heroic name
To person or to poem. Me of these
Nor skilled nor studious, higher argument
Remains, sufficient of itself to raise
That name, unless an age too late, or cold
Climate, or years damp my intended wing
Depressed, and much they may, if all be mine,
Not hers, who brings it nightly to my ear.

    The sun was sunk, and after him the star
Of Hesperus, whose office is to bring
Twilight upon the earth, short arbiter
Twixt day and night, and now from end to end
Night's hemisphere had veiled the horizon round;
When Satan who late fled before the threats
Of Gabriel out of Eden, now improved
In meditated fraud and malice, bent
On man's destruction, maugre what might hap
Of heavier on himself, fearless returned.
By night he fled, and at midnight returned
From compassing the earth, cautious of day,
Since Uriel regent of the sun descried
His entrance, and forewarned the Cherubim
That kept their watch; thence full of anguish driven,
The space of seven continued nights he rode
With darkness; thrice the equinoctial line

He circled, four times crossed the car of night
From pole to pole, traversing each colure;
On the eighth returned, and on the coast averse
From entrance or cherubic watch, by stealth
Found unsuspected way. There was a place,
Now not, though sin, not time, first wrought the change,
Where Tigris at the foot of Paradise
Into a gulf shot underground, till part
Rose up a fountain by the Tree of Life;
In with the river sunk, and with it rose
Satan involved in rising mist, then sought
Where to lie hid; sea he had searched and land
From Eden over Pontus, and the pool
Maeotis, up beyond the river Ob;
Downward as far antarctic; and in length
West from Orontes to the Ocean barred
At Darien, thence to the land where flows
Ganges and Indus: thus the orb he roamed
With narrow search; and with inspection deep
Considered every creature, which of all
Most opportune might serve his wiles, and found
The serpent subtlest beast of all the field.
Him after long debate, irresolute
Of thoughts revolved, his final sentence chose
Fit vessel, fittest imp of fraud, in whom
To enter, and his dark suggestions hide
From sharpest sight: for in the wily snake,
Whatever sleights none would suspicious mark,
As from his wit and native subtlety
Proceeding, which in other beasts observed
Doubt might beget of diabolic power
Active within beyond the sense of brute.
Thus he resolved, but first from inward grief
His bursting passion into plaints thus poured:

O Earth, how like to Heaven, if not preferred
More justly, seat worthier of gods, as built
With second thoughts, reforming what was old!
For what God after better worse would build?
Terrestrial Heaven, danced round by other Heavens
That shine, yet bear their bright officious lamps,
Light above light, for thee alone, as seems,
In thee concentring all their precious beams
Of sacred influence: as God in Heaven
Is centre, yet extends to all, so thou
Centring receiv'st from all those orbs; in thee,
Not in themselves, all their known virtue appears
Productive in herb, plant, and nobler birth
Of creatures animate with gradual life
Of growth, sense, reason, all summed up in man.
With what delight could I have walked thee round
If I could joy in aught, sweet interchange
Of hill and valley, rivers, woods and plains,
Now land, now sea, and shores with forests crowned,
Rocks, dens, and caves; but I in none of these
Find place or refuge; and the more I see
Pleasures about me, so much more I feel
Torment within me, as from the hateful siege
Of contraries; all good to me becomes
Bane, and in Heaven much worse would be my state.
But neither here seek I, no nor in Heaven
To dwell, unless by mastering Heaven's supreme;
Nor hope to be myself less miserable
By what I seek, but others to make such
As I, though thereby worse to me redound:
For only in destroying I find ease
To my relentless thoughts; and him destroyed,
Or won to what may work his utter loss,
For whom all this was made, all this will soon

Follow, as to him linked in weal or woe;
In woe then; that destruction wide may range.
To me shall be the glory sole among
The infernal powers, in one day to have marred
What he, Almighty styled, six nights and days
Continued making, and who knows how long
Before had been contriving, though perhaps
Not longer than since I in one night freed
From servitude inglorious wellnigh half
Th'angelic name, and thinner left the throng
Of his adorers: he to be avenged,
And to repair his numbers thus impaired,
Whether such virtue spent of old now failed
More angels to create, if they at least
Are his created or to spite us more,
Determined to advance into our room
A creature formed of earth, and him endow,
Exalted from so base original,
With heavenly spoils, our spoils; what he decreed
He effected; man he made, and for him built
Magnificent this world, and earth his seat,
Him lord pronounced, and, O indignity!
Subjected to his service angel wings,
And flaming ministers to watch and tend
Their earthy charge: Of these the vigilance
I dread, and to elude, thus wrapt in mist
Of midnight vapour glide obscure, and pry
In every bush and brake, where hap may find
The serpent sleeping, in whose mazy folds
To hide me, and the dark intent I bring.
O foul descent! That I who erst contended
With gods to sit the highest, am now constrained
Into a beast, and mixed with bestial slime,
This essence to incarnate and imbrute,

That to the height of deity aspired;
But what will not ambition and revenge
Descend to? Who aspires must down as low
As high he soared, obnoxious first or last
To basest things. Revenge, at first though sweet,
Bitter ere long back on itself recoils;
Let it; I reck not, so it light well aimed,
Since higher I fall short, on him who next
Provokes my envy, this new favourite
Of Heaven, this man of clay, son of despite,
Whom us the more to spite his maker raised
From dust: spite then with spite is best repaid.

So saying, through each thicket dank or dry,
Like a black mist low creeping, he held on
His midnight search, where soonest he might find
The serpent: him fast sleeping soon he found
In labyrinth of many a round self-rolled,
His head the midst, well stored with subtle wiles:
Not yet in horrid shade or dismal den,
Not nocent yet, but on the grassy herb
Fearless unfeared he slept: in at his mouth
The Devil entered, and his brutal sense,
In heart or head, possessing soon inspired
With act intelligential; but his sleep
Disturbed not, waiting close th'approach of morn.
Now whenas sacred light began to dawn
In Eden on the humid flowers, that breathed
Their morning incense, when all things that breathe,
From th'earth's great altar send up silent praise
To the Creator, and his nostrils fill
With grateful smell, forth came the human pair
And joined their vocal worship to the quire
Of creatures wanting voice; that done, partake
The season, prime for sweetest scents and airs:

Then commune how that day they best may ply
Their growing work: for much their work outgrew
The hand's dispatch of two gardening so wide.
And Eve first to her husband thus began.

    Adam well may we labour still to dress
This garden, still to tend plant, herb and flower.
Our pleasant task enjoined, but till more hands
Aid us, the work under our labour grows,
Luxurious by restraint: what we by day
Lop overgrown, or prune, or prop, or bind,
One night or two with wanton growth derides
Tending to wild. Thou therefore now advise
Or hear what to my mind first thoughts present,
Let us divide our labours, thou where choice
Leads thee, or where most needs, whether to wind
The woodbine round this arbour, or direct
The clasping ivy, where to climb, while I
In yonder spring of roses intermixed
With myrtle, find what to redress till noon:
For while so near each other thus all day
Our task we choose, what wonder if so near
Looks intervene and smiles, or object new
Casual discourse draw on, which intermits
Our day's work brought to little, though begun
Early, and th'hour of supper comes unearned.

    To whom mild answer Adam thus returned.
Sole Eve, associate sole, to me beyond
Compare above all living creatures dear,
Well hast thou motioned, well thy thoughts employed
How we might best fulfil the work which here
God hath assigned us, nor of me shalt pass
Unpraised; for nothing lovelier can be found
In woman, than to study household good,
And good works in her husband to promote.

Yet not so strictly hath our Lord imposed
Labour, as to debar us when we need
Refreshment, whether food, or talk between,
Food of the mind, or this sweet intercourse
Of looks and smiles, for smiles from reason flow,
To brute denied, and are of love the food,
Love not the lowest end of human life.
For not to irksome toil, but to delight
He made us, and delight to reason joined.
These paths and bowers doubt not, but our joint hands
Will keep from wilderness with ease, as wide
As we need walk, till younger hands ere long
Assist us: but if much converse perhaps
Thee satiate, to short absence I could yield.
For solitude sometimes is best society,
And short retirement urges sweet return.
But other doubt possesses me, lest harm
Befall thee severed from me; for thou knowest
What hath been warned us, what malicious foe
Envying our happiness, and of his own
Despairing, seeks to work us woe and shame
By sly assault; and somewhere nigh at hand
Watches, no doubt, with greedy hope to find
His wish and best advantage, us asunder,
Hopeless to circumvent us joined, where each
To other speedy aid might lend at need;
Whether his first design be to withdraw
Our fealty from God, or to disturb
Conjugal love, than which perhaps no bliss
Enjoyed by us excites his envy more;
Or this, or worse, leave not the faithful side
That gave thee being, still shades thee and protects.
The wife, where danger or dishonour lurks,
Safest and seemliest by her husband stays,

Who guards her, or with her the worst endures.
    To whom the virgin majesty of Eve,
As one who loves, and some unkindness meets,
With sweet austere composure thus replied:
    Offspring of Heaven, and earth, and all earth's lord,
That such an enemy we have, who seeks
Our ruin, both by thee informed I learn,
And from the parting angel overheard
As in a shady nook I stood behind,
Just then returned at shut of evening flowers.
But that thou shouldst my firmness therefore doubt
To God or thee, because we have a foe
May tempt it, I expected not to hear.
His violence thou fearst not, being such,
As we, not capable of death or pain,
Can either not receive, or can repel.
His fraud is then thy fear, which plain infers
Thy equal fear that my firm faith and love
Can by his fraud be shaken or seduced;
Thoughts, which how found they harbour in thy breast,
Adam, misthought of her to thee so dear?
    To whom with healing words Adam replied.
Daughter of God and man, immortal Eve,
For such thou art, from sin and blame entire:
Not diffident of thee do I dissuade
Thy absence from my sight, but to avoid
Th'attempt itself, intended by our foe.
For he who tempts, though in vain, at least asperses
The tempted with dishonour foul, supposed
Not incorruptible of faith, not proof
Against temptation: thou thyself with scorn
And anger wouldst resent the offered wrong,
Though ineffectual found: misdeem not then,
If such affront I labour to avert

From thee alone, which on us both at once
The enemy, though bold, will hardly dare,
Or daring, first on me th'assault shall light.
Nor thou his malice and false guile contemn;
Subtle he needs must be, who could seduce
Angels, nor think superfluous others' aid.
I from the influence of thy looks receive
Access in every virtue, in thy sight
More wise, more watchful, stronger, if need were
Of outward strength; while shame, thou looking on,
Shame to be overcome or over-reached
Would utmost vigour raise, and raised unite.
Why shouldst not thou like sense within thee feel
When I am present, and thy trial choose
With me, best witness of thy virtue tried.

   So spake domestic Adam in his care
And matrimonial love, but Eve, who thought
Less attributed to her faith sincere,
Thus her reply with accent sweet renewed.

   If this be our condition, thus to dwell
In narrow circuit straitened by a foe,
Subtle or violent, we not endued
Single with like defence, wherever met,
How are we happy, still in fear of harm?
But harm precedes not sin: only our foe
Tempting affronts us with his foul esteem
Of our integrity: his foul esteem
Sticks no dishonour on our front, but turns
Foul on himself. Then wherefore shunned or feared
By us? Who rather double honour gain
From his surmise proved false, find peace within,
Favour from Heaven, our witness from th'event.
And what is faith, love, virtue unassayed
Alone, without exterior help sustained?

Let us not then suspect our happy state
Left so imperfect by the Maker wise,
As not secure to single or combined.
Frail is our happiness, if this be so,
And Eden were no Eden thus exposed.

    To whom thus Adam fervently replied.
O woman, best are all things as the will
Of God ordained them, his creating hand
Nothing imperfect or deficient left
Of all that he created, much less man,
Or ought that might his happy state secure,
Secure from outward force; within himself
The danger lies, yet lies within his power:
Against his will he can receive no harm.
But God left free the will, for what obeys
Reason, is free, and reason he made right
But bid her well beware, and still erect,
Lest by some fair appearing good surprised
She dictate false, and misinform the will
To do what God expressly hath forbid.
Not then mistrust, but tender love enjoins,
That I should mind thee oft, and mind thou me.
Firm we subsist, yet possible to swerve,
Since reason not impossibly may meet
Some specious object by the foe suborned,
And fall into deception unaware,
Not keeping strictest watch, as she was warned.
Seek not temptation then, which to avoid
Were better, and most likely if from me
Thou sever not: trial will come unsought.
Wouldst thou approve thy constancy, approve
First thy obedience; th'other who can know,
Not seeing thee attempted, who attest?
But if thou think trial unsought may find

Us both securer than thus warned thou seemst,
Go: for thy stay, not free, absents thee more:
Go in thy native innocence, rely
On what thou hast of virtue, summon all,
For God towards thee hath done his part, do thine.

  So spake the Patriarch of mankind, but Eve
Persisted: yet submiss, though last, replied.

  With thy permission then, and thus forewarned
Chiefly by what thy own last reasoning words
Touched only, that our trial, when least sought,
May find us both perhaps far less prepared,
The willinger I go, nor much expect
A foe so proud will first the weaker seek:
So bent, the more shall shame him his repulse.
Thus saying, from her husband's hand her hand
Soft she withdrew, and like a wood-nymph light
Oread or Dryad, or of Delia's train,
Betook her to the groves, but Delia's self
In gait surpassed and goddess-like deport,
Though not as she with bow and quiver armed,
But with such gardening tools as art yet rude,
Guiltless of fire had formed, or angels brought.
To Pales, or Pomona, thus adorned,
Likest she seemed, Pomona when she fled
Vertumnus, or to Ceres in her prime,
Yet virgin of Proserpina from Jove.
Her long with ardent look his eye pursued
Delighted, but desiring more her stay.
Oft he to her his charge of quick return
Repeated, she to him as oft engaged
To be returned by noon amid the bower,
And all things in best order to invite
Noontide repast, or afternoon's repose.
O much deceived, much failing, hapless Eve,

Of thy presumed return! Event perverse!
Thou never from that hour in Paradise
Foundst either sweet repast, or sound repose;
Such ambush hid among sweet flowers and shades
Waited with hellish rancour imminent
To intercept thy way, or send thee back
Despoiled of innocence, of faith, of bliss.
For now, and since first break of dawn, the fiend,
Mere serpent in appearance, forth was come,
And on his quest, where likeliest he might find
The only two of mankind, but in them
The whole included race, his purposed prey.
In bower and field he sought, where any tuft
Of grove or garden-plot more pleasant lay,
Their tendance or plantation for delight;
By fountain or by shady rivulet
He sought them both, but wished his hap might find
Eve separate, he wished, but not with hope
Of what so seldom chanced, when to his wish,
Beyond his hope, Eve separate he spies,
Veiled in a cloud of fragrance, where she stood,
Half spied, so thick the roses blushing round
About her glowed, oft stooping to support
Each flower of slender stalk, whose head though gay
Carnation, purple, azure, or spect with gold,
Hung drooping unsustained, them she upstays
Gently with myrtle band, mindless the while,
Herself, though fairest unsupported flower,
From her best prop so far, and storm so nigh.
Nearer he drew, and many a walk traversed
Of stateliest covert, cedar, pine, or palm:
Then voluble and bold, now hid, now seen
Among thick-woven arborets and flowers
Imbordered on each bank, the hand of Eve:

Spot more delicious than those gardens feigned
Or of revived Adonis, or renowned
Alcinous, host of old Laertes son,
Or that, not mystic, where the sapient king
Held dalliance with his fair Egyptian spouse.
Much he the place admired, the person more.
As one who long in populous city pent,
Where houses thick and sewers annoy the air,
Forth issuing on a summer's morn to breathe
Among the pleasant villages and farms
Adjoined, from each thing met conceives delight,
The smell of grain, or tedded grass, or kine,
Or dairy, each rural sight, each rural sound:
If chance with nymphlike step fair virgin pass,
What pleasing seemed, for her now pleases more,
She most, and in her looks sums all delight.
Such pleasure took the serpent to behold
This flowery plat, the sweet recess of Eve
Thus early, thus alone; her heavenly form
Angelic, but more soft, and feminine,
Her graceful innocence, her every air
Of gesture or least action overawed
His malice, and with rapine sweet bereaved
His fierceness of the fierce intent it brought:
That space the evil one abstracted stood
From his own evil, and for the time remained
Stupidly good, of enmity disarmed,
Of guile, of hate, of envy, of revenge:
But the hot Hell that always in him burns,
Though in mid Heaven, soon ended his delight,
And tortures him now more, the more he sees
Of pleasure not for him ordained: then soon
Fierce hate he recollects, and all his thoughts
Of mischief, gratulating, thus excites.

Thoughts, whither have ye led me, with what sweet
Compulsion thus transported to forget
What hither brought us, hate, not love, nor hope
Of Paradise for Hell, hope here to taste
Of pleasure, but all pleasure to destroy,
Save what is in destroying, other joy
To me is lost. Then let me not let pass
Occasion which now smiles, behold alone
The woman, opportune to all attempts,
Her husband, for I view far round, not nigh,
Whose higher intellectual more I shun,
And strength, of courage haughty, and of limb
Heroic built, though of terrestrial mould,
Foe not informidable, exempt from wound,
I not; so much hath Hell debased, and pain
Infeebled me, to what I was in Heaven.
She fair, divinely fair, fit love for gods,
Not terrible, though terror be in love
And beauty, not approached by stronger hate,
Hate stronger, under show of love well feigned,
The way which to her ruin now I tend.
    So spake the enemy of mankind, enclosed
In serpent, inmate bad, and toward Eve
Addressed his way, not with indented wave,
Prone on the ground, as since, but on his rear,
Circular base of rising folds, that towered
Fold above fold a surging maze, his head
Crested aloft, and carbuncle his eyes;
With burnished neck of verdant gold, erect
Amidst his circling spires, that on the grass
Floated redundant: pleasing was his shape,
And lovely, never since of serpent kind
Lovelier, not those that in Illyria changed
Hermione, and Cadmus, or the god

In Epidaurus; nor to which transformed
Ammonian Jove, or Capitoline was seen,
He with Olympias, this with her who bore
Scipio the highth of Rome. With tract oblique
At first, as one who sought access, but feared
To interrupt, side-long he works his way.
As when a ship by skilful steersman wrought
Nigh river's mouth or foreland, where the wind
Veers oft, as oft so steers, and shifts her sail:
So varied he, and of his tortuous train
Curled many a wanton wreath in sight of Eve,
To lure her eye: she busied heard the sound
Of rustling leaves, but minded not, as used
To such disport before her through the field,
From every beast, more duteous at her call,
Than at Circean call the herd disguised.
He bolder now, uncalled before her stood:
But as in gaze admiring; oft he bowed
His turret crest, and sleek enamelled neck,
Fawning, and licked the ground whereon she trod.
His gentle dumb expression turned at length
The eye of Eve to mark his play: he glad
Of her attention gained, with serpent tongue
Organic, or impulse of vocal air,
His fraudulent temptation thus began.

　　Wonder not, sovereign mistress, if perhaps
Thou canst, who art sole wonder, much less arm
Thy looks, the Heaven of mildness, with disdain,
Displeased that I approach thee thus, and gaze
Insatiate, I thus single, nor have feared
Thy awful brow, more awful thus retired.
Fairest resemblance of thy Maker fair,
Thee all things living gaze on, all things thine
By gift, and thy celestial beauty adore

With ravishment beheld, there best beheld
Where universally admired: but here
In this enclosure wild, these beasts among,
Beholders rude, and shallow to discern
Half what in thee is fair, one man except,
Who sees thee? (and what is one?) who shouldst be seen
A goddess among gods, adored and served
By angels numberless, thy daily train.

So glozed the tempter, and his proem tuned;
Into the heart of Eve his words made way,
Though at the voice much marvelling: at length
Not unamazed she thus in answer spake.
What may this mean? Language of man pronounced
By tongue of brute, and human sense expressed?
The first at least of these I thought denied
To beasts, whom God on their creation day
Created mute to all articulate sound;
The latter I demur, for in their looks
Much reason, and in their actions oft appears.
Thee, serpent, subtlest beast of all the field
I knew, but not with human voice endued:
Redouble then this miracle, and say,
How cam'st thou speakable of mute, and how
To me so friendly grown above the rest
Of brutal kind, that daily are in sight?
Say, for such wonder claims attention due.

To whom the guileful Tempter thus replied.
Empress of this fair world, resplendent Eve,
Easy to me it is to tell thee all
What thou commandst and right thou shouldst be obeyed:
I was at first as other beasts that graze
The trodden herb, of abject thoughts and low,
As was my food, nor aught but food discerned
Or sex, and apprehended nothing high:

Till on a day roving the field, I chanced
A goodly tree far distant to behold
Loaden with fruit of fairest colours mixt,
Ruddy and gold; I nearer drew to gaze:
When from the boughs a savoury odour blown,
Grateful to appetite, more pleased my sense
Than smell of sweetest fennel, or the teats
Of ewe or goat dropping with milk at even,
Unsucked of lamb or kid, that tend their play.
To satisfy the sharp desire I had
Of tasting those fair apples, I resolved
Not to defer: hunger and thirst at once,
Powerful persuaders, quickened at the scent
Of that alluring fruit, urged me so keen.
About the mossy trunk I wound me soon,
For high from ground the branches would require
Thy utmost reach, or Adam's: round the tree
All other beasts that saw, with like desire
Longing and envying stood, but could not reach.
Amid the tree now got, where plenty hung
Tempting so nigh, to pluck and eat my fill
I spared not, for such pleasure till that hour
At feed or fountain never had I found.
Sated at length, ere long I might perceive
Strange alteration in me, to degree
Of reason in my inward powers, and speech
Wanted not long, though to this shape retained.
Thenceforth to speculations high or deep
I turned my thoughts, and with capacious mind
Considered all things visible in Heaven,
Or earth, or middle, all things fair and good:
But all that fair and good in thy divine
Semblance, and in thy beauty's heavenly ray
United I beheld: no fair to thine

G 2

Equivalent or second, which compelled
Me thus, though importune perhaps, to come
And gaze, and worship thee of right declared
Sovereign of creatures, universal dame.

So talked the spirited sly snake: and Eve
Yet more amazed unwary thus replied.

Serpent, thy overpraising leaves in doubt
The virtue of that fruit, in thee first proved:
But say, where grows the tree, from hence how far?
For many are the trees of God that grow
In Paradise, and various, yet unknown
To us, in such abundance lies our choice,
As leaves a greater store of fruit untouched,
Still hanging incorruptible, till men
Grow up to their provision, and more hands
Help to disburden nature of her bearth.

To whom the wily adder, blithe and glad.
Empress, the way is ready, and not long,
Beyond a row of myrtles, on a flat,
Fast by a fountain, one small thicket past
Of blowing myrrh and balm: if thou accept
My conduct, I can bring thee thither soon.

Lead then, said Eve. He leading swiftly rolled
In tangles, and made intricate seem straight,
To mischief swift. Hope elevates, and joy
Brightens his crest, as when a wandering fire
Compact of unctuous vapour, which the night
Condenses, and the cold environs round,
Kindled through agitation to a flame,
Which oft, they say, some evil spirit attends,
Hovering and blazing with delusive light,
Misleads th'amazed night-wanderer from his way
To bogs and mires, and oft through pond or pool,
There swallowed up and lost, from succour far.

So glistered the dire snake, and into fraud
Led Eve our credulous mother, to the tree
Of prohibition, root of all our woe:
Which when she saw, thus to her guide she spake.

    Serpent, we might have spared our coming hither,
Fruitless to me, though fruit be here to excess,
The credit of whose virtue rests with thee,
Wondrous indeed, if cause of such effects.
But of this tree we may not taste nor touch:
God so commanded, and left that command
Sole daughter of his voice; the rest, we live
Law to ourselves, our reason is our law.

    To whom the Tempter guilefully replied.
Indeed? Hath God then said that of the fruit
Of all these garden trees ye shall not eat,
Yet lords declared of all in earth or air?

    To whom thus Eve yet sinless. Of the fruit
Of each tree in the garden we may eat,
But of the fruit of this fair tree amidst
The garden, God hath said, Ye shall not eat
Thereof, nor shall ye touch it, lest ye die.

    She scarce had said, though brief, when now more bold,
The tempter, but with show of zeal and love
To man, and indignation at his wrong,
New part puts on, and as to passion moved,
Fluctuates disturbed, yet comely, and in act
Raised, as of some great matter to begin.
As when of old some orator renowned
In Athens or free Rome, where eloquence
Flourished, since mute, to some great cause addressed,
Stood in himself collected, while each part,
Motion, each act won audience ere the tongue,
Sometimes in highth began, as no delay
Of preface brooking, through his zeal of right.

So standing, moving, or to highth upgrown
The tempter all impassioned thus began.

O sacred, wise and wisdom-giving plant,
Mother of science, now I feel thy power
Within me clear, not only to discern
Things in their causes, but to trace the ways
Of highest agents, deemed however wise.
Queen of this universe, do not believe
Those rigid threats of death: ye shall not die;
How should ye? By the fruit? it gives you life
To knowledge: by the threatner? look on me,
Me who have touched and tasted, yet both live,
And life more perfect have attained than fate
Meant me, by venturing higher than my lot.
Shall that be shut to man, which to the beast
Is open? Or will God incense his ire
For such a petty trespass, and not praise
Rather your dauntless virtue, whom the pain
Of death denounced, whatever thing death be,
Deterred not from achieving what might lead
To happier life, knowledge of good and evil:
Of good, how just! Of evil, if what is evil
Be real, why not known, since easier shunned?
God therefore cannot hurt ye, and be just;
Not just, not God; not feared then, nor obeyed:
Your fear itself of death removes the fear.
Why then was this forbid? Why but to awe,
Why but to keep ye low and ignorant,
His worshippers; he knows that in the day
Ye eat thereof, your eyes shall seem so clear,
Yet are but dim, shall perfectly be then
Opened and cleared, and ye shall be as gods,
Knowing both good and evil, as they know.
That ye should be as gods, since I as man,

Internal man, is but proportion meet,
I of brute human, ye of human gods.
So ye shall die perhaps, by putting off
Human, to put on gods: death to be wished,
Though threatened, which no worse than this can bring.
And what are gods that man may not become
As they, participating godlike food?
The gods are first, and that advantage use
On our belief, that all from them proceeds;
I question it, for this fair earth I see,
Warmed by the sun, producing every kind,
Them nothing: If they all things, who enclosed
Knowledge of good and evil in this tree,
That whoso eats thereof forthwith attains
Wisdom without their leave? And wherein lies
Th'offence, that man should thus attain to know?
What can your knowledge hurt him, or this tree
Impart against his will if all be his?
Or is it envy, and can envy dwell
In heavenly breasts? These, these, and many more
Causes import your need of this fair fruit.
Goddess humane, reach then, and freely taste.

    He ended, and his words replete with guile
Into her heart too easy entrance won:
Fixed on the fruit she gazed, which to behold
Might tempt alone, and in her ears the sound
Yet rung of his persuasive words, impregned
With reason, to her seeming, and with truth;
Meanwhile the hour of noon drew on, and waked
An eager appetite, raised by the smell
So savoury of that fruit, which with desire,
Inclinable now grown to touch or taste,
Solicited her longing eye; yet first
Pausing a while, thus to herself she mused.

Great are thy virtues, doubtless, best of fruits,
Though kept from man, and worthy to be admired,
Whose taste, too long forborn, at first assay
Gave elocution to the mute, and taught
The tongue not made for speech to speak thy praise:
Thy praise he also who forbids thy use,
Conceals not from us, naming thee the tree
Of knowledge, knowledge both of good and evil;
Forbids us then to taste, but his forbidding
Commends thee more, while it infers the good
By thee communicated, and our want:
For good unknown, sure is not had, or had
And yet unknown, is as not had at all.
In plain then, what forbids he but to know,
Forbids us good, forbids us to be wise?
Such prohibitions bind not. But if death
Bind us with after-bands, what profits then
Our inward freedom? In the day we eat
Of this fair fruit, our doom is, we shall die.
How dies the serpent? He hath eaten and lives,
And knows, and speaks, and reasons, and discerns,
Irrational till then. For us alone
Was death invented? Or to us denied
This intellectual food, for beasts reserved?
For beasts it seems: yet that one beast which first
Hath tasted, envies not, but brings with joy
The good befallen him, author unsuspect,
Friendly to man, far from deceit or guile.
What fear I then, rather what know to fear
Under this ignorance of good and evil,
Of God or death, of law or penalty?
Here grows the cure of all, this fruit divine,
Fair to the eye, inviting to the taste,
Of virtue to make wise: what hinders then

To reach, and feed at once both body and mind?
  So saying, her rash hand in evil hour,
Forth reaching to the fruit, she plucked, she ate:
Earth felt the wound, and Nature from her seat
Sighing through all her works gave signs of woe,
That all was lost. Back to the thicket slunk
The guilty serpent, and well might, for Eve
Intent now wholly on her taste, naught else
Regarded, such delight till then, as seemed,
In fruit she never tasted, whether true
Or fancied so, through expectation high
Of knowledge, nor was godhead from her thought.
Greedily she ingorged without restraint,
And knew not eating death: satiate at length,
And heightened as with wine, jocund and boon,
Thus to herself she pleasingly began.

  O sovereign, virtuous, precious of all trees
In Paradise, of operation blest
To sapience, hitherto obscured, infamed,
And thy fair fruit let hang, as to no end
Created; but henceforth my early care,
Not without song each morning, and due praise
Shall tend thee, and the fertile burden ease
Of thy full branches offered free to all;
Till dieted by thee I grow mature
In knowledge, as the gods who all things know;
Though others envy what they cannot give:
For had the gift been theirs, it had not here
Thus grown. Experience, next to thee I owe,
Best guide; not following thee I had remained
In ignorance; thou op'nst wisdom's way,
And giv'st access, though secret she retire.
And I perhaps am secret; Heaven is high,
High and remote to see from thence distinct

Each thing on earth; and other care perhaps
May have diverted from continual watch
Our great Forbidder, safe with all his spies
About him. But to Adam in what sort
Shall I appear? Shall I to him make known
As yet my change, and give him to partake
Full happiness with me, or rather not,
But keep the odds of knowledge in my power
Without copartner? So to add what wants
In female sex, the more to draw his love,
And render me more equal, and perhaps,
A thing not undesirable, sometime
Superior: for inferior who is free?
This may be well: but what if God have seen
And death ensue? Then I shall be no more,
And Adam wedded to another Eve,
Shall live with her enjoying, I extinct;
A death to think. Confirmed then I resolve,
Adam shall share with me in bliss or woe:
So dear I love him, that with him all deaths
I could endure, without him live no life.

So saying, from the tree her step she turned,
But first low reverence done, as to the power
That dwelt within, whose presence had infused
Into the plant sciental sap, derived
From nectar, drink of gods. Adam the while
Waiting desirous her return, had wove
Of choicest flowers a garland to adorn
Her tresses, and her rural labours crown,
As reapers oft are wont their harvest queen.
Great joy he promised to his thoughts, and new
Solace in her return, so long delayed:
Yet oft his heart, divine of something ill,
Misgave him; he the faltering measure felt;

And forth to meet her went, the way she took
That morn when first they parted; by the tree
Of knowledge he must pass, there he her met,
Scarce from the tree returning; in her hand
A bough of fairest fruit that downy smiled,
New gathered, and ambrosial smell diffused.
To him she hasted, in her face excuse
Came prologue, and apology to prompt,
Which with bland words at will she thus addressed.

   Hast thou not wondered, Adam, at my stay?
Thee I have missed, and thought it long, deprived
Thy presence, agony of love till now
Not felt, nor shall be twice, for never more
Mean I to try, what rash untried I sought,
The pain of absence from thy sight. But strange
Hath been the cause, and wonderful to hear:
This tree is not as we are told, a tree
Of danger tasted, nor to evil unknown
Opening the way, but of divine effect
To open eyes, and make them gods who taste;
And hath been tasted such: the serpent wise,
Or not restrained as we, or not obeying,
Hath eaten of the fruit, and is become,
Not dead, as we are threatened, but thenceforth
Endued with human voice and human sense,
Reasoning to admiration, and with me
Persuasively hath so prevailed, that I
Have also tasted, and have also found
Th'effects to correspond, opener mine eyes
Dim erst, dilated spirits, ampler heart,
And growing up to godhead; which for thee
Chiefly I sought, without thee can despise.
For bliss, as thou hast part, to me is bliss,
Tedious, unshared with thee, and odious soon.

Thou therefore also taste, that equal lot
May join us, equal joy, as equal love;
Lest thou not tasting, different degree
Disjoin us, and I then too late renounce
Deity for thee, when fate will not permit.

    Thus Eve with countenance blithe her story told;
But in her cheek distemper flushing glowed.
On th'other side, Adam, soon as he heard
The fatal trespass done by Eve, amazed,
Astonished stood and blank, while horror chill
Ran through his veins, and all his joints relaxed;
From his slack hand the garland wreathed for Eve
Down dropped, and all the faded roses shed.
Speechless he stood and pale, till thus at length
First to himself he inward silence broke.

    O fairest of creation, last and best
Of all God's works, creature in whom excelled
Whatever can to sight or thought be formed,
Holy, divine, good, amiable, or sweet!
How art thou lost, how on a sudden lost,
Defaced, deflowered, and now to death devote?
Rather how hast thou yielded to transgress
The strict forbiddance, how to violate
The sacred fruit forbidden! Some cursed fraud
Of enemy hath beguiled thee, yet unknown,
And me with thee hath ruined, for with thee
Certain my resolution is to die.
How can I live without thee, how forgo
Thy sweet converse and love so dearly joined,
To live again in these wild woods forlorn?
Should God create another Eve, and I
Another rib afford, yet loss of thee
Would never from my heart; no no, I feel
The link of nature draw me: flesh of flesh,

Bone of my bone thou art, and from thy state
Mine never shall be parted, bliss or woe.

    So having said, as one from sad dismay
Recomforted, and after thoughts disturbed
Submitting to what seemed remediless,
Thus in calm mood his words to Eve he turned.

    Bold deed thou hast presumed, adventurous Eve
And peril great provoked, who thus hast dared
Had it been only coveting to eye
That sacred fruit, sacred to abstinence,
Much more to taste it under ban to touch.
But past who can recall, or done undo?
Not God omnipotent, nor fate, yet so
Perhaps thou shalt not die, perhaps the fact
Is not so heinous now, foretasted fruit,
Profaned first by the serpent, by him first
Made common and unhallowed ere our taste;
Nor yet on him found deadly, he yet lives,
Lives, as thou saidst, and gains to live as man
Higher degree of life, inducement strong
To us, as likely tasting to attain
Proportional ascent, which cannot be
But to be gods, or angels demi-gods.
Nor can I think that God, Creator wise,
Though threatening, will in earnest so destroy
Us his prime creatures, dignified so high,
Set over all his works, which in our fall,
For us created, needs with us must fail,
Dependent made; so God shall uncreate,
Be frustrate, do, undo, and labour lose,
Not well conceived of God, who though his power
Creation could repeat, yet would be loath
Us to abolish, lest the adversary
Triumph and say: Fickle their state whom God

Most favours, who can please him long? Me first
He ruined, now mankind; whom will he next?
Matter of scorn, not to be given the foe.
However I with thee have fixed my lot,
Certain to undergo like doom, if death
Consort with thee, death is to me as life;
So forcible within my heart I feel
The bond of nature draw me to my own,
My own in thee, for what thou art is mine;
Our state cannot be severed, we are one,
One flesh; to lose thee were to lose myself.
　　So Adam, and thus Eve to him replied.
O glorious trial of exceeding love,
Illustrious evidence, example high!
Ingaging me to emulate, but short
Of thy perfection, how shall I attain,
Adam, from whose dear side I boast me sprung,
And gladly of our union hear thee speak,
One heart, one soul in both; whereof good proof
This day affords, declaring thee resolved,
Rather than death or aught than death more dread
Shall separate us, linked in love so dear,
To undergo with me one guilt, one crime,
If any be, of tasting this fair fruit,
Whose virtue, for of good still good proceeds,
Direct, or by occasion hath presented
This happy trial of thy love, which else
So eminently never had been known.
Were it I thought death menaced would ensue
This my attempt, I would sustain alone
The worst, and not persuade thee, rather die
Deserted, than oblige thee with a fact
Pernicious to thy peace, chiefly assured
Remarkably so late of thy so true,

So faithful love unequalled; but I feel
Far otherwise th'event, not death, but life
Augmented, opened eyes, new hopes, new joys,
Taste so divine, that what of sweet before
Hath touched my sense, flat seems to this, and harsh.
On my experience, Adam, freely taste,
And fear of death deliver to the winds.

　　So saying, she embraced him, and for joy
Tenderly wept, much won that he his love
Had so ennobled, as of choice to incur
Divine displeasure for her sake, or death.
In recompense (for such compliance bad
Such recompense best merits) from the bough
She gave him of that fair enticing fruit
With liberal hand: he scrupled not to eat
Against his better knowledge, not deceived,
But fondly overcome with female charm.
Earth trembled from her entrails, as again
In pangs, and nature gave a second groan,
Sky lowered, and muttering thunder, some sad drops
Wept at completing of the mortal sin
Original; while Adam took no thought,
Eating his fill, nor Eve to iterate
Her former trespass feared, the more to soothe
Him with her loved society, that now
As with new wine intoxicated both
They swim in mirth, and fancy that they feel
Divinity within them breeding wings
Wherewith to scorn the earth: but that false fruit
Far other operation first displayed,
Carnal desire inflaming, he on Eve
Began to cast lascivious eyes, she him
As wantonly repaid; in lust they burn:
Till Adam thus 'gan Eve to dalliance move.

Eve now I see thou art exact of taste,
And elegant, of sapience no small part,
Since to each meaning savour we apply,
And palate call judicious; I the praise
Yield thee, so well this day thou hast purveyed.
Much pleasure we have lost, while we abstained
From this delightful fruit, nor known till now
True relish, tasting; if such pleasure be
In things to us forbidden, it might be wished,
For this one tree had been forbidden ten.
But come, so well refreshed, now let us play,
As meet is, after such delicious fare;
For never did thy beauty since the day
I saw thee first and wedded thee, adorned
With all perfections, so enflame my sense
With ardour to enjoy thee, fairer now
Than ever, bounty of this virtuous tree.

So said he, and forbore not glance or toy
Of amorous intent, well understood
Of Eve, whose eye darted contagious fire.
Her hand he seized, and to a shady bank,
Thick overhead with verdant roof imbowered
He led her nothing loath; flowers were the couch,
Pansies, and violets, and asphodel,
And hyacinth, earth's freshest, softest lap.
There they their fill of love and love's disport
Took largely, of their mutual guilt the seal,
The solace of their sin, till dewy sleep
Oppressed them, wearied with their amorous play.
Soon as the force of that fallacious fruit,
That with exhilarating vapour bland
About their spirits had played, and inmost powers
Made err, was now exhaled, and grosser sleep
Bred of unkindly fumes, with conscious dreams

Encumbered, now had left them, up they rose
As from unrest, and each the other viewing,
Soon found their eyes how opened, and their minds
How darkened; innocence, that as a veil
Had shadowed them from knowing ill, was gone,
Just confidence, and native righteousness,
And honour from about them, naked left
To guilty shame he covered, but his robe
Uncovered more. So rose the Danite strong
Herculean Samson from the harlot-lap
Of Philistean Dalilah, and waked
Shorn of his strength, they destitute and bare
Of all their virtue: silent, and in face
Confounded long they sat, as strucken mute,
Till Adam, though not less than Eve abashed,
At length gave utterance to these words constrained.

    O Eve, in evil hour thou didst give ear
To that false worm, of whomsoever taught
To counterfeit man's voice, true in our fall,
False in our promised rising; since our eyes
Opened we find indeed, and find we know
Both good and evil, good lost, and evil got,
Bad fruit of knowledge, if this be to know,
Which leaves us naked thus, of honour void,
Of innocence, of faith, of purity,
Our wonted ornaments now soiled and stained,
And in our faces evident the signs
Of foul concupiscence; whence evil store;
Even shame, the last of evils; of the first
Be sure then. How shall I behold the face
Henceforth of God or angel, erst with joy
And rapture so oft beheld? Those heavenly shapes
Will dazzle now this earthly, with their blaze
Insufferably bright. O might I here

In solitude live savage, in some glade
Obscured, where highest woods impenetrable
To star or sunlight, spread their umbrage broad,
And brown as evening: cover me ye pines,
Ye cedars, with innumerable boughs
Hide me, where I may never see them more.
But let us now, as in bad plight, devise
What best may for the present serve to hide
The parts of each from other, that seem most
To shame obnoxious, and unseemliest seen;
Some trees whose broad smooth leaves together sowed,
And girded on our loins, may cover round
Those middle parts, that this new comer, shame,
There sit not, and reproach us as unclean.

So counselled he, and both together went
Into the thickest wood, there soon they chose
The figtree, not that kind for fruit renowned,
But such as at this day to Indians known
In Malabar or Deccan spreads her arms
Branching so broad and long, that in the ground
The bended twigs take root, and daughters grow
About the mother tree, a pillared shade
High overarched, and echoing walks between;
There oft the Indian herdsman shunning heat
Shelters in cool, and tends his pasturing herds
At loopholes cut through thickest shade: those leaves
They gathered, broad as Amazonian targe,
And with what skill they had, together sowed,
To gird their waist, vain covering if to hide
Their guilt and dreaded shame; O how unlike
To that first naked glory. Such of late
Columbus found th'American so girt
With feathered cincture, naked else and wild
Among the trees on isles and woody shores.

Thus fenced, and as they thought, their shame in part
Covered, but not at rest or ease of mind,
They sat them down to weep, nor only tears
Rained at their eyes, but high winds worse within
Began to rise, high passions, anger, hate,
Mistrust, suspicion, discord, and shook sore
Their inward state of mind, calm region once
And full of peace, now tossed and turbulent:
For understanding ruled not, and the will
Heard not her lore, both in subjection now
To sensual appetite, who from beneath
Usurping over sovereign reason claimed
Superior sway. From thus distempered breast,
Adam, estranged in look and altered style,
Speech intermitted thus to Eve renewed.

Would thou hadst hearkened to my words, and stayed
With me, as I besought thee, when that strange
Desire of wandering this unhappy morn,
I know not whence possessed thee; we had then
Remained still happy, not as now, despoiled
Of all our good, shamed, naked, miserable.
Let none henceforth seek needless cause to approve
The faith they owe; when earnestly they seek
Such proof, conclude, they then begin to fail.

To whom soon moved with touch of blame thus Eve.
What words have passed thy lips, Adam severe?
Imput'st thou that to my default, or will
Of wandering, as thou call'st it, which who knows
But might as ill have happ'n'd thou being by,
Or to thyself perhaps: hadst thou been there,
Or here th'attempt, thou couldst not have discerned
Fraud in the serpent, speaking as he spake;
No ground of enmity between us known,
Why he should mean me ill, or seek to harm.

Was I to have never parted from thy side?
As good have grown there still a liveless rib.
Being as I am, why didst not thou the head
Command me absolutely not to go,
Going into such danger as thou saidst?
Too facile then thou didst not much gainsay,
Nay, didst permit, approve, and fair dismiss.
Hadst thou been firm and fixed in thy dissent,
Neither had I transgressed, nor thou with me.

    To whom then first incensed Adam replied.
Is this the love, is this the recompense
Of mine to thee, ingrateful Eve, expressed
Immutable when thou were lost, not I,
Who might have lived and joyed immortal bliss,
Yet willingly chose rather death with thee:
And am I now upbraided as the cause
Of thy transgressing? not enough severe,
It seems, in thy restraint: what could I more?
I warned thee, I admonished thee, foretold
The danger, and the lurking enemy
That lay in wait; beyond this had been force,
And force upon free will hath here no place.
But confidence then bore thee on, secure
Either to meet no danger, or to find
Matter of glorious trial; and perhaps
I also erred in overmuch admiring
What seemed in thee so perfect, that I thought
No evil durst attempt thee, but I rue
That error now, which is become my crime,
And thou th'accuser. Thus it shall befall
Him who to worth in women overtrusting
Lets her will rule; restraint she will not brook,
And left to herself, if evil thence ensue,
She first his weak indulgence will accuse.

Thus they in mutual accusation spent
The fruitless hours, but neither self-condemning,
And of their vain contest appeared no end.

*

BOOK X

The Argument

MAN's transgression known, the guardian angels forsake Paradise, and return up to Heaven to approve their vigilance, and are approved, God declaring that the entrance of Satan could not be by them prevented. He sends his Son to judge the transgressors, who descends and gives sentence accordingly; then in pity clothes them both, and reascends. Sin and Death sitting till then at the gates of Hell, by wondrous sympathy feeling the success of Satan in this new world, and the sin by man there committed, resolve to sit no longer confined in Hell, but to follow Satan their Sire up to the place of man: to make the way easier from Hell to this world to and fro, they pave a broad highway or bridge over chaos, according to the track that Satan first made; then preparing for earth, they meet him proud of his success returning to Hell; their mutual gratulation. Satan arrives at Pandemonium, in full assembly relates with boasting his success against man; instead of applause is entertained with a general hiss by all his audience, transformed with himself also suddenly into serpents, according to his doom given in Paradise; then deluded with a show of the forbidden tree springing up before them, they greedily reaching to take of the fruit, chew dust and bitter ashes. The proceedings of Sin and Death; God foretells the final victory of his Son over them, and the renewing of all things; but for the present commands his angels to make several alterations in the Heavens and elements. Adam more and more perceiving his fallen condition

heavily bewails, rejects the condolement of Eve; she persists, and
at length appeases him: then to evade the curse likely to fall on
their offspring, proposes to Adam violent ways, which he approves
not, but conceiving better hope, puts her in mind of the late
promise made them, that her seed should be revenged on the
serpent, and exhorts her with him to seek peace of the offended
Deity, by repentance and supplication.

MEANWHILE the heinous and despiteful act
Of Satan done in Paradise, and how
He in the serpent had perverted Eve,
Her husband she, to taste the fatal fruit,
Was known in Heaven; for what can scape the eye
Of God all-seeing, or deceive his heart
Omniscient, who in all things wise and just,
Hindered not Satan to attempt the mind
Of man with strength entire, and free will armed,
Complete to have discovered and repulsed
Whatever wiles of foe or seeming friend?
For still they knew, and ought to have still remembered
The high injunction not to taste that fruit,
Whoever tempted; which they not obeying,
Incurred (what could they less?) the penalty,
And manifold in sin, deserved to fall.
Up into Heaven from Paradise in haste
Th'angelic guards ascended, mute and sad
For man, for of his state by this they knew,
Much wondering how the subtle fiend had stolen
Entrance unseen. Soon as th'unwelcome news
From earth arrived at Heaven gate, displeased
All were who heard, dim sadness did not spare
That time celestial visages, yet mixt
With pity, violated not their bliss.
About the new arrived, in multitudes

Th'ethereal people ran, to hear and know
How all befell: they towards the throne supreme
Accountable made haste to make appear
With righteous plea, their utmost vigilance,
And easily approved; when the most high
Eternal Father from his secret cloud,
Amidst in thunder uttered thus his voice.

    Assembled angels, and ye powers returned
From unsuccessful charge, be not dismayed,
Nor troubled at these tidings from the earth,
Which your sincerest care could not prevent,
Foretold so lately what would come to pass;
When first this tempter crossed the gulf from Hell
I told ye then he should prevail and speed
On his bad errand, man should be seduced
And flattered out of all, believing lies
Against his maker; no decree of mine
Concurring to necessitate his fall,
Or touch with lightest moment of impulse
His free will, to her own inclining left
In even scale. But fallen he is, and now
What rests, but that the mortal sentence pass
On his transgression, death denounced that day,
Which he presumes already vain and void,
Because not yet inflicted, as he feared,
By some immediate stroke; but soon shall find
Forbearance no acquittance ere day end.
Justice shall not return as bounty scorned.
But whom send I to judge them? Whom but thee
Viceregent son, to thee I have transferred
All judgement, whether in Heaven, or earth, or Hell.
Easy it may be seen that I intend
Mercy colleague with justice, sending thee
Man's friend, his mediator, his designed

Both Ransom and Redeemer voluntary,
And destined man himself to judge man fallen.
    So spake the Father, and unfolding bright
Toward the right hand his glory, on the Son
Blazed forth unclouded Deity; he full
Resplendent all his Father manifest
Expressed, and thus divinely answered mild.
    Father eternal, thine is to decree,
Mine both in Heaven and earth to do thy will
Supreme, that thou in me thy Son beloved
Mayest ever rest well pleased. I go to judge
On earth these thy transgressors, but thou knowst
Whoever judged, the worst on me must light,
When time shall be, for so I undertook
Before thee; and not repenting, this obtain
Of right, that I may mitigate their doom
On me derived, yet I shall temper so
Justice with mercy, as may illustrate most
Them fully satisfied, and thee appease.
Attendance none shall need, nor train, where none
Are to behold the judgement, but the judged,
Those two; the third best absent is condemned,
Convict by flight, and rebel to all law.
Conviction to the serpent none belongs.
    Thus saying, from his radiant seat he rose
Of high collateral glory: him Thrones and Powers,
Princedoms, and Dominations ministrant
Accompanied to Heaven gate, from whence
Eden and all the coast in prospect lay.
Down he descended straight; the speed of gods
Time counts not, though with swiftest minute winged.
Now was the sun in western cadence low
From noon, and gentle airs due at their hour
To fan the earth now waked, and usher in

The evening cool when he from wrath more cool
Came the mild judge and intercessor both
To sentence man: the voice of God they heard
Now walking in the garden, by soft winds
Brought to their ears, while day declined, they heard
And from his presence hid themselves among
The thickest trees, both man and wife, till God
Approaching, thus to Adam called aloud.

Where art thou Adam, wont with joy to meet
My coming seen far off? I miss thee here,
Not pleased, thus entertained with solitude,
Where obvious duty erewhile appeared unsought:
Or come I less conspicuous, or what change
Absents thee, or what chance detains? come forth.
He came, and with him Eve, more loath, though first
To offend, discountenanced both, and discomposed;
Love was not in their looks, either to God
Or to each other, but apparent guilt,
And shame, and perturbation, and despair,
Anger, and obstinacy, and hate, and guile.
Whence Adam faltering long, thus answered brief.

I heard thee in the garden, and of thy voice
Afraid, being naked, hid myself. To whom
The gracious judge without revile replied.

My voice thou oft hast heard, and hast not feared,
But still rejoiced, how is it now become
So dreadful to thee? That thou art naked, who
Hath told thee? Hast thou eaten of the tree
Whereof I gave thee charge thou shouldst not eat?

To whom thus Adam sore beset replied.
O Heaven! in evil strait this day I stand
Before my judge, either to undergo
Myself the total crime, or to accuse
My other self, the partner of my life;

Whose failing, while her faith to me remains,
I should conceal, and not expose to blame
By my complaint; but strict necessity
Subdues me, and calamitous constraint,
Lest on my head both sin and punishment,
However insupportable, be all
Devolved; though should I hold my peace, yet thou
Wouldst easily detect what I conceal.
This woman whom thou mad'st to be my help,
And gav'st me as thy perfect gift, so good,
So fit, so acceptable, so divine,
That from her mind I could suspect no ill,
And what she did, whatever in itself,
Her doing seemed to justify the deed;
She gave me of the tree and I did eat.

　　To whom the sovereign Presence thus replied.
Was she thy God, that her thou didst obey
Before his voice, or was she made thy guide,
Superior, or but equal, that to her
Thou didst resign thy manhood, and the place
Wherein God set thee above her made of thee,
And for thee, whose perfection far excelled
Hers in all real dignity; adorned
She was indeed, and lovely to attract
Thy love, not thy subjection, and her gifts
Were such as under government well seemed,
Unseemly to bear rule, which was thy part
And person, hadst thou known thyself aright.

　　So having said, he thus to Eve in few:
Say woman, what is this which thou hast done?

　　To whom sad Eve with shame nigh overwhelmed,
Confessing soon, yet not before her judge
Bold or loquacious, thus abashed replied.

　　The serpent me beguiled, and I did eat.

Which when the Lord God heard, without delay
To judgement he proceeded on th'accused
Serpent though brute, unable to transfer
The guilt on him who made him instrument
Of mischief, and polluted from the end
Of his creation; justly then accurst,
As vitiated in nature; more to know
Concerned not man (since he no further knew)
Nor altered his offence; yet God at last
To Satan first in sin his doom applied
Though in mysterious terms, judged as then best:
And on the serpent thus his curse let fall.

Because thou hast done this, thou art accurst
Above all cattle, each beast of the field;
Upon thy belly grovelling thou shalt go,
And dust shalt eat all the days of thy life.
Between thee and the woman I will put
Enmity, and between thine and her seed;
Her seed shall bruise thy head, thou bruise his heel.

So spake this oracle, then verified
When Jesus son of Mary, second Eve,
Saw Satan fall like lightning down from Heaven,
Prince of the air; then rising from his grave
Spoiled principalities and powers, triumphed
In open show, and with ascension bright
Captivity led captive through the air,
The realm itself of Satan long usurped,
Whom he shall tread at last under our feet;
Even he who now foretold his fatal bruise,
And to the woman thus his sentence turned.

Thy sorrow I will greatly multiply
By thy conception; children thou shalt bring
In sorrow forth, and to thy husband's will
Thine shall submit, he over thee shall rule.

On Adam last thus judgement he pronounced.
Because thou hast hearkened to the voice of thy wife,
And eaten of the tree concerning which
I charged thee, saying: Thou shalt not eat thereof,
Cursed is the ground for thy sake, thou in sorrow
Shalt eat thereof all the days of thy life;
Thorns also and thistles it shall bring thee forth
Unbid, and thou shalt eat the herb of the field,
In the sweat of thy face shalt thou eat bread,
Till thou return unto the ground, for thou
Out of the ground wast taken, know thy birth,
For dust thou art, and shalt to dust return.
So judged he man, both Judge and Saviour sent,
And th'instant stroke of death denounced that day
Removed far off; then pitying how they stood
Before him naked to the air, that now
Must suffer change, disdained not to begin
Thenceforth the form of servant to assume,
As when he washed his servant's feet, so now
As Father of his family, he clad
Their nakedness with skins of beasts, or slain,
Or as the snake with youthful coat repaid;
And thought not much to clothe his enemies:
Nor he their outward only with the skins
Of beasts, but inward nakedness, much more
Opprobrious, with his robe of righteousness,
Arraying covered from his Father's sight.
To him with swift ascent he up returned,
Into his blissful bosom reassumed
In glory as of old, to him appeased
All, though all-knowing, what had passed with man
Recounted, mixing intercession sweet.
Meanwhile ere thus was sinned and judged on earth,
Within the gates of Hell sat Sin and Death,

In counterview within the gates, that now
Stood open wide, belching outrageous flame
Far into chaos, since the Fiend passed through,
Sin opening, who thus now to Death began.

    O son, why sit we here each other viewing
Idly, while Satan our great author thrives
In other worlds, and happier seat provides
For us his offspring dear? It cannot be
But that success attends him; if mishap,
Ere this he had returned, with fury driv'n
By his Avenger, since no place like this
Can fit his punishment, or their revenge.
Methinks I feel new strength within me rise,
Wings growing, and dominion giv'n me large
Beyond this deep; whatever draws me on,
Or sympathy, or some connatural force
Powerful at greatest distance to unite
With secret amity things of like kind
By secretest conveyance. Thou my shade
Inseparable must with me along;
For Death from Sin no power can separate.
But lest the difficulty of passing back
Stay his return perhaps over this gulf
Impassable, impervious, let us try
Adventurous work, yet to thy power and mine
Not unagreeable, to found a path
Over this main from Hell to that new world
Where Satan now prevails, a monument
Of merit high to all th'infernal host,
Easing their passage hence, for intercourse,
Or transmigration, as their lot shall lead
Nor can I miss the way, so strongly drawn
By this new felt attraction and instinct.

    Whom thus the meagre shadow answered soon.

Go whither fate and inclination strong
Leads thee, I shall not lag behind, nor err
The way, thou leading, such a scent I draw
Of carnage, prey innumerable, and taste
The savour of death from all things here that live:
Nor shall I to the work thou enterprisest
Be wanting, but afford thee equal aid.

    So saying, with delight he snuffed the smell
Of mortal change on earth. As when a flock
Of ravenous fowl, though many a league remote,
Against the day of battle, to a field,
Where armies lie encampt, come flying, lured
With scent of living carcasses designed
For death the following day in bloody fight.
So scented the grim feature, and upturned
His nostril wide into the murky air,
Sagacious of his quarry from so far.
Then both from out Hell gates into the waste
Wide anarchy of chaos damp and dark
Flew divers, and with power (their power was great)
Hovering upon the waters, what they met
Solid or slimy, as in raging sea
Tossed up and down, together crowded drove
From each side shoaling towards the mouth of Hell.
As when two polar winds blowing adverse
Upon the Cronian sea, together drive
Mountains of ice, that stop th'imagined way
Beyond Petsora eastward, to the rich
Cathaian coast. The aggregated soil
Death with his mace petrific, cold and dry,
As with a trident smote, and fixed as firm
As Delos floating once; the rest his look
Bound with Gorgonian rigour not to move,
And with asphaltic slime; broad as the gate,

Deep to the roots of Hell the gathered beach
They fastened, and the mole immense wrought on
Over the foaming deep high arched, a bridge
Of length prodigious joining to the wall
Immoveable of this now fenceless world
Forfeit to Death; from hence a passage broad,
Smooth, easy, inoffensive down to Hell.
So if great things to small may be compared,
Xerxes, the liberty of Greece to yoke,
From Susa his Memnonian palace high
Came to the sea, and over Hellespont
Bridging his way, Europe with Asia joined,
And scourged with many a stroke th'indignant waves.
Now had they brought the work by wondrous art
Pontifical, a ridge of pendant rock
Over the vexed abyss, following the track
Of Satan, to the self-same place where he
First lighted from his wing, and landed safe
From out of chaos to the outside bare
Of this round world: with pins of adamant
And chains they made all fast, too fast they made
And durable; and now in little space
The confines met of empyrean Heaven
And of this world, and on the left hand Hell
With long reach interposed; three several ways
In sight, to each of these three places led.
And now their way to earth they had descried,
To Paradise first tending, when behold
Satan in likeness of an angel bright
Betwixt the Centaur and the Scorpion steering
His zenith, while the sun in Aries rose:
Disguised he came, but those his children dear
Their parent soon discerned, though in disguise.
He, after Eve seduced, unminded slunk

Into the wood fast by, and changing shape
To observe the sequel, saw his guileful act
By Eve, though all unweeting, seconded
Upon her husband, saw their shame that sough
Vain covertures; but when he saw descend
The Son of God to judge them, terrified
He fled, not hoping to escape, but shun
The present, fearing guilty what his wrath
Might suddenly inflict; that past, returned
By night, and listening where the hapless pair
Sat in their sad discourse, and various plaint,
Thence gathered his own doom, which understood
Not instant, but of future time. With joy
And tidings fraught, to Hell he now returned,
And at the brink of chaos, near the foot
Of this new wondrous pontifice, unhoped
Met who to meet him came, his offspring dear.
Great joy was at their meeting, and at sight
Of that stupendious bridge his joy increased.
Long he admiring stood, till Sin, his fair
Inchanting daughter, thus the silence broke.

  O Parent, these are thy magnific deeds,
Thy trophies, which thou view'st as not thine own,
Thou art their author and prime architect:
For I no sooner in my heart divined,
My heart which by a secret harmony
Still moves with thine, joined in connexion sweet,
That thou on earth hadst prospered, which thy looks
Now also evidence, but straight I felt
Though distant from thee worlds between, yet felt
That I must after thee with this thy son;
Such fatal consequence unites us three.
Hell could no longer hold us in her bounds,
Nor this unvoyagable gulf obscure

Detain from following thy illustrious track.
Thou hast achieved our liberty, confined
Within Hell gates till now, thou us impowered
To fortify thus far, and overlay
With this portentous bridge the dark abyss.
Thine now is all this world, thy virtue hath won
What thy hands builded not, thy wisdom gained
With odds what war hath lost, and fully avenged
Our foil in Heaven; here thou shalt monarch reign,
There didst not; there let him still victor sway,
As battle hath adjudged, from this new world
Retiring, by his own doom alienated,
And henceforth monarchy with thee divide
Of all things, parted by th'empyreal bounds,
His quadrature, from thy orbicular world,
Or try thee now more dangerous to his throne.

    Whom thus the Prince of Darkness answered glad.
Fair daughter, and thou son and grandchild both,
High proof ye now have given to be the race
Of Satan (for I glory in the name,
Antagonist of Heaven's almighty King)
Amply have merited of me, of all
Th'infernal empire, that so near Heaven's door
Triumphal with triumphal act have met,
Mine with this glorious work, and made one realm
Hell and this world, one realm, one continent,
Of easy thoroughfare. Therefore while I
Descend through darkness, on your road with ease
To my associate powers, them to acquaint
With these successes, and with them rejoice,
You two this way, among those numerous orbs
All yours, right down to Paradise descend;
There dwell and reign in bliss, thence on the earth
Dominion exercise and in the air,

Chiefly on man, sole lord of all declared,
Him first make sure your thrall, and lastly kill.
My substitutes I send ye, and create
Plenipotent on earth, of matchless might
Issuing from me: on your joint vigour now
My hold of this new kingdom all depends,
Through Sin to Death exposed by my exploit.
If your joint power prevail, th'affairs of Hell
No detriment need fear, go and be strong.

So saying he dismissed them, they with speed
Their course through thickest constellations held,
Spreading their bane; the blasted stars looked wan,
And planets, planet-strook, real eclipse
Then suffered. Th'other way Satan went down
The causey to Hell gate; on either side
Disparted chaos over built exclaimed,
And with rebounding surge the bars assailed,
That scorned his indignation. Through the gate,
Wide open and unguarded, Satan passed,
And all about found desolate; for those
Appointed to sit there, had left their charge,
Flown to the upper world; the rest were all
Far to the inland retired, about the walls
Of Pandemonium, city and proud seat
Of Lucifer, so by allusion called,
Of that bright star to Satan paragoned.
There kept their watch the legions, while the grand
In council sat, solicitous what chance
Might intercept their emperor sent, so he
Departing gave command, and they observed.
As when the Tartar from his Russian foe
By Astracan over the snowy plains
Retires, or Bactrian Sophi from the horns
Of Turkish crescent, leaves all waste beyond

The realm of Aladule, in his retreat
To Tauris or Casbeen. So these the late
Heaven-banished host, left desert utmost Hell
Many a dark league, reduced in careful watch
Round their metropolis, and now expecting
Each hour their great adventurer from the search
Of foreign worlds: he through the midst unmarked,
In show plebeian angel militant
Of lowest order, passed; and from the door
Of that Plutonian hall, invisible,
Ascended his high throne, which under state
Of richest texture spread, at th'upper end
Was placed in regal lustre. Down a while
He sat, and round about him saw unseen:
At last as from a cloud his fulgent head
And shape star-bright appeared, or brighter, clad
With what permissive glory since his fall
Was left him, or false glitter: All amazed
At that so sudden blaze the Stygian throng
Bent their aspect, and whom they wished beheld,
Their mighty chief returned: loud was th'acclaim:
Forth rushed in haste the great consulting peers,
Raised from their dark divan, and with like joy
Congratulant approached him, who with hand
Silence, and with these words attention won.

    Thrones, Dominations, Princedoms, Virtues, Powers,
For in possession such, not only of right,
I call ye, and declare ye now, returned
Successful beyond hope, to lead ye forth
Triumphant out of this infernal pit
Abominable, accurst, the house of woe,
And dungeon of our tyrant: Now possess
As lords a spacious world, to our native Heaven
Little inferior, by my adventure hard

H 2

With peril great achieved. Long were to tell
What I have done, what suffered, with what pain
Voyaged th'unreal, vast, unbounded deep
Of horrible confusion, over which
By Sin and Death a broad way now is paved
To expedite your glorious march; but I
Toiled out my uncouth passage, forced to ride
Th'untractable abyss, plunged in the womb
Of unoriginal night and chaos wild,
That jealous of their secrets fiercely opposed
My journey strange, with clamorous uproar
Protesting fate supreme; thence how I found
The new created world, which fame in Heaven
Long had foretold, a fabric wonderful
Of absolute perfection, therein man
Placed in a paradise, by our exile
Made happy: him by fraud I have seduced
From his Creator, and the more to increase
Your wonder, with an apple; he thereat
Offended, worth your laughter, hath given up
Both his beloved man and all his world,
To Sin and Death a prey, and so to us,
Without our hazard, labour, or alarm,
To range in, and to dwell, and over man
To rule, as over all he should have ruled.
True is, me also he hath judged, or rather
Me not, but the brute serpent, in whose shape
Man I deceived: that which to me belongs
Is enmity, which he will put between
Me and mankind; I am to bruise his heel;
His seed, when is not set, shall bruise my head:
A world who would not purchase with a bruise,
Or much more grievous pain? Ye have th'account
Of my performance; what remains, ye gods,

But up and enter now into full bliss.
   So having said, awhile he stood, expecting
Their universal shout and high applause
To fill his ear, when contrary he hears
On all sides, from innumerable tongues
A dismal universal hiss, the sound
Of public scorn; he wondered, but not long
Had leisure, wondering at himself now more;
His visage drawn he felt to sharp and spare,
His arms clung to his ribs, his legs entwining
Each other, till supplanted down he fell
A monstrous serpent on his belly prone,
Reluctant, but in vain: a greater power
Now ruled him, punished in the shape he sinned,
According to his doom: he would have spoke,
But hiss for hiss returned with forked tongue
To forked tongue, for now were all transformed
Alike, to serpents all as accessories
To his bold riot: dreadful was the din
Of hissing through the hall, thick swarming now
With complicated monsters, head and tail,
Scorpion and asp, and Amphisboena dire,
Cerastes horned, Hydrus and Ellops drear,
And Dipsas (not so thick swarmed once the soil
Bedropped with blood of Gorgon, or the isle
Ophiusa) but still greatest he the midst,
Now dragon grown, larger than whom the sun
Ingendered in the Pythian vale on slime,
Huge Python, and his power no less he seemed
Above the rest still to retain; they all
Him followed, issuing forth to th' open field,
Where all yet left of that revolted rout
Heaven-fallen, in station stood or just array,
Sublime with expectation when to see

In triumph issuing forth their glorious chief.
They saw, but other sight instead, a crowd
Of ugly serpents; horror on them fell,
And horrid sympathy; for what they saw,
They felt themselves now changing; down their arms,
Down fell both spear and shield, down they as fast,
And the dire hiss renewed, and the dire form
Catched by contagion, like in punishment,
As in their crime. Thus was th'applause they meant,
Turned to exploding hiss, triumph to shame
Cast on themselves from their own mouths. There stood
A grove hard by, sprung up with this their change,
His will who reigns above, to aggravate
Their penance, laden with fair fruit, like that
Which grew in Paradise, the bait of Eve
Used by the Tempter; on that prospect strange
Their earnest eyes they fixed, imagining
For one forbidden tree a multitude
Now risen, to work them further woe or shame;
Yet parched with scalding thirst and hunger fierce,
Though to delude them sent, could not abstain,
But on they rolled in heaps, and up the trees
Climbing, sat thicker than the snaky locks
That curled Megoera: greedily they plucked
The fruitage fair to sight, like that which grew
Near that bituminous lake where Sodom flamed;
This more delusive, not the touch, but taste
Deceived: they fondly thinking to allay
Their appetite with gust, instead of fruit
Chewed bitter ashes, which th'offended taste
With spattering noise rejected. Oft they assayed,
Hunger and thirst constraining, drugged as oft,
With hatefullest disrelish writhed their jaws
With soot and cinders filled; so oft they fell

Into the same illusion, not as man
Whom they triumphed once lapst. Thus were they plagued
And worn with famine, long and ceaseless hiss,
Till their lost shape, permitted, they resumed,
Yearly enjoined, some say, to undergo
This annual humbling certain numbered days,
To dash their pride, and joy for man seduced.
However some tradition they dispersed
Among the heathen of their purchase got,
And fabled how the serpent, whom they called
Ophion with Eurynome, the wide-
Encroaching Eve perhaps, had first the rule
Of high Olympus, thence by Saturn driven
And Ops, ere yet Dictaean Jove was born.
Meanwhile in Paradise the hellish pair
Too soon arrived, Sin there in power before,
Once actual, now in body, and to dwell
Habitual habitant; behind her Death
Close following pace for pace, not mounted yet
On his pale horse: to whom Sin thus began.

  Second of Satan sprung, all conquering Death,
What thinkst thou of our empire now, though earned
With travail difficult, not better far
Than still at Hell's dark threshold to have sat watch,
Unnamed, undreaded, and thy self half starved?

  Whom thus the Sin-born monster answered soon.
To me, who with eternal famine pine,
Alike is Hell, or Paradise, or Heaven,
There best, where most with ravine I may meet;
Which here, though plenteous, all too little seems
To stuff this maw, this vast unhide-bound corpse.

  To whom th'incestuous mother thus replied.
Thou therefore on these herbs, and fruits, and flowers
Feed first, on each beast next, and fish, and fowl,

No homely morsels, and whatever thing
The scythe of Time mows down, devour unspared,
Till I in man residing through the race,
His thoughts, his looks, words, actions, all infect,
And season him thy last and sweetest prey.

　　This said, they both betook them several ways,
Both to destroy, or unimmortal make
All kinds, and for destruction to mature
Sooner or later; which th'Almighty seeing
From his transcendent seat the saints among,
To those bright orders uttered thus his voice.

　　See with what heat these dogs of Hell advance
To waste and havoc yonder world, which I
So fair and good created, and had still
Kept in that state, had not the folly of man
Let in these wasteful furies, who impute
Folly to me, so doth the Prince of Hell
And his adherents, that with so much ease
I suffer them to enter and possess
A place so heavenly, and conniving seem
To gratify my scornful enemies,
That laugh, as if transported with some fit
Of passion, I to them had quitted all,
At random yielded up to their misrule;
And know not that I called and drew them thither
My Hell-hounds, to lick up the draff and filth
Which man's polluting sin with taint hath shed
On what was pure, till crammed and gorged, nigh burst
With sucked and glutted offal, at one sling
Of thy victorious arm, well-pleasing Son,
Both Sin and Death, and yawning grave at last
Through chaos hurled, obstruct the mouth of Hell
For ever, and seal up his ravenous jaws.
Then Heaven and Earth renewed shall be made pure

To sanctity that shall receive no stain:
Till then the curse pronounced on both proceeds.
    He ended, and the heavenly audience loud
Sung Halleluia, as the sound of seas,
Through multitude that sung: Just are thy ways,
Righteous are thy decrees on all thy works;
Who can extenuate thee? Next, to the Son,
Destined restorer of mankind, by whom
New Heaven and Earth shall to the ages rise,
Or down from Heaven descend. Such was their song,
While the Creator calling forth by name
His mighty angels gave them several charge,
As sorted best with present things. The sun
Had first his precept so to move, so shine,
As might affect the earth with cold and heat
Scarce tolerable, and from the north to call
Decrepit winter, from the south to bring
Solstitial summer's heat. To the blank moon
Her office they prescribed, to th'other five
Their planetary motions and aspects
In sextile, square and trine, and opposite,
Of noxious efficacy, and when to join
In Synod unbenign, and taught the fixed
Their influence malignant when to shower,
Which of them rising with the sun, or falling,
Should prove tempestuous: to the winds they set
Their corners, when with bluster to confound
Sea, air, and shore, the thunder when to roll
With terror through the dark aerial hall.
Some say he bid his angels turn askance
The poles of earth twice ten degrees and more
From the sun's axle; they with labour pushed
Oblique the centric globe. Some say the sun
Was bid turn reins from th'equinoctial road

Like distant breadth to Taurus with the seven
Atlantic sisters, and the Spartan twins
Up to the tropic Crab; thence down amain
By Leo and the Virgin and the Scales,
As deep as Capricorn, to bring in change
Of seasons to each clime; else had the spring
Perpetual smiled on earth with vernant flowers,
Equal in days and nights, except to those
Beyond the Polar circles; to them day
Had unbenighted shone, while the low sun
To recompense his distance, in their sight
Had rounded still th'horizon, and not known
Or east or west, which had forbid the snow
From cold Estotiland, and south as far
Beneath Magellan. At that tasted fruit
The sun, as from Thyestean banquet, turned
His course intended; else how had the world
Inhabited, though sinless, more than now,
Avoided pinching cold and scorching heat?
These changes in the heavens, though slow, produced
Like change on sea and land, sideral blast,
Vapour, and mist, and exhalation hot,
Corrupt and pestilent. Now from the north
Of Norumbega and the Samoed shore
Bursting their brazen dungeon, armed with ice
And snow and hail and stormy gust and flaw,
Boreas and Caecias and Argestes loud
And Thrascias rend the woods and seas upturn;
With adverse blasts upturns them from the south
Notus and Afer black with thundrous clouds
From Serraliona; thwart of these as fierce
Forth rush the Levant and the Ponent winds
Eurus and Zephyr with their lateral noise,
Sirocco, and Libecchio. Thus began

Outrage from liveless things; but discord first
Daughter of Sin, among th'irrational,
Death introduced through fierce antipathy:
Beast now with beast gan war, and fowl with fowl,
And fish with fish: to graze the herb all leaving,
Devoured each other; nor stood much in awe
Of man, but fled him, or with countenance grim
Glared on him passing: these were from without
The growing miseries, which Adam saw
Already in part, though hid in gloomiest shade,
To sorrow abandoned, but worse felt within,
And in a troubled sea of passion tossed,
Thus to disburden sought with sad complaint.

   O miserable of happy! Is this the end
Of this new glorious world, and me so late
The glory of that glory, who now become
Accursed of blessed, hide me from the face
Of God, whom to behold was then my highth
Of happiness: yet well, if here would end
The misery, I deserved it, and would bear
My own deservings: but this will not serve.
All that I eat or drink, or shall beget,
Is propagated curse. O voice once heard
Delightfully, Increase and multiply,
Now death to hear! for what can I increase
Or multiply, but curses on my head?
Who of all ages to succeed, but feeling
The evil on him brought by me, will curse
My head: Ill fare our ancestor impure,
For this we may thank Adam; but his thanks
Shall be the execration; so besides
Mine own that bide upon me, all from me
Shall with a fierce reflux on me redound,
On me as on their natural centre light

Heavy, though in their place. O fleeting joys
Of paradise, dear bought with lasting woes!
Did I request thee, Maker, from my clay
To mould me man, did I solicit thee
From darkness to promote me, or here place
In this delicious garden? As my will
Concurred not to my being, it were but right
And equal to reduce me to my dust,
Desirous to resign, and render back
All I received, unable to perform
Thy terms too hard, by which I was to hold
The good I sought not. To the loss of that,
Sufficient penalty, why hast thou added
The sense of endless woes? Inexplicable
Thy justice seems; yet to say truth, too late,
I thus contest; then should have been refused
Those terms whatever, when they were proposed:
Thou didst accept them; wilt thou enjoy the good,
Then cavil the conditions? And though God
Made thee without thy leave, what if thy son
Prove disobedient, and reproved, retort,
Wherefore didst thou beget me? I sought it not.
Wouldst thou admit for his contempt of thee
That proud excuse? Yet him not thy election,
But natural necessity begot.
God made thee of choice his own, and of his own
To serve him, thy reward was of his grace,
Thy punishment then justly is at his will.
Be it so, for I submit, his doom is fair,
That dust I am and shall to dust return.
O welcome hour whenever! Why delays
His hand to execute what his decree
Fixed on this day? Why do I overlive,
Why am I mocked with death, and lengthened out

To deathless pain? How gladly would I meet
Mortality my sentence, and be earth
Insensible, how glad would lay me down
As in my mother's lap? There I should rest
And sleep secure; his dreadful voice no more
Would thunder in my ears, no fear of worse
To me and to my offspring would torment me
With cruel expectation. Yet one doubt
Pursues me still, lest all I cannot die,
Lest that pure breath of life, the spirit of man
Which God inspired, cannot together perish
With this corporeal clod; then in the grave,
Or in some other dismal place, who knows
But I shall die a living death? O thought
Horrid, if true! Yet why? It was but breath
Of life that sinned; what dies but what had life
And sin? the body properly hath neither.
All of me then shall die: let this appease
The doubt, since human reach no further knows.
For though the Lord of all be infinite,
Is his wrath also? Be it, man is not so,
But mortal doomed. How can he exercise
Wrath without end on man whom death must end?
Can he make deathless death? That were to make
Strange contradiction, which to God himself
Impossible is held, as argument
Of weakness, not of power. Will he draw out,
For anger's sake, finite to infinite
In punished man, to satisfy his rigour
Satisfied never; that were to extend
His sentence beyond dust and nature's law,
By which all causes else according still
To the reception of their matter act,
Not to th'extent of their own sphere. But say

That death be not one stroke, as I supposed,
Bereaving sense, but endless misery
From this day onward, which I feel begun
Both in me, and without me, and so last
To perpetuity; aye me, that fear
Comes thundering back with dreadful revolution
On my defenceless head; both death and I
Am found eternal, and incorporate both,
Nor I on my part single, in me all
Posterity stands curst: fair patrimony
That I must leave ye, sons. O were I able
To waste it all myself, and leave ye none!
So disinherited how would ye bless
Me now your curse! Ah why should all mankind
For one man's fault thus guiltless be condemned,
If guiltless? But from me what can proceed,
But all corrupt, both mind and will depraved,
Not to do only, but to will the same
With me; how can they acquitted stand
In sight of God? Him after all disputes
Forced I absolve. All my evasions vain
And reasonings, though through mazes, lead me still
But to my own conviction: first and last
On me, me only, as the source and spring
Of all corruption, all the blame lights due;
So might the wrath. Fond wish! Couldst thou support
That burden heavier than the earth to bear,
Than all the world much heavier, though divided
With that bad woman? Thus what thou desir'st,
And what thou fearst, alike destroys all hope
Of refuge, and concludes thee miserable
Beyond all past example and future,
To Satan only like both crime and doom.
O conscience, into what abyss of fears

And horrors hast thou driven me; out of which
I find no way, from deep to deeper plunged!
    Thus Adam to himself lamented loud
Through the still night, not now, as ere man fell,
Wholesome and cool, and mild, but with black air
Accompanied, with damps and dreadful gloom,
Which to his evil conscience represented
All things with double terror. On the ground
Outstretched he lay, on the cold ground, and oft
Cursed his creation, death as oft accused
Of tardy execution, since denounced
The day of his offence. Why comes not death,
Said he, with one thrice acceptable stroke
To end me? Shall truth fail to keep her word,
Justice divine not hasten to be just?
But death comes not at call, justice divine
Mends not her slowest pace for prayers or cries.
O woods, O fountains, hillocks, dales and bowers,
With other echo late I taught your shades
To answer, and resound far other song.
Whom thus afflicted when sad Eve beheld,
Desolate where she sat, approaching nigh,
Soft words to his fierce passion she assayed:
But her with stern regard he thus repelled.
    Out of my sight, thou serpent, that name best
Befits thee with him leagued, thyself as false
And hateful; nothing wants, but that thy shape,
Like his, and colour serpentine may shew
Thy inward fraud, to warn all creatures from thee
Henceforth; lest that too heavenly form, pretended
To hellish falsehood, snare them. But for thee
I had persisted happy, had not thy pride
And wandering vanity, when least was safe,
Rejected my forewarning, and disdained

Not to be trusted, longing to be seen
Though by the devil himself, him overweening
To overreach, but with the serpent meeting
Fooled and beguiled, by him thou, I by thee,
To trust thee from my side, imagined wise,
Constant, mature, proof against all assaults,
And understood not all was but a show
Rather than solid virtue, all but a rib
Crooked by nature, bent, as now appears,
More to the part sinister from me drawn,
Well if thrown out, as supernumerary,
To my just number found. O why did God,
Creator wise, that peopled highest Heaven
With spirits masculine, create at last
This novelty on earth, this fair defect
Of nature, and not fill the world at once
With men as angels without feminine,
Or find some other way to generate
Mankind? This mischief had not then befallen,
And more that shall befall, innumerable
Disturbances on earth through female snares,
And straight conjunction with this sex: for either
He never shall find out fit mate, but such
As some misfortune brings him, or mistake,
Or whom he wishes shall most seldom gain
Through her perverseness, but shall see her gained
By a far worse, or if she love, withheld
By parents, or his happiest choice too late
Shall meet, already linked and wedlock-bound
To a fell adversary, his hate or shame:
Which infinite calamity shall cause
To human life, and household peace confound.

    He added not, and from her turned, but Eve
Not so repulsed, with tears that ceased not flowing,

And tresses all disordered, at his feet
Fell humble, and embracing them, besought
His peace, and thus proceeded in her plaint.

   Forsake me not thus, Adam, witness Heaven
What love sincere, and reverence in my heart
I bear thee, and unweeting have offended,
Unhappily deceived; thy suppliant
I beg, and clasp thy knees; bereave me not,
Whereon I live, thy gentle looks, thy aid,
Thy counsel in this uttermost distress,
My only strength and stay: forlorn of thee,
Whither shall I betake me, where subsist?
While yet we live, scarce one short hour perhaps,
Between us two let there be peace, both joining,
As joined in injuries, one enmity
Against a foe by doom express assigned us,
That cruel serpent. On me exercise not
Thy hatred for this misery befallen,
On me already lost, me, than thyself
More miserable; both have sinned, but thou
Against God only, I against God and thee,
And to the place of judgement will return,
There with my cries importune heaven, that all
The sentence from thy head removed may light
On me, sole cause to thee of all this woe,
Me me only just object of his ire.

   She ended weeping, and her lowly plight,
Immovable till peace obtained from fault
Acknowledged, and deplored, in Adam wrought
Commiseration; soon his heart relented
Towards her, his life so late and sole delight,
Now at his feet submissive in distress,
Creature so fair his reconcilement seeking,
His counsel whom she had displeased, his aid;

As one disarmed, his anger all he lost,
And thus with peaceful words upraised her soon.
    Unwary, and too desirous, as before,
So now of what thou knowst not, who desir'st
The punishment all on thyself; alas,
Bear thine own first, ill able to sustain
His full wrath whose thou feelst as yet least part,
And my displeasure bearst so ill. If prayers
Could alter high decrees, I to that place
Would speed before thee, and be louder heard,
That on my head all might be visited,
Thy frailty and infirmer sex forgiven,
To me committed and by me exposed.
But rise, let us no more contend, nor blame
Each other, blamed enough elsewhere, but strive
In offices of love, how we may light'n
Each other's burden in our share of woe;
Since this day's death denounced, if ought I see,
Will prove no sudden, but a slow-paced evil,
A long day's dying to augment our pain,
And to our seed (O hapless seed!) derived.
    To whom thus Eve, recovering heart, replied.
Adam, by sad experiment I know
How little weight my words with thee can find,
Found so erroneous, thence by just event
Found so unfortunate; nevertheless,
Restored by thee, vile as I am, to place
Of new acceptance, hopeful to regain
Thy love, the sole contentment of my heart,
Living or dying from thee I will not hide
What thoughts in my unquiet breast are risen,
Tending to some relief of our extremes,
Or end, though sharp and sad, yet tolerable,
As in our evils, and of easier choice.

If care of our descent perplex us most,
Which must be born to certain woe, devoured
By death at last, and miserable it is
To be to others cause of misery,
Our own begotten, and of our loins to bring
Into this cursed world a woeful race,
That after wretched life must be at last
Food for so foul a monster, in thy power
It lies, yet ere conception to prevent
The race unblest, to being yet unbegot.
Childless thou art, childless remain : so Death
Shall be deceived his glut, and with us two
Be forced to satisfy his rav'nous maw.
But if thou judge it hard and difficult,
Conversing, looking, loving, to abstain
From love's due rites, nuptial embraces sweet,
And with desire to languish without hope,
Before the present object languishing
With like desire, which would be misery
And torment less than none of what we dread,
Then both ourselves and seed at once to free
From what we fear for both, let us make short,
Let us seek death, or he not found, supply
With our own hands his office on ourselves ;
Why stand we longer shivering under fears,
That shew no end but death, and have the power,
Of many ways to die the shortest choosing,
Destruction with destruction to destroy.

    She ended here, or vehement despair
Broke off the rest; so much of death her thoughts
Had entertained, as dyed her cheeks with pale.
But Adam with such counsel nothing swayed,
To better hopes his more attentive mind
Labouring had raised, and thus to Eve replied.

Eve, thy contempt of life and pleasure seems
To argue in thee something more sublime
And excellent than what thy mind contemns;
But self-destruction therefore sought, refutes
That excellence thought in thee, and implies,
Not thy contempt, but anguish and regret
For loss of life and pleasure overloved.
Or if thou covet death, as utmost end
Of misery, so thinking to evade
The penalty pronounced, doubt not but God
Hath wiselier armed his vengeful ire than so
To be forestalled; much more I fear lest death
So snatched will not exempt us from the pain
We are by doom to pay; rather such acts
Of contumacy will provoke the highest
To make death in us live. Then let us seek
Some safer resolution, which methinks
I have in view, calling to mind with heed
Part of our sentence, that thy seed shall bruise
The serpent's head; piteous amends, unless
Be meant, whom I conjecture, our grand foe
Satan, who in the serpent hath contrived
Against us this deceit: to crush his head
Would be revenge indeed; which will be lost
By death brought on ourselves, or childless days
Resolved, as thou proposest; so our foe
Shall scape his punishment ordained, and we
Instead shall double ours upon our heads.
No more be mentioned then of violence
Against ourselves, and wilful barrenness,
That cuts us off from hope, and savours only
Rancour and pride, impatience and despite,
Reluctance against God and his just yoke
Laid on our necks. Remember with what mild

And gracious temper he both heard and judged
Without wrath or reviling; we expected
Immediate dissolution, which we thought
Was meant by death that day, when lo, to thee
Pains only in child-bearing were foretold,
And bringing forth, soon recompensed with joy,
Fruit of thy womb: on me the curse aslope
Glanced on the ground, with labour I must earn
My bread; what harm? Idleness had been worse;
My labour will sustain me; and lest cold
Or heat should injure us, his timely care
Hath unbesought provided, and his hands
Clothed us unworthy, pitying while he judged;
How much more, if we pray him, will his ear
Be open, and his heart to pity incline,
And teach us further by what means to shun
Th'inclement seasons, rain, ice, hail and snow,
Which now the sky with various face begins
To shew us in this mountain, while the winds
Blow moist and keen, shattering the graceful locks
Of these fair spreading trees; which bid us seek
Some better shroud, some better warmth to cherish
Our limbs benumbed, ere this diurnal star
Leave cold the night, how we his gathered beams
Reflected, may with matter sere foment,
Or by collision of two bodies grind
The air attrite to fire, as late the clouds
Justling or pushed with winds rude in their shock
Tine the slant lightning, whose thwart flame driv'n down
Kindles the gummy bark of fir or pine,
And sends a comfortable heat from far,
Which might supply the sun. Such fire to use,
And what may else be remedy or cure
To evils which our own misdeeds have wrought,

He will instruct us praying, and of grace
Beseeching him, so as we need not fear
To pass commodiously this life, sustained
By him with many comforts, till we end
In dust, our final rest and native home.
What better can we do, than to the place
Repairing where he judged us, prostrate fall
Before him reverent, and there confess
Humbly our faults, and pardon beg, with tears
Watering the ground, and with our sighs the air
Frequenting, sent from hearts contrite, in sign
Of sorrow unfeigned, and humiliation meek.
Undoubtedly he will relent and turn
From his displeasure; in whose look serene,
When angry most he seemed and most severe,
What else but favour, grace and mercy shone?
　So spake our father penitent, nor Eve
Felt less remorse; they forthwith to the place
Repairing where he judged them prostrate fell
Before him reverent, and both confessed
Humbly their faults, and pardon begged, with tears
Watering the ground, and with their sighs the air
Frequenting, sent from hearts contrite, in sign
Of sorrow unfeigned, and humiliation meek.

*

BOOK XI

The Argument

THE Son of God presents to his Father the prayers of our first parents now repenting, and intercedes for them: God accepts them, but declares that they must no longer abide in Paradise;

sends Michael with a band of cherubim to dispossess them; but
first to reveal to Adam future things: Michael's coming down.
Adam shows to Eve certain ominous signs; he discerns Michael's
approach, goes out to meet him: the angel denounces their departure. Eve's lamentation. Adam pleads, but submits: the angel
leads him up a high hill, sets before him in vision what shall
happen till the flood.

Michael tells Adam about Death

(*Adam is speaking*)

BUT is there yet no other way, besides
These painful passages, how we may come
To death, and mix with our connatural dust?
     There is, said Michael, if thou well observe
The rule of not too much, by temperance taught
In what thou eatst and drinkst, seeking from thence
Due nourishment, not gluttonous delight,
Till many years over thy head return:
So mayst thou live, till like ripe fruit thou drop
Into thy mother's lap, or be with ease
Gathered, not harshly plucked, for death mature:
This is old age; but then thou must outlive
Thy youth, thy strength, thy beauty, which will change
To withered weak and grey; thy senses then
Obtuse, all taste of pleasure must forego,
To what thou hast, and for the air of youth
Hopeful and cheerful, in thy blood will reign
A melancholy damp of cold and dry
To weigh thy spirits down, and last consume
The balm of life. To whom our ancestor.
     Henceforth I fly not death, nor would prolong
Life much, bent rather how I may be quit

Fairest and easiest of this cumbrous charge,
Which I must keep till my appointed day
Of rendering up. Michael to him replied.

Nor love thy life, nor hate; but what thou livst
Live well, how long or short permit to Heaven.

(Lines 524–550)

*

BOOK XII

The Argument

THE angel Michael continues from the flood to relate what shall succeed; then, in the mention of Abraham, comes by degrees to explain, who that seed of the woman shall be, which was promised Adam and Eve in the Fall; his Incarnation, Death, Resurrection and Ascension; the state of the church till his second coming. Adam greatly satisfied and recomforted by these relations and promises descends the hill with Michael; wakens Eve, who all this while had slept, but with gentle dreams composed to quietness of mind and submission. Michael in either hand leads them out of Paradise, the fiery sword waving behind them, and the cherubim taking their stations to guard the place.

The Departure from Eden

HE ended, and they both descend the hill;
Descended, Adam to the bower where Eve
Lay sleeping ran before, but found her waked;
And thus with words not sad she him received.

Whence thou returnst, and whither wentst, I know
For God is also in sleep, and dreams advise,

Which he hath sent propitious, some great good
Presaging, since with sorrow and heart's distress
Wearied I fell asleep: but now lead on.
In me is no delay; with thee to go,
Is to stay here; without thee here to stay
Is to go hence unwilling; thou to me
Art all things under Heaven, all places thou,
Who for my wilful crime art banisht hence.
This further consolation yet secure
I carry hence; though all by me is lost,
Such favour I unworthy am vouchsafed,
By me the promised seed shall all restore.

   So spake our mother Eve, and Adam heard
Well pleased, but answered not; for now too nigh
Th'archangel stood, and from the other hill
To their fixed station, all in bright array
The cherubim descended; on the ground
Gliding meteorous, as evening mist
Risen from a river o'er the marish glides,
And gathers ground fast at the labourer's heel
Homeward returning. High in front advanced,
The brandished sword of God before them blazed
Fierce as a comet; which with torrid heat,
And vapour as the Libyan air adust,
Began to parch that temperate clime; whereat
In either hand the hastening angel caught
Our lingering parents, and to th'Eastern gate
Led them direct, and down the cliff as fast
To the subjected plain; then disappeared.
They looking back, all th'eastern side beheld
Of Paradise, so late their happy seat,
Waved over by that flaming brand, the gate
With dreadful faces thronged and fiery arms.
Some natural tears they dropped, but wiped them soon;

The world was all before them, where to choose
Their place of rest, and providence their guide:
They hand in hand with wandering steps and slow
Through Eden took their solitary way.

(Lines 606–649)

Paradise Regained

BOOK II

Satan tempts Christ in the Wilderness: the Banquet

He spake no dream, for as his words had end,
Our saviour lifting up his eyes beheld
In ample space under the broadest shade
A table richly spread, in regal mode,
With dishes piled, and meats of noblest sort
And savour, beasts of chase, or fowl of game,
In pastry built, or from the spit, or boiled,
Gris-amber-steamed; all fish from sea or shore,
Freshet, or purling brook, of shell or fin,
And exquisitest name, for which was drained
Pontus and Lucrine bay, and Afric coast.
Alas how simple, to these cates compared,
Was that crude apple that diverted Eve!
And at a stately sideboard by the wine
That fragrant smell diffused, in order stood
Tall stripling youths rich clad, of fairer hue
Than Ganymede or Hylas; distant more
Under the trees now tripped, now solemn stood
Nymphs of Diana's train, and Naiades
With fruits and flowers from Amalthea's horn,
And ladies of the Hesperides, that seemed
Fairer than feigned of old, or fabled since
Of fairy damsels met in forest wide,
By knights of Logres, or of Lyoness,
Lancelot or Pelleas, or Pellenore,
And all the while harmonious airs were heard,
Of chiming strings, or charming pipes and winds

Of gentlest gale Arabian odours fanned
From their soft wings, and Flora's earliest smells.

(Lines 337–365)

*

BOOK III

The Kingdoms of the World

WITH that (such power was given him then) he took
The Son of God up to a mountain high.
It was a mountain at whose verdant feet
A spacious plain outstretched in circuit wide
Lay pleasant; from his side two rivers flowed,
Th'one winding, the other straight, and left between
Fair champaign with less rivers interveined,
Then meeting joined their tribute to the sea:
Fertile of corn the glebe, of oil and wine,
With herds the pastures thronged, with flocks the hills,
Huge cities and high towered, that well might seem
The seats of mightiest monarchs, and so large
The prospect was, that here and there was room
For barren desert fountainless and dry.
To this high mountain top the Tempter brought
Our Saviour, and new train of words began.

Well have we speeded, and o'er hill and dale,
Forest and field, and flood, temples and towers
Cut shorter many a league; here thou behold'st
Assyria and her empire's ancient bounds,
Araxes and the Caspian lake, thence on
As far as Indus east, Euphrates west,
And oft beyond; to south the Persian bay,
And inaccessible the Arabian drouth:

Here Nineveh, of length within her wall
Several days' journey, built by Ninus old,
Of that first golden monarchy the seat,
And seat of Salmanassar, whose success
Israel in long captivity still mourns;
There Babylon the wonder of all tongues,
As ancient, but rebuilt by him who twice
Judah and all thy father David's house
Led captive, and Jerusalem laid waste,
Till Cyrus set them free; Persepolis
His city there thou seest, and Bactra there;
Ecbatana her structure vast there shows,
And Hecatompylos her hundred gates;
There Susa, by Choaspes, amber stream,
The drink of none but kings. Of later fame
Built by Emathian, or by Parthian hands,
The great Seleucia, Nisibis, and there
Artaxata, Teredon, Tesiphon,
Turning with easy eye thou may'st behold.
All these the Parthian, now some ages past,
By great Arsaces led, who founded first
That empire, under his dominion holds
From the luxurious kings of Antioch won.
And just in time thou com'st to have a view
Of his great power; for now the Parthian king
In Ctesiphon hath gathered all his host
Against the Scythian, whose incursions wild
Have wasted Sogdiana; to her aid
He marches now in haste; see, though from far,
His thousands, in what martial equipage
They issue forth, steel bows, and shafts their arms
Of equal dread in flight, or in pursuit;
All horsemen, in which fight they most excel;
See how in warlike muster they appear,

In rhombs and wedges, and half moons, and wings.
    He looked, and saw what numbers numberless
The city gates out poured, light armed troops
In coats of mail and military pride;
In mail their horses clad, yet fleet and strong,
Prancing their riders bore, the flower and choice
Of many provinces from bound to bound;
From Arachosia, from Candaor east,
And Margiana to the Hyrcanian cliffs
Of Caucasus, and dark Iberian dales,
From Atropatia and the neighbouring plains
Of Adiabene, Media, and the south
Of Susiana to Balsara's haven.
He saw them in their forms of battle ranged,
How quick they wheeled, and flying behind them shot
Sharp sleet of arrowy showers against the face
Of their pursuers, and overcame by flight;
The field all iron cast a gleaming brown,
Nor wanted clouds of foot, nor on each horn,
Cuirassiers all in steel for standing fight;
Chariots or elephants endorsed with towers
Of archers, nor of labouring pioneers
A multitude with spades and axes armed
To lay hills plain, fell woods, or valleys fill,
Or where plain was raise hill, or over-lay
With bridges rivers proud, as with a yoke.
Mules after these, camels and dromedaries,
And waggons fraught with utensils of war.
Such forces met not, nor so wide a camp,
When Agrican with all his northern powers
Beseiged Albracca, as romances tell,
The city of Gallaphrone, from thence to win
The fairest of her sex, Angelica
His daughter, sought by many prowest knights,

Both Paynim, and the peers of Charlemagne.
Such and so numerous was their chivalry.

(Lines 251–344)

*

BOOK IV

The Rejection of Classical Culture

(Satan speaks)

LOOK once more ere we leave this specular mount
Westward, much nearer by southwest, behold
Where on the Aegean shore a city stands
Built nobly, pure the air, and light the soil,
Athens the eye of Greece, mother of arts
And eloquence, native to famous wits
Or hospitable, in her sweet recess,
City or suburban, studious walks and shades;
See there the olive grove of Academe,
Plato's retirement, where the Attic bird
Trills her thick-warbled notes the summer long;
There flowery hill Hymettus with the sound
Of bees' industrious murmur oft invites
To studious musing; there Ilissus rolls
His whispering stream; within the walls then view
The schools of ancient sages; his who bred
Great Alexander to subdue the world,
Lyceum there, and painted Stoa next.
There thou shalt hear and learn the secret power
Of harmony in tones and numbers hit
By voice or hand, and various-measured verse,
Aeolian charms and Dorian lyric odes,
And his who gave them breath, but higher sung,

Blind Melesigenes thence Homer called,
Whose poem Phoebus challenged for his own.
Thence what the lofty grave tragedians taught
In chorus or iambic, teachers best
Of moral prudence, with delight received
In brief sententious precepts, while they treat
Of fate, and chance, and change in human life;
High actions, and high passions best describing.
Thence to the famous orators repair,
Those ancient, whose resistless eloquence
Wielded at will that fierce democracy,
Shook the arsenal and fulmined over Greece,
To Macedon, and Artaxerxes' throne;
To sage philosophy next lend thine ear,
From Heaven descended to the low-roofed house
Of Socrates, see there his tenement,
Whom well-inspired the oracle pronounced
Wisest of men; from whose mouth issued forth
Mellifluous streams that watered all the schools
Of Academics old and new, with those
Surnamed Peripatetics, and the sect
Epicurean, and the Stoic severe.
These here revolve, or, as thou lik'st, at home,
Till time mature thee to a kingdom's weight;
These rules will render thee a king complete
Within thyself, much more with empire joined.

   To whom our Saviour sagely thus replied.
Think not but that I know these things, or think
I know them not; not therefore am I short
Of knowing what I ought; he who receives
Light from above, from the fountain of light,
No other doctrine needs, though granted true;
But these are false, or little else but dreams,
Conjectures, fancies, built on nothing firm.

The first and wisest of them all professed
To know this only, that he nothing knew;
The next to fabling fell, and smooth conceits;
A third sort doubted all things, though plain sense;
Others in virtue placed felicity,
But virtue joined with riches and long life;
In corporal pleasure he, and careless ease;
The Stoic last in philosophic pride,
By him called virtue; and his virtuous man,
Wise, perfect in himself, and all possessing
Equal to God, oft shames not to prefer,
As fearing God nor man, contemning all
Wealth, pleasure, pain or torment, death and life,
Which when he lists, he leaves, or boasts he can,
For all his tedious talk is but vain boast,
Or subtle shifts conviction to evade.
Alas what can they teach, and not mislead;
Ignorant of themselves, of God much more,
And how the world began, and how man fell
Degraded by himself, on grace depending?
Much of the soul they talk, but all awry,
And in themselves seek virtue, and to themselves
All glory arrogate, to God give none;
— Rather accuse him under usual names,
Fortune and fate, as one regardless quite
Of mortal things. Who therefore seeks in these
True wisdom, finds her not, or by delusion
Far worse, her false resemblance only meets,
An empty cloud. However, many books
Wise men have said are wearisome; who reads
Incessantly, and to his reading brings not
A spirit and judgement equal or superior,
(And what he brings, what needs he elsewhere seek?)
Uncertain and unsettled still remains,

Deep versed in books and shallow in himself,
Crude or intoxicate, collecting toys,
And trifles for choice matters, worth a sponge,
As children gathering pebbles on the shore.
Or if I would delight my private hours
With music or with poem, where so soon
As in our native language can I find
That solace? All our law and story strewed
With hymns, our psalms with artful terms inscribed,
Our Hebrew songs and harps in Babylon,
That pleased so well our victors' ear, declare
That rather Greece from us these arts derived;
Ill imitated, while they loudest sing
The vices of their deities, and their own
In fable, hymn, or song, so personating
Their gods ridiculous, and themselves past shame.
Remove their swelling epithets thick laid
As varnish on a harlot's cheek, the rest
Thin sown with aught of profit or delight,
Will far be found unworthy to compare
With Sion's songs to all true tastes excelling,
Where God is praised aright, and godlike men,
The holiest of holies, and his saints;
Such are from God inspired, not such from thee;
Unless where moral virtue is expressed
By light of nature not in all quite lost.
Their orators thou then extoll'st, as those
The top of eloquence, statists indeed,
And lovers of their country, as may seem
But herein to our prophets far beneath,
As men divinely taught, and better teaching
The solid rules of civil government
In their majestic unaffected style,
Than all the oratory of Greece and Rome.

In them is plainest taught, and easiest learnt,
What makes a nation happy, and keeps it so,
What ruins kingdoms, and lays cities flat,
These only with our law best form a king.

(Lines 236–364)

Satan sets Storms raging while Christ sleeps

So saying he took (for still he knew his power
Not yet expired) and to the wilderness
Brought back the Son of God, and left him there,
Feigning to disappear. Darkness now rose,
As daylight sunk, and brought in lowering night
Her shadowy offspring unsubstantial both,
Privation mere of light and absent day.
Our Saviour meek and with untroubled mind
After his airy jaunt, though hurried sore,
Hungry and cold betook him to his rest,
Wherever, under some concourse of shades
Whose branching arms thick intertwined might shield
From dews and damps of night his sheltered head,
But sheltered slept in vain, for at his head
The Tempter watched, and soon with ugly dreams
Disturbed his sleep; and either tropic now
'Gan thunder, and both ends of Heaven; the clouds
From many a horrid rift abortive poured
Fierce rain with lightning mixed, water with fire
In ruin reconciled: nor slept the winds
Within their stony caves, but rushed abroad
From the four hinges of the world, and fell
On the vexed wilderness, whose tallest pines,
Though rooted deep as high, and sturdiest oaks
Bowed their stiff necks, loaden with stormy blasts,
Or torn up sheer: ill wast thou shrouded then,

O patient Son of God, yet only stoodst
Unshaken. Nor yet stayed the terror there,
Infernal ghosts, and hellish furies, round
Environed thee, some howled, some yelled, some shrieked,
Some bent at thee their fiery darts, while thou
Sat'st unappalled in calm and sinless peace.
Thus passed the night so foul till morning fair
Came forth with pilgrim steps in amice grey.

(Lines 394–427)

Samson Agonistes

A DRAMATIC POEM

The Argument

SAMSON made captive, blind, and now in the prison at Gaza, there to labour as in a common workhouse, on a festival day, in the general cessation from labour, comes forth into the open air, to a place nigh, somewhat retired there to sit a while and bemoan his condition. Where he happens at length to be visited by certain friends and equals of his tribe, which make the Chorus, who seek to comfort him what they can; then by his old father Manoa, who endeavours the like, and withal tells him his purpose to procure his liberty by ransom; lastly, that this feast was proclaimed by the Philistines as a day of thanksgiving for their deliverance from the hands of Samson, which yet more troubles him. Manoa then departs to prosecute his endeavour with the Philistian lords for Samson's redemption; who in the meanwhile is visited by other persons; and lastly by a public officer to require his coming to the feast before the lords and people, to play or show his strength in their presence; he at first refuses, dismissing the public officer with absolute denial to come; at length persuaded inwardly that this was from God, he yields to go along with him, who came now the second time with great threatenings to fetch him; the Chorus yet remaining on the place, Manoa returns full of joyful hope, to procure ere long his son's deliverance: in the midst of which discourse an Ebrew comes in haste confusedly at first; and afterward more distinctly relating the catastrophe, what Samson had done to the Philistines, and by accident to himself; wherewith the tragedy ends.

*

THE PERSONS

Samson
Manoa, the father of Samson
Dalila, his wife
Harapha of Gath
Public officer
Messenger
Chorus of Danites

The scene before the prison in Gaza

＊

Samson. A little onward lend thy guiding hand
To these dark steps, a little further on.
For yonder bank hath choice of sun or shade;
There I am wont to sit, when any chance
Relieves me from my task of servile toil,
Daily in the common prison else enjoined me,
Where I a prisoner chained, scarce freely draw
The air imprisoned also, close and damp,
Unwholesome draught: but here I feel amends,
The breath of Heaven fresh-blowing, pure and sweet,
With dayspring born; here leave me to respire.
This day a solemn feast the people hold
To Dagon their sea-idol, and forbid
Laborious works, unwillingly this rest
Their superstition yields me; hence with leave
Retiring from the popular noise, I seek
This unfrequented place to find some ease,
Ease to the body some, none to the mind
From restless thoughts, that like a deadly swarm
Of hornets armed, no sooner found alone,

But rush upon me thronging, and present
Times past, what once I was, and what am now.
O wherefore was my birth from Heaven foretold
Twice by an angel, who at last in sight
Of both my parents all in flames ascended
From off the altar, where an offering burned,
As in a fiery column charioting
His godlike presence, and from some great act
Or benefit revealed to Abraham's race?
Why was my breeding ordered and prescribed
As of a person separate to God,
Designed for great exploits; if I must die
Betrayed, captived, and both my eyes put out,
Made of my enemies the scorn and gaze;
To grind in brazen fetters under task
With this Heaven-gifted strength? O glorious strength
Put to the labour of a beast, debased
Lower than bondslave! Promise was that I
Should Israel from Philistian yoke deliver;
Ask for this great deliverer now, and find him
Eyeless in Gaza at the mill with slaves,
Himself in bonds under Philistian yoke;
Yet stay, let me not rashly call in doubt
Divine prediction; what if all foretold
Had been fulfilled but through mine own default,
Whom have I to complain of but my self?
Who this high gift of strength committed to me,
In what part lodged, how easily bereft me,
Under the seal of silence could not keep,
But weakly to a woman must reveal it
O'ercome with importunity and tears.
O impotence of mind, in body strong!
But what is strength without a double share
Of wisdom, vast, unwieldy, burdensome,

Proudly secure, yet liable to fall
By weakest subtleties, not made to rule,
But to subserve where wisdom bears command.
God, when he gave me strength, to shew withal
How slight the gift was, hung it in my hair.
But peace, I must not quarrel with the will
Of highest dispensation, which herein
Hap'ly had ends above my reach to know.
Suffices that to me strength is my bane,
And proves the source of all my miseries;
So many and so huge, that each apart
Would ask a life to wail, but chief of all,
O loss of sight, of thee I most complain!
Blind among enemies, O worse than chains,
Dungeon, or beggary, or decrepit age!
Light the prime work of God to me is extinct,
And all her various objects of delight
Annulled, which might in part my grief have eased,
Inferior to the vilest now become
Of man or worm; the vilest here excel me,
They creep, yet see, I dark in light exposed
To daily fraud, contempt, abuse and wrong,
Within doors, or without, still as a fool,
In power of others, never in my own;
Scarce half I seem to live, dead more than half.
O dark, dark, dark, amid the blaze of noon,
Irrecoverably dark, total eclipse
Without all hope of day!
O first created beam, and thou great Word,
Let there be light, and light was over all;
Why am I thus bereaved thy prime decree?
The sun to me is dark
And silent as the moon,
When she deserts the night

264

Hid in her vacant interlunar cave.
Since light so necessary is to life,
And almost life itself, if it be true
That light is in the soul,
She all in every part; why was the sight
To such a tender ball as th'eye confined?
So obvious and so easy to be quenched,
And not as feeling through all parts diffused,
That she might look at will through every pore?
Then had I not been thus exiled from light;
As in the land of darkness yet in light,
To live a life half dead, a living death,
And buried; but O yet more miserable!
Myself, my sepulchre, a moving grave,
Buried, yet not exempt
By privilege of death and burial
From worst of other evils, pains and wrongs,
But made hereby obnoxious more
To all the miseries of life,
Life in captivity
Among inhuman foes.
But who are these? for with joint pace I hear
The tread of many feet steering this way;
Perhaps my enemies who come to stare
At my affliction, and perhaps to insult,
Their daily practice to afflict me more.
   Chorus. This, this is he; softly awhile,
Let us not break in upon him;
O change beyond report, thought, or belief!
See how he lies at random, carelessly diffused,
With languished head unpropt,
As one past hope, abandoned
And by himself given over;
In slavish habit, ill-fitted weeds

O'er worn and soiled;
Or do my eyes misrepresent? Can this be he,
That heroic, that renowned,
Irresistible Samson? Whom unarmed
No strength of man, or fiercest wild beast could withstand;
Who tore the lion, as the lion tears the kid,
Ran on imbattled armies clad in iron,
And weaponless himself,
Made arms ridiculous, useless the forgery
Of brazen shield and spear, the hammered cuirass,
Chalybean tempered steel, and frock of mail
Adamantean proof;
But safest he who stood aloof,
When insupportably his foot advanced,
In scorn of their proud arms and warlike tools,
Spurned them to death by troops. The bold Ascalonite
Fled from his lion ramp, old warriors turned
Their plated backs under his heel;
Or grovelling soiled their crested helmets in the dust.
Then with what trivial weapon came to hand,
The jaw of a dead ass, his sword of bone,
A thousand foreskins fell, the flower of Palestine
In Ramath-lechi famous to this day.
Then by main force pulled up, and on his shoulders bore
The gates of Azza, post, and massy bar
Up to the hill by Hebron, seat of giants old,
No journey of a sabbath day, and loaded so;
Like whom the gentiles feign to bear up Heaven.
Which shall I first bewail,
Thy bondage or lost sight,
Prison within prison
Inseparably dark?
Thou art become (O worst imprisonment!)
The dungeon of thyself; thy soul

(Which men enjoying sight oft without cause complain)
Imprisoned now indeed,
In real darkness of the body dwells,
Shut up from outward light
To incorporate with gloomy night;
For inward light alas
Puts forth no visual beam.
O mirror of our fickle state,
Since man on earth unparalleled!
The rarer thy example stands,
By how much from the top of wondrous glory,
Strongest of mortal men,
To lowest pitch of abject fortune thou art fallen.
For him I reckon not in high estate
Whom long descent of birth
Or the sphere of fortune raises;
But thee whose strength, while virtue was her mate
Might have subdued the earth,
Universally crowned with highest praises.

    Samson. I hear the sound of words, their sense the air
Dissolves unjointed, ere it reach my ear.

    Chorus. He speaks, let us draw nigh. Matchless in might,
The glory late of Israel, now the grief;
We come thy friends and neighbours not unknown
From Eshtaol and Zora's fruitful vale
To visit or bewail thee, or if better,
Counsel or consolation we may bring,
Salve to thy sores, apt words have power to suage
The tumours of a troubled mind,
And are as balm to festered wounds.

    Samson. Your coming, friends, revives me, for I learn
Now of my own experience, not by talk,
How counterfeit a coin they are who friends
Bear in their superscription (of the most

I would be understood). In prosperous days
They swarm, but in adverse withdraw their head
Not to be found, though sought. Ye see, O friends,
How many evils have enclosed me round;
Yet that which was the worst now least afflicts me,
Blindness, for had I sight, confused with shame,
How could I once look up, or heave the head,
Who like a foolish pilot have shipwrackt
My vessel trusted to me from above,
Gloriously rigged; and for a word, a tear,
Fool, have divulged the secret gift of God
To a deceitful woman. Tell me friends,
Am I not sung and proverbed for a fool
In every street, do they not say, how well
Are come upon him his deserts? yet why?
Immeasurable strength they might behold
In me, of wisdom nothing more than mean;
This with the other should, at least, have paired,
These two proportioned ill drove me transverse.

    Chorus. Tax not divine disposal, wisest men
Have erred, and by bad women been deceived;
And shall again, pretend they ne'er so wise.
Deject not then so overmuch thyself,
Who hast of sorrow thy full load besides;
Yet truth to say, I oft have heard men wonder
Why thou shouldst wed Philistian women rather
Than of thine own tribe fairer, or as fair,
At least of thy own nation, and as noble.

    Samson. The first I saw at Timna, and she pleased
Me, not my parents, that I sought to wed,
The daughter of an infidel: they knew not
That what I motioned was of God; I knew
From intimate impulse, and therefore urged
The marriage on; that by occasion hence

I might begin Israel's deliverance,
The work to which I was divinely called;
She proving false, the next I took to wife
(O that I never had! fond wish too late)
Was in the vale of Sorec, Dalila,
That specious monster, my accomplished snare.
I thought it lawful from my former act,
And the same end; still watching to oppress
Israel's oppressors. Of what now I suffer
She was not the prime cause, but I myself,
Who vanquished with a peal of words (O weakness!)
Gave up my fort of silence to a woman.
    Chorus. In seeking just occasion to provoke
The Philistine, thy country's enemy,
Thou never wast remiss, I bear thee witness:
Yet Israel still serves with all his sons.
    Samson. That fault I take not on me, but transfer
On Israel's governors, and heads of tribes,
Who seeing those great acts which God had done
Singly by me against their conquerors
Acknowledged not, or not at all considered
Deliverance offered: I on th'other side
Used no ambition to commend my deeds,
The deeds themselves, though mute, spoke loud the doer;
But they persisted deaf, and would not seem
To count them things worth notice, till at length
Their lords the Philistines with gathered powers
Entered Judea seeking me, who then
Safe to the rock of Etham was retired,
Not flying, but forecasting in what place
To set upon them, what advantaged best.
Meanwhile the men of Judah to prevent
The harass of their land, beset me round;
I willingly on some conditions came

Into their hands, and they as gladly yield me
To the uncircumcised a welcome prey,
Bound with two cords; but cords to me were threads
Touched with the flame: on their whole host I flew
Unarmed, and with a trivial weapon felled
Their choicest youth; they only lived who fled.
Had Judah that day joined, or one whole tribe,
They had by this possessed the towers of Gath,
And lorded over them whom now they serve;
But what more oft in nations grown corrupt,
And by their vices brought to servitude,
Than to love bondage more than liberty,
Bondage with ease than strenuous liberty;
And to despise, or envy, or suspect
Whom God hath of his special favour raised
As their deliverer; if he aught begin,
How frequent to desert him, and at last
To heap ingratitude on worthiest deeds?
    Chorus. Thy words to my remembrance bring
How Succoth and the fort of Penuel
Their great deliverer contemned,
The matchless Gideon in pursuit
Of Madian and her vanquished kings;
And how ingrateful Ephraim
Had dealt with Jephtha, who by argument,
Not worse than by his shield and spear
Defended Israel from the Ammonite,
Had not his prowess quelled their pride
In that sore battle when so many died,
Without reprieve adjudged to death,
For want of well pronouncing Shibboleth.
    Samson. Of such examples add me to the roll,
Me easily indeed mine may neglect,
But God's proposed deliverance not so.

Chorus. Just are the ways of God,
And justifiable to men;
Unless there be who think not God at all.
If any be, they walk obscure;
For of such doctrine never was there school,
But the heart of the fool,
And no man therein doctor but himself.

Yet more there be who doubt his ways not just,
As to his own edicts, found contradicting,
Then give the reins to wandering thought,
Regardless of his glory's diminution;
Till by their own perplexities involved
They ravel more, still less resolved,
But never find self-satisfying solution.

As if they would confine th'interminable,
And tie him to his own prescript,
Who made our laws to bind us, not himself,
And hath full right to exempt
Whom so it pleases him by choice
From national obstriction, without taint
Of sin, or legal debt;
For with his own laws he can best dispense.

He would not else who never wanted means,
Nor in respect of the enemy just cause
To set his people free,
Have prompted this heroic Nazarite,
Against his vow of strictest purity,
To seek in marriage that fallacious bride,
Unclean, unchaste.

Down Reason then, at least vain reasonings down,
Though Reason here aver
That moral verdict quits her of unclean:
Unchaste was subsequent, her stain not his.

But see here comes thy reverend sire

With careful steps, locks white as down,
Old Manoa: advise
Forthwith how thou oughtst to receive him.

 Samson. Ay me, another inward grief awaked,
With mention of that name renews th'assault.

 Manoa. Brethren and men of Dan, for such ye seem,
Though in this uncouth place; if old respect,
As I suppose, towards your once gloried friend,
My son now captive, hither hath informed
Your younger feet, while mine cast back with age
Came lagging after; say if he be here.

 Chorus. As signal now in low dejected state,
As erst in highest, behold him where he lies.

 Manoa. O miserable change! Is this the man,
That invincible Samson, far renowned,
The dread of Israel's foes, who with a strength
Equivalent to angels walked their streets,
None offering fight; who single combatant
Duelled their armies ranked in proud array,
Himself an army, now unequal match
To save himself against a coward armed
At one spear's length. O ever failing trust
In mortal strength! And oh what not in man
Deceivable and vain! Nay what thing good
Prayed for, but often proves our woe, our bane?
I prayed for children, and thought barrenness
In wedlock a reproach; I gained a son,
And such a son as all men hailed me happy;
Who would be now a father in my stead?
O wherefore did God grant me my request,
And as a blessing with such pomp adorned?
Why are his gifts desirable, to tempt
Our earnest prayers, then given with solemn hand
As graces, draw a scorpion's tail behind?

For this did the angel twice descend? for this
Ordained thy nurture holy, as of a plant;
Select and sacred, glorious for a while,
The miracle of men: then in an hour
Ensnared, assaulted, overcome, led bound,
Thy foes' derision, captive, poor, and blind,
Into a dungeon thrust, to work with slaves?
Alas methinks whom God hath chosen once
To worthiest deeds, if he through frailty err.
He should not so o'erwhelm, and as a thrall
Subject him to so foul indignities,
Be it but for honour's sake of former deeds.

    Samson. Appoint not heavenly disposition, father.
Nothing of all these evils hath befall'n me
But justly; I myself have brought them on,
Sole author I, sole cause: if aught seem vile,
As vile hath been my folly, who have profaned
The mystery of God giv'n me under pledge
Of vow, and have betrayed it to a woman,
A Canaanite, my faithless enemy.
This well I knew, nor was at all surprised,
But warned by oft experience: did not she
Of Timna first betray me, and reveal
The secret wrested from me in her highth
Of nuptial love professed, carrying it straight
To them who had corrupted her, my spies,
And rivals? In this other was there found
More faith? Who also in her prime of love,
Spousal embraces, vitiated with gold,
Though offered only, by the scent conceived
Her spurious first-born, treason against me?
Thrice she assayed with flattering prayers and sighs,
And amorous reproaches to win from me
My capital secret, in what part my strength

Lay stored, in what part summed, that she might know:
Thrice I deluded her, and turned to sport
Her importunity, each time perceiving
How openly, and with what impudence
She purposed to betray me, and (which was worse
Than undissembled hate) with what contempt
She sought to make me traitor to myself.
Yet the fourth time, when mustering all her wiles,
With blandished parlies, feminine assaults,
Tongue-batteries, she surceased not day nor night
To storm me overwatched and wearied out.
At times when men seek most repose and rest,
I yielded, and unlocked her all my heart,
Who with a grain of manhood well resolved
Might easily have shook off all her snares.
But foul effeminacy held me yoked
To her bond-slave. O indignity, O blot
To honour and religion! Servile mind
Rewarded well with servile punishment!
The base degree to which I now am fallen,
These rags, this grinding, is not yet so base
As was my former servitude, ignoble,
Unmanly, ignominious, infamous,
True slavery, and that blindness worse than this,
That saw not how degenerately I served.

    Manoa. I cannot praise thy marriage choices, son,
Rather approved them not; but thou didst plead
Divine impulsion prompting how thou might'st
Find some occasion to infest our foes.
I state not that; this I am sure: our foes
Found soon occasion thereby to make thee
Their captive, and their triumph; thou the sooner
Temptation found'st, or over-potent charms
To violate the sacred trust of silence

Deposited within thee; which to have kept
Tacit, was in thy power. True: and thou bear'st
Enough, and more, the burden of that fault.
Bitterly hast thou paid, and still art paying
That rigid score. A worse thing yet remains;
This day the Philistines a popular feast
Here celebrate in Gaza; and proclaim
Great pomp, and sacrifice, and praises loud
To Dagon, as their God who hath delivered
Thee Samson bound and blind into their hands,
Them out of thine, who slew'st them many a slain
So Dagon shall be magnified, and God,
Besides whom is no God, compared with idols,
Disglorified, blasphemed, and had in scorn
By th'idolatrous rout amidst their wine.
Which to have come to pass by means of thee,
Samson, of all thy sufferings think the heaviest,
Of all reproach the most with shame that ever
Could have befall'n thee and thy father's house.
    Samson. Father, I do acknowledge and confess
That I this honour, I this pomp have brought
To Dagon, and advanced his praises high
Among the Heathen round; to God have brought
Dishonour, obloquy, and oped the mouths
Of idolists, and atheists; have brought scandal
To Israel, diffidence of God, and doubt
In feeble hearts, propense enough before
To waver, or fall off and join with idols:
Which is my chief affliction, shame and sorrow,
The anguish of my soul, that suffers not
Mine eye to harbour sleep, or thoughts to rest.
This only hope relieves me, that the strife
With me hath end; all the contest is now
'Twixt God and Dagon; Dagon hath presumed,

Me overthrown, to enter lists with God
His deity comparing and preferring
Before the God of Abraham. He, be sure,
Will not connive, or linger, thus provoked,
But will arise and his great name assert.
Dagon must stoop, and shall ere long receive
Such a discomfit, as shall quite despoil him
Of all these boasted trophies won on me,
And with confusion blank his worshippers.

 Manoa. With cause this hope relieves thee, and these words
I as a prophecy receive: for God,
Nothing more certain, will not long defer
To vindicate the glory of his name
Against all competition, nor will long
Endure it, doubtful whether God be Lord,
Or Dagon. But for thee what shall be done?
Thou must not in the meanwhile here forgot
Lie in this miserable loathsome plight
Neglected. I already have made way
To some Philistian lords, with whom to treat
About thy ransom: well they may by this
Have satisfied their utmost of revenge
By pains and slaveries, worse than death inflicted
On thee, who now no more canst do them harm.

 Samson. Spare that proposal, father, spare the trouble
Of that solicitation; let me here,
As I deserve, pay on my punishment;
And expiate, if possible, my crime,
Shameful garrulity. To have revealed
Secrets of men, the secrets of a friend,
How heinous had the fact been, how deserving
Contempt, and scorn of all, to be excluded
All friendship, and avoided as a blab,
The mark of fool set on his front?

But I God's counsel have not kept, his holy secret
Presumptuously have published, impiously,
Weakly at least, and shamefully: a sin
That Gentiles in their parables condemn
To their abyss and horrid pains confined.

   Manoa. Be penitent and for thy fault contrite,
But act not in thy own affliction, son,
Repent the sin, but if the punishment
Thou canst avoid, self-preservation bids;
Or th'execution leave to high disposal,
And let another hand, not thine, exact
Thy penal forfeit from thyself; perhaps
God will relent, and quit thee all his debt,
Who evermore approves and more accepts
(Best pleased with humble and filial submission)
Him who imploring mercy sues for life,
Than who self-rigorous chooses death as due,
Which argues over-just, and self-displeased
For self-offence, more than for God offended.
Reject not then what offered means, who knows
But God hath set before us, to return thee
Home to thy country, and his sacred house,
Where thou mayst bring thy offerings, to avert
His further ire, with prayers and vows renewed.

   Samson. His pardon I implore; but as for life,
To what end should I seek it? When in strength
All mortals I excelled, and great in hopes
With youthful courage and magnanimous thoughts
Of birth from Heaven foretold and high exploits,
Full of divine instinct, after some proof
Of acts indeed heroic, far beyond
The sons of Anac, famous now and blazed,
Fearless of danger, like a petty God
I walked about admired of all and dreaded

On hostile ground, none daring my affront.
Then swoll'n with pride into the snare I fell
Of fair fallacious looks, venereal trains,
Softened with pleasure and voluptuous life;
At length to lay my head and hallowed pledge
Of all my strength in the lascivious lap
Of a deceitful concubine who shore me
Like a tame wether, all my precious fleece,
Then turned me out ridiculous, despoiled,
Shav'n, and disarmed among my enemies.

   Chorus. Desire of wine and all delicious drinks,
Which many a famous warrior overturns,
Thou couldst repress, nor did the dancing ruby
Sparkling, outpoured, the flavour or the smell,
Or taste that cheers the heart of gods and men,
Allure thee from the cool crystalline stream.

   Samson. Where ever fountain or fresh current flowed
Against the eastern ray, translucent, pure,
With touch ethereal of Heaven's fiery rod
I drank, from the clear milky juice allaying
Thirst, and refreshed; nor envied them the grape
Whose heads that turbulent liquor fills with fumes.

   Chorus. O madness, to think use of strongest wines
And strongest drinks our chief support of health,
When God with these forbidden made choice to rear
His mighty champion, strong above compare,
Whose drink was only from the liquid brook.

   Samson. But what availed this temperance, not complete
Against another object more enticing?
What boots it at one gate to make defence
And at another to let in the foe
Effeminately vanquished? By which means,
Now blind, disheartened, shamed, dishonoured, quelled,
To what can I be useful, wherein serve

My nation, and the work from Heaven imposed,
But to sit idle on the household hearth,
A burdenous drone; to visitants a gaze,
Or pitied object, these redundant locks
Robustious to no purpose clustering down,
Vain monument of strength; till length of years
And sedentary numbness craze my limbs
To a contemptible old age obscure.
Here rather let me drudge and earn my bread,
Till vermin or the draff of servile food
Consume me, and oft-invocated death
Hast'n the welcome end of all my pains.

    Manoa. Wilt thou then serve the Philistines with that gift
Which was expressly giv'n thee to annoy them?
Better at home lie bed-rid, not only idle,
Inglorious, unemployed, with age out-worn.
But God who caused a fountain at thy prayer
From the dry ground to spring, thy thirst to allay
After the brunt of battle, can as easy
Cause light again within thy eyes to spring,
Wherewith to serve him better than thou hast.
And I persuade me so: why else this strength
Miraculous yet remaining in those locks?
His might continues in thee not for naught,
Nor shall his wondrous gifts be frustrate thus.

    Samson. All otherwise to me my thoughts portend,
That these dark orbs no more shall treat with light,
Nor th'other light of life continue long,
But yield to double darkness nigh at hand:
So much I feel my genial spirits droop,
My hopes all flat, nature within me seems
In all her functions weary of herself;
My race of glory run, and race of shame,
And I shall shortly be with them that rest.

Manoa. Believe not these suggestions which proceed
From anguish of the mind and humours black,
That mingle with thy fancy. I however
Must not omit a father's timely care
To prosecute the means of thy deliverance
By ransom or how else: meanwhile be calm,
And healing words from these thy friends admit.

   Samson. O that torment should not be confined
To the body's wounds and sores
With maladies innumerable
In heart, head, breast, and reins;
But must secret passage find
To th'inmost mind,
There exercise all his fierce accidents,
And on her purest spirits prey,
As on entrails, joints, and limbs,
With answerable pains, but more intense,
Though void of corporal sense.
   My griefs not only pain me
As a lingering disease,
But finding no redress, ferment and rage,
Nor less than wounds immedicable
Rankle, and fester, and gangrene,
To black mortification.
Thoughts my tormentors armed with deadly stings
Mangle my apprehensive tenderest parts,
Exasperate, exulcerate, and raise
Dire inflammation which no cooling herb
Or medicinal liquor can assuage,
Nor breath of vernal air from snowy alp.
Sleep hath forsook and given me o'er
To death's benumbing opium as my only cure.
Thence faintings, swoonings of despair,
And sense of heaven's desertion.

I was his nursling once and choice delight,
His destined from the womb,
Promised by heavenly message twice descending.
Under his special eye
Abstemious I grew up and thrived amain;
He led me on to mightiest deeds
Above the nerve of mortal arm
Against the uncircumcised, our enemies.
But now hath cast me off as never known,
And to those cruel enemies,
Whom I by his appointment had provoked,
Left me all helpless with th'irreparable loss
Of sight, reserved alive to be repeated
The subject of their cruelty, or scorn.
Nor am I in the list of them that hope;
Hopeless are all my evils, all remediless;
This one prayer yet remains, might I be heard,
No long petition, speedy death,
The close of all my miseries, and the balm.

   Chorus. Many are the sayings of the wise
In ancient and in modern books enrolled;
Extolling patience as the truest fortitude;
And to the bearing well of all calamities,
All chances incident to man's frail life
Consolatories writ
With studied argument, and much persuasion sought
Lenient of grief and anxious thought:
But with th'afflicted in his pangs their sound
Little prevails, or rather seems a tune,
Harsh, and of dissonant mood from his complaint,
Unless he feel within
Some source of consolation from above
— Secret refreshings that repair his strength,
And fainting spirits uphold.

God of our fathers, what is man!
That thou towards him with hand so various,
Or might I say contrarious,
Temper'st thy providence through his short course,
Not evenly, as thou rul'st
The angelic orders and inferior creatures mute,
Irrational and brute.
Nor do I name of men the common rout,
That wandering loose about
Grow up and perish, as the summer fly,
Heads without name no more remembered,
But such as thou hast solemnly elected,
With gifts and graces eminently adorned
To some great work, thy glory,
And people's safety, which in part they effect:
Yet toward these thus dignified, thou oft
Amidst their highth of noon,
Changest thy countenance, and thy hand with no regard
Of highest favours past
From thee on them, or them to thee of service.
    Nor only dost degrade them, or remit
To life obscured, which were a fair dismission,
But throw'st them lower than thou didst exalt them high,
Unseemly falls in human eye,
Too grievous for the trespass or omission,
Oft leavst them to the hostile sword
Of heathen and profane, their carcasses
To dogs and fowls a prey, or else captived,
Or to the unjust tribunals, under change of times,
And condemnation of the ingrateful multitude.
If these they scape, perhaps in poverty
With sickness and disease thou bow'st them down,
Painful diseases and deformed,
In crude old age:

Though not disordinate, yet causeless suffering
The punishment of dissolute days, in fine,
Just or unjust, alike seem miserable,
For oft alike, both come to evil end.

    So deal not with this once thy glorious champion,
The image of thy strength, and mighty minister.
What do I beg? How hast thou dealt already?
Behold him in this state calamitous, and turn
His labours, for thou canst, to peaceful end.

    But who is this, what thing of sea or land?
Female of sex it seems,
That so bedecked, ornate, and gay,
Comes this way sailing
Like a stately ship
Of Tarsus, bound for th'isles
Of Javan or Gadier
With all her bravery on, and tackle trim,
Sails filled, and streamers waving,
Courted by all the winds that hold them play,
An amber scent of odorous perfume
Her harbinger, a damsel train behind.
Some rich Philistian matron she may seem,
And now at nearer view, no other certain
Than Dalila thy wife.

    Samson. My wife, my traitress, let her not come near me.

    Chorus. Yet on she moves, now stands and eyes thee fixt,
About t'have spoke, but now, with head declined
Like a fair flower surcharged with dew, she weeps
And words addressed seem into tears dissolved,
Wetting the borders of her silken veil;
But now again she makes address to speak.

    Dalila. With doubtful feet and wavering resolution
I came, still dreading thy displeasure, Samson,
Which to have merited, without excuse,

I cannot but acknowledge; yet if tears
May expiate (though the fact more evil drew
In the perverse event than I foresaw)
My penance hath not slackened, though my pardon
No way assured. But conjugal affection
Prevailing over fear, and timorous doubt,
Hath led me on desirous to behold
Once more thy face, and know of thy estate.
If aught in my ability may serve
To lighten what thou suffer'st, and appease
Thy mind with what amends is in my power,
Though late, yet in some part to recompense
My rash but more unfortunate misdeed.

Samson. Out, out, Hyaena. These are thy wonted arts,
And arts of every woman false like thee,
To break all faith, all vows, deceive, betray,
Then as repentant to submit, beseech,
And reconcilement move with feigned remorse,
Confess, and promise wonders in her change,
Not truly penitent, but chief to try
Her husband, how far urged his patience bears,
His virtue or weakness which way to assail:
Then with more cautious and instructed skill
Again transgresses, and again submits.
That wisest and best men full oft beguiled
With goodness principled not to reject
The penitent, but ever to forgive,
Are drawn to wear out miserable days,
Entangled with a poisonous bosom snake,
If not by quick destruction soon cut off
As I by thee, to ages an example.

Dalila. Yet hear me Samson: not that I endeavour
To lessen or extenuate my offence,
But that on th'other side if it be weighed

By itself, with aggravations not surcharged,
Or else with just allowance counterpoised
I may, if possible, thy pardon find
The easier towards me, or thy hatred less.
First granting, as I do, it was a weakness
In me, but incident to all our sex,
Curiosity, inquisitive, importune
Of secrets, then with like infirmity
To publish them, both common female faults:
Was it not weakness also to make known
For importunity, that is for naught,
Wherein consisted all thy strength and safety?
To what I did thou showdst me first the way.
But I to enemies revealed, and should not.
Nor shouldst thou have trusted that to woman's frailty.
Ere I to thee, thou to thyself wast cruel.
Let weakness then with weakness come to parl
So near related, or the same of kind,
Thine forgive mine: that men may censure thine
The gentler, if severely thou exact not
More strength from me, than in thyself was found.
And what if love, which thou interpret'st hate,
The jealousy of love, powerful of sway
In human hearts, nor less in mine towards thee,
Caused what I did? I saw thee mutable
Of fancy, feared lest one day thou wouldst leave me
As her at Timna, sought by all means therefore
How to endear, and hold thee to me firmest.
No better way I saw than by importuning
To learn thy secrets, get into my power
Thy key of strength and safety: thou wilt say,
Why then revealed? I was assured by those
Who tempted me, that nothing was designed
Against thee but safe custody, and hold.

That made for me, I knew that liberty
Would draw thee forth to perilous enterprises,
While I at home sat full of cares and fears
Wailing thy absence in my widowed bed;
Here I should still enjoy thee day and night
Mine and love's prisoner, not the Philistines';
Whole to myself, unhazarded abroad,
Fearless at home of partners in my love.
These reasons in love's law have passed for good,
Though fond and reasonless to some perhaps.
And love hath oft, well meaning, wrought much woe,
Yet always pity or pardon hath obtained.
Be not unlike all others, not austere
As thou art strong, inflexible as steel.
If thou in strength all mortals dost exceed,
In uncompassionate anger do not so.

   Samson. How cunningly the sorceress displays
Her own transgressions, to upbraid me mine!
That malice not repentance brought thee hither,
By this appears. I gave, thou sayst, th'example,
I led the way; bitter reproach, but true,
I to myself was false ere thou to me;
Such pardon therefore as I give my folly,
Take to thy wicked deed: which when thou seest
Impartial, self-severe, inexorable,
Thou wilt renounce thy seeking, and much rather
Confess it feigned. Weakness is thy excuse,
And I believe it, weakness to resist
Philistian gold: if weakness may excuse,
What murderer, what traitor, parricide,
Incestuous, sacrilegious, but may plead it?
All wickedness is weakness: that plea therefore
With God or man will gain thee no remission.
But love constrained thee: call it furious rage

To satisfy thy lust: love seeks to have love.
My love how couldst thou hope, who tookst the way
To raise in me inexpiable hate,
Knowing, as needs I must, by thee betrayed?
In vain thou striv'st to cover shame with shame,
Or by evasions thy crime uncoverst more.

    Dalila. Since thou determinst weakness for no plea
In man or woman, though to thy own condemning,
Hear what assaults I had, what snares besides,
What sieges girt me round, ere I consented;
Which might have awed the best resolved of men,
The constantest to have yielded without blame.
It was not gold, as to my charge thou lay'st,
That wrought with me: thou know'st the magistrates
And princes of my country came in person,
Solicited, commanded, threatened, urged,
Adjured by all the bonds of civil duty
And of religion, pressed how just it was,
How honourable, how glorious to entrap
A common enemy, who had destroyed
Such numbers of our nation: and the priest
Was not behind, but ever at my ear,
Preaching how meritorious with the gods
It would be to ensnare an irreligious
Dishonourer of Dagon: what had I
To oppose against such powerful arguments?
Only my love of thee held long debate;
And combated in silence all these reasons
With hard contest: at length that grounded maxim
So rife and celebrated in the mouths
Of wisest men — that to the public good
Private respects must yield — with grave authority
Took full possession of me and prevailed;
Virtue, as I thought, truth, duty so enjoining.

Samson. I thought where all thy circling wiles would end;
In feigned religion, smooth hypocrisy.
But had thy love, still odiously pretended,
Been, as it ought, sincere, it would have taught thee
Far other reasonings, brought forth other deeds.
I before all the daughters of my tribe
And of my nation chose thee from among
My enemies, loved thee, as too well thou knew'st,
Too well, unbosomed all my secrets to thee,
Not out of levity, but overpowered
By thy request, who could deny thee nothing;
Yet now am judged an enemy. Why then
Didst thou at first receive me for thy husband?
Then, as since then, thy country's foe professed.
Being once a wife, for me thou wast to leave
Parents and country; nor was I their subject,
Nor under their protection but my own,
Thou mine, not theirs: if aught against my life
Thy country sought of thee, it sought unjustly,
Against the law of nature, law of nations,
No more thy country, but an impious crew
Of men conspiring to uphold their state
By worse than hostile deeds, violating the ends
For which our country is a name so dear;
Not therefore to be obeyed. But zeal moved thee;
To please thy gods thou didst it; gods unable
To acquit themselves and prosecute their foes
But by ungodly deeds, the contradiction
Of their own deity, gods cannot be:
Less therefore to be pleased, obeyed, or feared.
These false pretexts and varnished colours failing,
Bare in thy guilt how foul must thou appear?
   Dalila. In argument with men a woman ever
Goes by the worse, whatever be her cause.

On both his wings, one black, th'other white,
Bears greatest names in his wild airy flight.
My name perhaps among the circumcised
In Dan, in Judah, and the bordering tribes,
To all posterity may stand defamed,
With malediction mentioned, and the blot
Of falsehood most unconjugal traduced.
But in my country where I most desire,
In Ecron, Gaza, Asdod, and in Gath
I shall be named among the famousest
Of women, sung at solemn festivals,
Living and dead recorded, who to save
Her country from a fierce destroyer, chose
Above the faith of wedlock-bands, my tomb
With odours visited and annual flowers.
Not less renowned than in Mount Ephraim,
Jael, who with inhospitable guile
Smote Sisera sleeping through the temples nailed.
Nor shall I count it heinous to enjoy
The public marks of honour and reward
Conferred upon me, for the piety
Which to my country I was judged to have shown.
At this whoever envies or repines
I leave him to his lot, and like my own.
    Chorus. She's gone, a manifest serpent by her sting
Discovered in the end, till now concealed.
    Samson. So let her go, God sent her to debase me,
And aggravate my folly who committed
To such a viper his most sacred trust
Of secrecy, my safety, and my life.
    Chorus. Yet beauty, though injurious, hath strange power,
After offence returning, to regain
Love once possessed, nor can be easily
Repulsed, without much inward passion felt

And secret sting of amorous remorse.

Samson. Love-quarrels oft in pleasing concord end,
Not wedlock treachery endangering life.

Chorus. It is not virtue, wisdom, valour, wit,
Strength, comeliness of shape, or amplest merit
That woman's love can win or long inherit;
But what it is, hard is to say,
Harder to hit,
(Which way soever men refer it)
Much like thy riddle, Samson, in one day
Or seven, though one should musing sit.
    If any of these or all, the Timnian bride
Had not so soon preferred
Thy paranymph, worthless to thee compared,
Successor in thy bed,
Nor both so loosely disallied
Their nuptials, nor this last so treacherously
Had shorn the fatal harvest of thy head.
Is it for that such outward ornament
Was lavished on their sex, that inward gifts
Were left for haste unfinished, judgement scant,
Capacity not raised to apprehend
Or value what is best
In choice, but oftest to affect the wrong?
Or was too much of self-love mixed,
Of constancy no root infixed,
That either they love nothing, or not long?
    Whate'er it be, to wisest men and best
Seeming at first all heavenly under virgin veil,
Soft, modest, meek, demure,
Once joined, the contrary she proves, a thorn
Intestine, far within defensive arms
A cleaving mischief, in his way to virtue
Adverse and turbulent, or by her charms

Draws him awry enslaved
With dotage, and his sense depraved
To folly and shameful deeds which ruin ends.
What pilot so expert but needs must wreck
Embarked with such a steersmate at the helm?
   Favoured of Heaven who finds
One virtuous rarely found,
That in domestic good combines;
Happy that house! His way to peace is smooth:
But virtue, which breaks through all opposition,
And all temptation can remove,
Most shines and most is acceptable above.
   Therefore God's universal law
Gave to the man despotic power
Over his female in due awe,
Nor from that right to part an hour,
Smile she or lower:
So shall he least confusion draw
On his whole life, not swayed
By female usurpation, nor dismayed.
   But had we best retire, I see a storm?
Samson. Fair days have oft contracted wind and rain.
Chorus. But this another kind of tempest brings.
Samson. Be less abstruse, my riddling days are past.
Chorus. Look now for no enchanting voice, nor fear
The bait of honied words; a rougher tongue
Draws hitherward, I know him by his stride,
The giant Harapha of Gath, his look
Haughty as is his pile high-built and proud.
Comes he in peace? What wind hath blown him hither
I less conjecture than when first I saw
The sumptuous Dalila floating this way.
His habit carries peace, his brow defiance.
   Samson. Or peace or not, alike to me he comes.

Chorus. His fraught we soon shall know, he now arrives.

Harapha. I come not Samson, to condole thy chance,
As these perhaps, yet wish it had not been,
Though for no friendly intent. I am of Gath,
Men call me Harapha, of stock renowned
As Og or Anak and the Emims old
That Kiriathaim held, thou knowest me now
If thou at all art known. Much I have heard
Of thy prodigious might and feats performed
Incredible to me, in this displeased,
That I was never present on the place
Of those encounters, where we might have tried
Each other's force in camp or listed field:
And now am come to see of whom such noise
Hath walked about, and each limb to survey,
If thy appearance answer loud report.

Samson. The way to know were not to see but taste.

Harapha. Dost thou already single me: I thought
Gyves and the mill had tamed thee? O that fortune
Had brought me to the field where thou art famed
To have wrought such wonders with an ass's jaw;
I should have forced thee soon with other arms,
Or left thy carcass where the ass lay thrown.
So had the glory of prowess been recovered
To Palestine, won by a Philistine
From the unforeskinned race, of whom thou bear'st
The highest name for valiant acts, that honour
Certain to have won by mortal duel from thee,
I lose, prevented by thy eyes put out.

Samson. Boast not of what thou wouldst have done, but do
What then thou would'st, thou seest it in thy hand.

Harapha. To combat with a blind man I disdain,
And thou hadst need much washing to be touched.

Samson. Such usage as your honourable lords

Afford me assassinated and betrayed,
Who durst not with their whole united powers
In fight withstand me single and unarmed,
Nor in the house with chamber ambushes
Close-banded durst attack me, no not sleeping,
Till they had hired a woman with their gold
Breaking her marriage faith to circumvent me.
Therefore without feigned shifts let be assigned
Some narrow place enclosed, where sight may give thee,
Or rather flight, no great advantage on me;
Then put on all thy glorious arms, thy helmet
And brigandine of brass, thy broad habergeon,
Vant-brass and greaves, and gauntlet, add thy spear
A weaver's beam, and seven-times-folded shield,
I only with an oaken staff will meet thee,
And raise such outcries on thy clattered iron,
Which long shall not with-hold me from thy head,
That in a little time while breath remains thee,
Thou oft shalt wish thyself at Gath to boast
Again in safety what thou wouldst have done
To Samson, but shalt never see Gath more.
   Harapha. Thou durst not thus disparage glorious arms
Which greatest heroes have in battle worn,
Their ornament and safety, had not spells
And black enchantments, some magician's art,
Armed thee or charmed thee strong, which thou from Heaven
Feignst at thy birth was given thee in thy hair,
Where strength can least abide, though all thy hairs
Were bristles ranged like those that ridge the back
Of chafed wild boars, or ruffled porcupines.
   Samson. I know no spells, use no forbidden arts;
My trust is in the living God who gave me
At my nativity this strength, diffused
No less through all my sinews, joints and bones,

Than thine, while I preserved these locks unshorn,
The pledge of my unviolated vow.
For proof hereof, if Dagon be thy god,
Go to his temple, invocate his aid
With solemnest devotion, spread before him
How highly it concerns his glory now
To frustrate and dissolve these magic spells,
Which I to be the power of Israel's God
Avow, and challenge Dagon to the test,
Offering to combat thee his champion bold,
With th'utmost of his godhead seconded:
Then thou shalt see, or rather to thy sorrow
Soon feel, whose God is strongest, thine or mine.

    Harapha. Presume not on thy God, whate'er he be,
Thee he regards not, owns not, hath cut off
Quite from his people, and delivered up
Into thy enemies' hand, permitted them
To put out both thine eyes, and fettered send thee
Into the common prison, there to grind
Among the slaves and asses thy comrades,
As good for nothing else, no better service
With those thy boisterous locks, no worthy match
For valour to assail, nor by the sword
Of noble warrior, so to stain his honour,
But by the barber's razor best subdued.

    Samson. All these indignities, for such they are
From thine, these evils I deserve and more,
Acknowledge them from God, inflicted on me
Justly, yet despair not of his final pardon
Whose ear is ever open; and his eye
Gracious to readmit the suppliant;
In confidence whereof I once again
Defy thee to the trial of mortal fight,
By combat to decide whose god is God,

Thine, or whom I with Israel's sons adore.

Harapha. Fair honour that thou dost thy God, in trusting
He will accept thee to defend his cause,
A murderer, a revolter, and a robber.

Samson. Tongue-doughty giant, how dost thou prove me
these?

Harapha. Is not thy nation subject to our lords?
Their magistrates confessed it, when they took thee
As a league-breaker and delivered bound
Into our hands: for hadst thou not committed
Notorious murder on those thirty men
At Askalon, who never did thee harm,
Then like a robber stripdst them of their robes?
The Philistines, when thou hadst broke the league,
Went up with armed powers thee only seeking,
To others did no violence nor spoil.

Samson. Among the daughters of the Philistines
I chose a wife, which argued me no foe;
And in your city held my nuptial feast.
But your ill-meaning politician lords,
Under pretence of bridal friends and guests,
Appointed to await me thirty spies,
Who threatening cruel death constrained the bride
To wring from me and tell to them my secret,
That solved the riddle which I had proposed.
When I perceived all set on enmity,
As on my enemies, where ever chanced,
I used hostility, and took their spoil
To pay my underminers in their coin.
My nation was subjected to your lords.
It was the force of conquest; force with force
Is well ejected when the conquered can.
But I a private person, whom my country
As a league-breaker gave up bound, presumed

Single rebellion and did hostile acts.
I was no private but a person raised
With strength sufficient and command from Heaven
To free my country; if their servile minds
Me their deliverer sent would not receive,
But to their masters gave me up for nought,
Th'unworthier they; whence to this day they serve.
I was to do my part from Heaven assigned,
And had performed it if my known offence
Had not disabled me, not all your force.
These shifts refuted, answer thy appellant
Though by his blindness maimed for high attempts,
Who now defies thee thrice to single fight,
As a petty enterprise of small enforce.

Harapha. With thee a man condemned, a slave enrolled,
Due by the law to capital punishment?
To fight with thee no man of arms will deign.

Samson. Cam'st thou for this, vain boaster, to survey me,
To descant on my strength, and give thy verdict?
Come nearer, part not hence so slight informed;
But take good heed my hand survey not thee.

Harapha. O Baal-zebub! can my ears unused
Hear these dishonours, and not render death?

Samson. No man withholds thee, nothing from thy hand
Fear I incurable; bring up thy van,
My heels are fettered, but my fist is free.

Harapha. This insolence other kind of answer fits.

Samson. Go baffled coward, lest I run upon thee,
Though in these chains, bulk without spirit vast,
And with one buffet lay thy structure low,
Or swing thee in the air, then dash thee down
To the hazard of thy brains and shattered sides.

Harapha. By Astaroth ere long thou shalt lament
These braveries in irons loaden on thee.

Chorus. His giantship is gone, somewhat crestfallen,
Stalking with less unconscionable strides,
And lower looks, but in a sultry chafe.

Samson. I dread him not, nor all his giant-brood,
Though fame divulge him father of five sons
All of gigantic size, Goliath chief.

Chorus. He will directly to the lords, I fear,
And with malicious counsel stir them up
Some way or other yet further to afflict thee.

Samson. He must allege some cause, and offered fight
Will not dare mention, lest a question rise
Whether he durst accept the offer or not,
And that he durst not plain enough appeared.
Much more affliction than already felt
They cannot well impose, nor I sustain;
If they intend advantage of my labours
The work of many hands, which earns my keeping
With no small profit daily to my owners.
But come what will, my deadliest foe will prove
My speediest friend, by death to rid me hence,
The worst that he can give, to me the best.
Yet so it may fall out, because their end
Is hate, not help to me, it may with mine
Draw their own ruin who attempt the deed.

Chorus. O how comely it is and how reviving
To the spirits of just men long oppressed!
When God into the hands of their deliverer
Puts invincible might
To quell the mighty of the earth, th'oppressor,
The brute and boisterous force of violent men
Hardy and industrious to support
Tyrannic power, but raging to pursue
The righteous and all such as honour truth.
He all their ammunition

And feats of war defeats
With plain heroic magnitude of mind
And celestial vigour armed;
Their armouries and magazines contemns,
Renders them useless, while
With winged expedition
Swift as the lightning glance he executes
His errand on the wicked, who surprised
Lose their defence distracted and amazed.

But patience is more oft the exercise
Of saints, the trial of their fortitude,
Making them each his own deliverer,
And victor over all
That tyranny or fortune can inflict.
Either of these is in thy lot,
Samson, with might endued
Above the sons of men; but sight bereaved
May chance to number thee with those
Whom patience finally must crown.
This idol's day hath been to thee no day of rest,
Labouring thy mind
More than the working day thy hands,
And yet perhaps more trouble is behind.
For I descry this way
Some other tending, in his hand
A sceptre or quaint staff he bears,
Comes on amain, speed in his look.
By his habit I discern him now
A public officer, and now at hand.
His message will be short and voluble.

Officer. Ebrews, the prisoner Samson here I seek.

Chorus. His manacles remark him, there he sits.

Officer. Samson, to thee our lords thus bid me say;
This day to Dagon is a solemn feast,

With sacrifices, triumph, pomp and games;
Thy strength they know surpassing human rate,
And now some public proof thereof require
To honour this great feast, and great assembly;
Rise therefore with all speed, and come along,
Where I will see thee heartened and fresh clad
To appear as fits before th'illustrious lords.

   Samson. Thou knowst I am an Ebrew, therefore tell them,
Our law forbids at their religious rites
My presence; for that cause I cannot come.

   Officer. This answer, be assured, will not content them.

   Samson. Have they not sword-players, and every sort
Of gymnic artists, wrestlers, riders, runners,
Jugglers and dancers, antics, mummers, mimics,
But they must pick me out with shackles tired,
And overlaboured at their public mill,
To make them sport with blind activity?
Do they not seek occasion of new quarrels
On my refusal to distress me more,
Or make a game of my calamities?
Return the way thou cam'st, I will not come.

   Officer. Regard thyself, this will offend them highly.

   Samson. My self? my conscience and internal peace.
Can they think me so broken, so debased
With corporal servitude, that my mind ever
Will condescend to such absurd commands?
Although their drudge, to be their fool or jester
And in my midst of sorrow and heart-grief
To show them feats, and play before their god,
The worst of all indignities, yet on me
Joined with extreme contempt? I will not come.

   Officer. My message was imposed on me with speed,
Brooks no delay: is this thy resolution?

   Samson. So take it with what speed thy message needs.

Officer. I am sorry what this stoutness will produce.

Samson. Perhaps thou shalt have cause to sorrow indeed.

Chorus. Consider, Samson; matters now are strained
Up to the highth, whether to hold or break;
He's gone, and who knows how he may report
Thy words by adding fuel to the flame?
Expect another message more imperious,
More lordly thundering than thou well wilt bear.

Samson. Shall I abuse this consecrated gift
Of strength, again returning with my hair
After my great transgression, so requite
Favour renewed, and add a greater sin
By prostituting holy things to idols;
A Nazarite in place abominable
Vaunting my strength in honour to their Dagon?
Besides, how vile, contemptible, ridiculous,
What act more execrably unclean, profane?

Chorus. Yet with this strength thou serv'st the Philistines,
Idolatrous, uncircumcised, unclean.

Samson. Not in their idol-worship, but by labour
Honest and lawful to deserve my food
Of those who have me in their civil power.

Chorus. Where the heart joins not, outward acts defile not.

Samson. Where outward force constrains, the sentence holds;
But who constrains me to the temple of Dagon,
Not dragging? The Philistian lords command.
Commands are no constraints. If I obey them,
I do it freely; venturing to displease
God for the fear of man, and man prefer,
Set God behind: which in his jealousy,
Shall never, unrepented, find forgiveness.
Yet that he may dispense with me or thee
Present in temples at idolatrous rites
For some important cause, thou needst not doubt.

Chorus. How thou wilt here come off surmounts my reach.

Samson. Be of good courage, I begin to feel
Some rousing motions in me which dispose
To something extraordinary my thoughts.
I with this messenger will go along,
Nothing to do, be sure. that may dishonour
Our law. or stain my vow of Nazarite.
If there be aught of presage in the mind,
This day will be remarkable in my life
By some great act, or of my days the last.

Chorus. In time thou hast resolved, the man returns.

Officer. Samson, this second message from our lords
To thee I am bid say. Art thou our slave,
Our captive, at the public mill our drudge,
And dar'st thou at our sending and command
Dispute thy coming? come without delay;
Or we shall find such engines to assail
And hamper thee, as thou shalt come of force,
Though thou wert firmlier fastened than a rock.

Samson. I could be well content to try their art,
Which to no few of them would prove pernicious.
Yet knowing their advantages too many,
Because they shall not trail me through their streets
Like a wild beast, I am content to go.
Masters' commands come with a power resistless
To such as owe them absolute subjection;
And for a life who will not change his purpose?
(So mutable are all the ways of men)
Yet this be sure, in nothing to comply
Scandalous or forbidden in our law.

Officer. I praise thy resolution, doff these links:
By this compliance thou wilt win the lords
To favour, and perhaps to set thee free.

Samson. Brethren farewell, your company along

I will not wish, lest it perhaps offend them
To see me girt with friends; and how the sight
Of me as of a common enemy,
So dreaded once, may now exasperate them
I know not. Lords are lordliest in their wine;
And the well-feasted priest then soonest fired
With zeal, if aught religion seem concerned.
No less the people on their holidays
Impetuous, insolent, unquenchable.
Happen what may, of me expect to hear
Nothing dishonourable, impure, unworthy
Our God, our law, my nation, or my self,
The last of me or no I cannot warrant.

   Chorus. Go, and the Holy One
Of Israel be thy guide
To what may serve his glory best, and spread his name
Great among the heathen round:
Send thee the angel of thy birth, to stand
Fast by thy side, who from thy father's field
Rode up in flames after his message told
Of thy conception, and be now a shield
Of fire; that spirit that first rushed on thee
In the camp of Dan
Be efficacious in thee now at need.
For never was from Heaven imparted
Measure of strength so great to mortal seed,
As in thy wondrous actions hath been seen.
But wherefore comes old Manoa in such haste
With youthful steps? much livelier than erewhile
He seems: supposing here to find his son,
Or of him bringing to us some glad news?

   Manoa. Peace with you brethren; my inducement hither
Was not at present here to find my son,
By order of the lords new parted hence

To come and play before them at their feast.
I heard all as I came, the city rings
And numbers thither flock, I had no will,
Lest I should see him forced to things unseemly.
But that which moved my coming now, was chiefly
To give ye part with me what hope I have
With good success to work his liberty.

   Chorus. That hope would much rejoice us to partake
With thee; say reverend sire, we thirst to hear.

   Manoa. I have attempted one by one the lords
Either at home, or through the high street passing,
With supplication prone and father's tears
To accept of ransom for my son their prisoner;
Some much averse I found and wondrous harsh,
Contemptuous, proud, set on revenge and spite;
That part most reverenced Dagon and his priests.
Others more moderate seeming, but their aim
Private reward, for which both God and state
They easily would set to sale: a third
More generous far and civil, who confessed
They had enough revenged, having reduced
Their foe to misery beneath their fears,
The rest was magnanimity to remit,
If some convenient ransom were proposed.
What noise or shout was that? It tore the sky.

   Chorus. Doubtless the people shouting to behold
Their one great dread, captive, and blind before them,
Or at some proof of strength before them shown.

   Manoa. His ransom, if my whole inheritance
May compass it, shall willingly be paid
And numbered down: much rather I shall choose
To live the poorest in my tribe, than richest,
And he in that calamitous prison left.
No, I am fixed not to part hence without him.

For his redemption all my patrimony,
If need be, I am ready to forgo
And quit: not wanting him, I shall want nothing.

 Chorus. Fathers are wont to lay up for their sons,
Thou for thy son art bent to lay out all;
Sons wont to nurse their parents in old age,
Thou in old age car'st how to nurse thy son,
Made older than thy age through eyesight lost.

 Manoa. It shall be my delight to tend his eyes,
And view him sitting in the house, ennobled
With all those high exploits by him achieved,
And on his shoulders waving down those locks,
That of a nation armed the strength contained:
And I persuade me God had not permitted
His strength again to grow up with his hair
Garrisoned round about him like a camp
Of faithful soldiery, were not his purpose
To use him further yet in some great service,
Not to sit idle with so great a gift
Useless, and thence ridiculous about him.
And since his strength with eyesight was not lost,
God will restore him eyesight to his strength.

 Chorus. Thy hopes are not ill founded nor seem vain
Of his delivery, and thy joy thereon
Conceived, agreeable to a father's love,
In both which we, as next participate.

 Manoa. I know your friendly minds and – O what noise!
Mercy of Heaven what hideous noise was that!
Horribly loud unlike the former shout.

 Chorus. Noise call you it or universal groan
As if the whole inhabitation perished,
Blood, death, and deathful deeds are in that noise,
Ruin, destruction at the utmost point.

 Manoa. Of ruin indeed methought I heard the noise,

Oh it continues, they have slain my son.

    Chorus. Thy son is rather slaying them, that outcry
From slaughter of one foe could not ascend.

    Manoa. Some dismal accident it needs must be;
What shall we do, stay here or run and see?

    Chorus. Best keep together here, lest running thither
We unawares run into danger's mouth.
This evil on the Philistines is fallen,
From whom could else a general cry be heard?
The sufferers then will scarce molest us here,
From other hands we need not much to fear.
What if his eyesight (for to Israel's God
Nothing is hard) by miracle restored,
He now be dealing dole among his foes,
And over heaps of slaughtered walk his way?

    Manoa. That were a joy presumptuous to be thought.

    Chorus. Yet God hath wrought things as incredible
For his people of old; what hinders now?

    Manoa. He can I know, but doubt to think he will;
Yet hope would fain subscribe, and tempts belief.
A little stay will bring some notice hither.

    Chorus. Of good or bad so great, of bad the sooner;
For evil news rides post, while good news baits.
And to our wish I see one hither speeding,
An Ebrew, as I guess, and of our tribe.

    Messenger. O whither shall I run, or which way fly
The sight of this so horrid spectacle
Which erst my eyes beheld and yet behold;
For dire imagination still pursues me.
But providence or instinct of nature seems,
Or reason though disturbed, and scarce consulted
To have guided me aright, I know not how,
To thee first reverend Manoa, and to these
My countrymen, whom here I knew remaining,

As at some distance from the place of horror,
So in the sad event too much concerned.
    Manoa. The accident was loud, and here before thee
With rueful cry, yet what it was we hear not;
No preface needs, thou seest we long to know.
    Messenger. It would burst forth, but I recover breath
And sense distract, to know well what I utter.
    Manoa. Tell us the sum, the circumstance defer.
    Messenger. Gaza yet stands, yet all her sons are fallen,
All in a moment overwhelmed and fallen.
    Manoa. Sad, but thou knowst to Israelites not saddest
The desolation of a hostile city.
    Messenger. Feed on that first, there may in grief be surfeit.
    Manoa. Relate by whom.
    Messenger.   By Samson.
    Manoa. That still lessens
The sorrow, and converts it nigh to joy.
    Messenger. Ah Manoa I refrain, too suddenly
To utter what will come at last too soon;
Lest evil tidings with too rude irruption
Hitting thy aged ear should pierce too deep.
    Manoa. Suspense in news is torture, speak them out.
    Messenger. Then take the worst in brief, Samson is dead.
    Manoa. The worst indeed, O all my hope's defeated
To free him hence! But death who sets all free
Hath paid his ransom now and full discharge.
What windy joy this day had I conceived
Hopeful of his delivery, which now proves
Abortive as the first-born bloom of spring
Nipt with the lagging rear of winter's frost.
Yet ere I give the reins to grief, say first,
How died he? death to life is crown or shame.
All by him fell thou say'st, by whom fell he,
What glorious hand gave Samson his death's **wound**?

Messenger. Unwounded of his enemies he fell.

Manoa. Wearied with slaughter then or how? explain.

Messenger. By his own hands.

Manoa.   Self-violence? what cause
Brought him so soon at variance with himself
Among his foes?

Messenger.   Inevitable cause
At once both to destroy and be destroyed;
The edifice where all were met to see him
Upon their heads and on his own he pulled.

Manoa. O lastly over-strong against thy self!
A dreadful way thou took'st to thy revenge.
More than enough we know; but while things yet
Are in confusion, give us if thou canst,
Eye-witness of what first or last was done,
Relation more particular and distinct.

Messenger. Occasions drew me early to this city,
And as the gates I entered with sunrise,
The morning trumpets festival proclaimed
Through each high street: little I had dispatched
When all abroad was rumoured that this day
Samson should be brought forth to show the people
Proof of his mighty strength in feats and games;
I sorrowed at his captive state, but minded
Not to be absent at that spectacle.
The building was a spacious theatre
Half round on two main pillars vaulted high,
With seats where all the lords and each degree
Of sort, might sit in order to behold;
The other side was open, where the throng
On banks and scaffolds under sky might stand;
I among these aloof obscurely stood.
The feast and noon grew high, and sacrifice
Had filled their hearts with mirth, high cheer, and wine,

When to their sports they turned. Immediately
Was Samson as a public servant brought,
In their state livery clad; before him pipes
And timbrels, on each side went armed guards,
Both horse and foot before him and behind
Archers and slingers, cataphracts and spears.
At sight of him the people with a shout
Rifted the air clamouring their god with praise,
Who had made their dreadful enemy their thrall.
He patient but undaunted where they led him,
Came to the place, and what was set before him
Which without help of eye, might be assayed,
To heave, pull, draw, or break, he still performed
All with incredible, stupendious force,
None daring to appear antagonist.
At length for intermission's sake they led him
Between the pillars; he his guide requested
(For so from such as nearer stood we heard)
As over-tired to let him lean awhile
With both his arms on those two massy pillars
That to the arched roof gave main support.
He unsuspicious led him; which when Samson
Felt in his arms, with head awhile inclined,
And eyes fast fixt he stood, as one who prayed,
Or some great matter in his mind revolved.
At last with head erect thus cried aloud,
Hitherto, lords, what your commands imposed
I have performed, as reason was, obeying,
Not without wonder or delight beheld.
Now of my own accord such other trial
I mean to show you of my strength, yet greater;
As with amaze shall strike all who behold.
This uttered, straining all his nerves he bowed,
As with the force of winds and waters pent,

When mountains tremble, those two massy pillars
With horrible convulsion to and fro,
He tugged, he shook, till down they came and drew
The whole roof after them, with burst of thunder
Upon the heads of all who sat beneath,
Lords, ladies, captains, counsellors, or priests,
Their choice nobility and flower, not only
Of this but each Philistian city round
Met from all parts to solemnize this feast.
Samson with these immixed, inevitably
Pulled down the same destruction on himself;
The vulgar only scaped who stood without.

 Chorus. O dearly-bought revenge, yet glorious!
Living or dying thou hast fulfilled
The work for which thou wast foretold
To Israel, and now li'st victorious
Among thy slain self-killed
Not willingly, but tangled in the fold
Of dire necessity, whose law in death conjoined
Thee with thy slaughtered foes in number more
Than all thy life had slain before.

 Semichorus. While their hearts were jocund and sublime,
Drunk with idolatry, drunk with wine,
And fat regorged of bulls and goats,
Chanting their idol, and preferring
Before our living Dread who dwells
In Silo his bright sanctuary.
Among them he a spirit of frenzy sent,
Who hurt their minds,
And urged them on with mad desire
To call in haste for their destroyer;
They only set on sport and play
Unweetingly importuned
Their own destruction to come speedy upon them.

So fond are mortal men
Fallen into wrath divine,
As their own ruin on themselves to invite,
Insensate left, or to sense reprobate,
And with blindness internal struck.

Semichorus. But he though blind of sight,
Despised and thought extinguished quite,
With inward eye illuminated
His fiery virtue roused
From under ashes into sudden flame,
And as an evening dragon came,
Assailant on the perched roosts,
And nests in order ranged
Of tame villatic fowl; but as an eagle
His cloudless thunder bolted on their heads.
So virtue given for lost,
Depressed, and overthrown, as seemed,
Like that self-begotten bird
In the Arabian woods embossed,
That no second knows nor third,
And lay erewhile a holocaust,
From out her ashy womb now teemed
Revives, reflourishes, then vigorous most
When most unactive deemed,
And though her body die, her fame survives,
A secular bird ages of lives.

Manoa. Come, come, no time for lamentation now,
Nor much more cause, Samson hath quit himself
Like Samson, and heroicly hath finished
A life heroic, on his enemies
Fully revenged, hath left them years of mourning,
And lamentation to the sons of Caphtor
Through all Philistian bounds. To Israel
Honour hath left, and freedom, let but them

Find courage to lay hold on this occasion,
To himself and father's house eternal fame;
And which is best and happiest yet, all this
With God not parted from him, as was feared,
But favouring and assisting to the end.
Nothing is here for tears, nothing to wail
Or knock the breast, no weakness, no contempt,
Dispraise, or blame, nothing but well and fair,
And what may quiet us in a death so noble.
Let us go find the body where it lies
Soaked in his enemies' blood, and from the stream
With lavers pure and cleansing herbs wash off
The clotted gore. I with what speed the while
(Gaza is not in plight to say us nay)
Will send for all my kindred, all my friends
To fetch him hence and solemnly attend
With silent obsequy and funeral train
Home to his father's house: there will I build him
A monument, and plant it round with shade
Of laurel ever green, and branching palm,
With all his trophies hung, and acts enrolled
In copious legend, or sweet lyric song.
Thither shall all the valiant youth resort,
And from his memory inflame their breasts
To matchless valour, and adventures high:
The virgins also shall on feastful days
Visit his tomb with flowers, only bewailing
His lot unfortunate in nuptial choice,
From whence captivity and loss of eyes.
 Chorus. All is best, though we oft doubt,
What th'unsearchable dispose
Of highest wisdom brings about,
And ever best found in the close.
Oft he seems to hide his face,

But unexpectedly returns
And to his faithful champion hath in place
Bore witness gloriously; whence Gaza mourns
And all that band them to resist
His uncontrollable intent;
His servants he with new acquist
Or true experience from this great event
With peace and consolation hath dismissed,
And calm of mind all passion spent.

Suggestions for Reading

THOSE interested in the seventeenth century as a whole will find that it has attracted some of the best of modern historians and critics. In addition to straight histories, such as Ogg's *Europe in the Seventeenth Century*, or the relevant volumes in the *Oxford History of England*, there are such original and fascinating works as G. N. Clark's *The Seventeenth Century*. Two excellent studies of the thought of the time, which have much to say on Milton, are Basil Willey's *Seventeenth-Century Background* and Grierson's *Cross Currents in English Literature of the Seventeenth Century*. On the visual arts, there is N. Pevsner's admirable *Outline of European Architecture*, in Pelican Books.

There are several good anthologies of seventeenth-century English poetry: here are three in descending order of price – *The Oxford Book of Seventeenth-Century Verse*; *Metaphysical Poems and Lyrics of the Seventeenth Century*, edited by H. J. C. Grierson, which has a justly famous introduction; and volume two of *The Centuries' Poetry*, edited by D. K. Roberts, in Penguins.

The best outline of the literature of the period is that of D. Bush (*English Literature in the Earlier Seventeenth Century*), which has a particularly good chapter on Milton. Much of the influential criticism of T. S. Eliot on seventeenth-century writers is to be found in a Penguin, *Selected Prose of T. S. Eliot:* this contains his essay on *The Metaphysical Poets*, an extract only from the excellent essay on Marvell, and both the famous essays on Milton.

Of the writing of books on Milton there is no end. Many of the best of recent works come from America, and include studies of him in relation to his historical background, such as those of Wolfe (*Milton in the Puritan Revolution*), or Barker (*Milton and the Puritan Dilemma*) as well as the more strictly critical work of the 'New Critics' in such periodicals as *Sewanee Review* and *Kenyon Review*. More readily obtainable are the following: *Milton, Man and Thinker*, by D. Saurat. This is interesting, but tries to overdramatize Milton as an arch-heretic, which he certainly was not. *Paradise Lost and the Seventeenth-Century Reader*, by B. Rajan, is an attempt to get back to the contemporary reader's attitude towards Milton. *Preface to Paradise Lost*, C. S. Lewis, hides some profound insight under a showy and polemical style. *Paradise Lost and its Critics*, by A. J. A. Waldock, attempts to do just the opposite to Rajan: to judge the poem entirely by modern standards. The criticism of F. R. Leavis, anti-Miltonic on the whole but perceptive and balanced, can be found in two of his books, *Revaluation* and *The Common Pursuit*. One older book must be mentioned: Dr Johnson's *Life of Milton* is a work which no-one will confess to agreeing with, and everyone insists on valuing highly.

The standard modern edition of Milton is the enormously expensive Columbia edition of the *Complete Works*, in eighteen volumes. The complete poems can be obtained in the Oxford edition (in the original spelling) or (with the famous if perhaps overrated introduction by Charles Williams) in the World's Classics. There is a nineteenth-century edition of the complete prose in Bohn's Standard Library, and a good selection, with rather a poor introduction, in Everyman's Library.

Coming Shortly

GERARD MANLEY HOPKINS
SELECTED POEMS AND PROSE

EDITED BY W. H. GARDNER

D 15

Since the posthumous works of Gerard Manley Hopkins first displayed their 'plumage of far wonder and heavenward flight' in the collection of 1918, which was edited by Robert Bridges, they have gone into a Third Edition and run through thirteen impressions. His prose has hitherto been published only in expensive volumes, two of which are now temporarily out of print. The present selection includes the forty-eight mature poems and thirteen of the best 'unfinished poems and fragments'. These are preceded by four early pieces and also by the 'Author's Preface', in which Hopkins explains his highly original prosody. Notes have been added to help the general reader to understand the poet's thought and to elucidate further his Sprung, Counterpoint and 'outriding' rhythms.

The prose passages have been taken mainly from the journals and letters, but they include also extracts from a Platonic dialogue, a sermon, and a commentary. They have been chosen with the purpose of filling in the portrait of this Victorian Jesuit, whose personality and vision are as significant as his brilliant poetic technique. The editor's critical and biographical Introduction stresses the importance of the poet's theory of 'inscape' and 'instress' and aims generally at giving a certain unity to the whole selection.

2s 6d

English Plays

THE PLAYS OF J. M. SYNGE
845

In the early part of the century Dublin's Abbey Theatre was the shrine of a great revival in Irish drama. The leading figure in that renaissance was J. M. Synge, whose six plays now appear in a single Penguin volume. They include that masterpiece of comedy, *The Playboy of the Western World*, which so enraged its first-night audience in 1907 that they wrecked the theatre, the beautiful unfinished drama, *Deirdre of the Sorrows*, and *Riders to the Sea*. (3s)

SHAKESPEARE AND SHAW

Eleven volumes of the Penguin Shakespeare are now available – *Hamlet, King Lear, Macbeth, Henry IV (Part II), Sonnets* and *A Lover's Complaint, The Taming of the Shrew, Antony and Cleopatra, Romeo and Juliet, A Midsummer Night's Dream, Love's Labour's Lost,* and *Henry V*.

Bernard Shaw's *Major Barbara, Androcles and the Lion, St Joan, The Doctor's Dilemma, Pygmalion, Man and Superman, Plays Pleasant, Plays Unpleasant* and *Three Plays for Puritans* are again available.

FOUR ENGLISH TRAGEDIES
EDITED BY J. M. MORRELL
956

These four plays have been selected to represent the variety in poetic tragedy of the kind made familiar by Shakespeare, and they make up a companion volume to the same editor's *Four English Comedies* (763). The tragedies are Marlowe's *Edward II*, Webster's *Duchess of Malfy*, Dryden's *All for Love*, and Heywood's *A Woman Killed with Kindness* (2s 6d); the comedies are Jonson's *Volpone*, Congreve's *Way of the World*, Goldsmith's *She Stoops to Conquer*, and Sheridan's *School for Scandal* (3s).

SOPHOCLES: ELECTRA AND OTHER PLAYS

TRANSLATED BY E. F. WATLING

(L28)

A new translation made by E. F. Watling, who has already translated the earlier *Theban Plays* for the Penguin Classics series. This volume includes *Electra*, *Ajax*, *The Women of Trachis*, and *Philoctetes*. Of the *Theban Plays*, *The Journal of Hellenic Studies* wrote: 'Mr Watling's translation of the dialogue into a "much resolved" form of iambic line and the choruses into rhyming verse is extremely successful; its great beauty and extreme speakability far outweigh the few mistakes.' (2s)

CHEHOV: THE CHERRY ORCHARD, IVANOV, THREE SISTERS

TRANSLATED BY ELISAVETA FEN

(L19)

A new translation of three of Chehov's greatest plays, two of which have been 'classics' in this country for a number of years, and the third, *Ivanov*, relatively little known. The translation is both idiomatic and true to the original, which makes it as suitable for stage-acting as for reading. (2s)

EURIPIDES: ALCESTIS AND OTHER PLAYS

TRANSLATED BY PHILIP VELLACOTT

(L31)

These, the first three of Euripides' plays to appear in the Penguin series, are: *Alcestis*, *Iphigenia in Tauris*, and *Hippolytus*. Other collections are in preparation. The translator's aim has been to consider impartially both the actor and the audience, both the scholar and the layman, and to use only language now current in English prose. 'These plays,' he says, 'were originally written to be acted first, then read; to raise dispute as well as tears, to fascinate, to irritate, to explode and to inspire.' (2s)

SELECTED PROSE OF
T. S. ELIOT

EDITED BY JOHN HAYWARD

873

The fame of T. S. Eliot as a poet has somewhat over-shadowed his distinguished reputation as a critic. The Penguin selection from his prose writings (a companion volume to his *Selected Poems* in the Penguin Poets) is designed to demonstrate the range and penetration of his criticism. Edited and introduced, with his approval, by Mr John Hayward, it provides a comprehensive intro-duction to one of the finest and most original critical minds of our time. The twelve essays and addresses printed here in full, and selected passages from some forty others, fall into two groups. In the first, literary criticism, chosen from Mr Eliot's continuous work in this field over the past thirty-five years, with particular emphasis on poetry and individual poets. In the second, social criticism, comprising his mature opinions on the human situation in general, and more especially his views on religion, culture, and educa-tion in contemporary life. The fact that some of the material in both groups is not readily accessible and is printed here for the first time in book-form, will increase the interest and value of this selection as a work of reference to a critic who has exercised a profound and exciting influence on the thought and sensibility of the age. (2s)

T. S. Eliot's *Selected Poems* has also been reprinted recently.